Home Made in the Kitchen

Also by Barry Bluestein and Kevin Morrissey

Dip It!

Light Sauces

Quick Breads

The Northern Exposure Cookbook

The 99% Fat-Free Cookbook

&

Barry Bluestein & Kevin Morrissey

Home Made
in the Kitchen

Traditional Recipes

and Household Projects

Updated and Made Easy

Illustrations by Jeanne Troxell Munson

VIKING
STUDIO
BOOKS

VIKING STUDIO BOOKS
Published by the Penguin Group
Penguin Books USA Inc., 375 Hudson Street,
New York, New York 10014, U.S.A.
Penguin Books Ltd, 27 Wrights Lane, London W8 5TZ, England
Penguin Books Australia Ltd, Ringwood,Victoria, Australia
Penguin Books Canada Ltd, 10 Alcorn Avenue,
Toronto, Ontario, Canada M4V 3B2
Penguin Books (N.Z.) Ltd, 182–190 Wairau Road,
Auckland 10, New Zealand

Penguin Books Ltd, Registered Offices:
Harmondsworth, Middlesex, England

First published in 1995 by Viking Penguin,
a division of Penguin Books USA Inc.

2 3 4 5 6 7 8 9 10

LIBRARY OF CONGRESS CATALOGING IN PUBLICATION DATA
Bluestein, Barry.
Home made in the kitchen: traditional recipes and
household projects updated and made easy /
by Barry Bluestein & Kevin Morrissey;
illustrations by Jeanne Troxell Munson.
p.   cm.
Includes index.
ISBN 0-670-84931-6
1. Cookery.   I. Morrissey, Kevin.   II. Title.
TX715.B6543   1994
641.5–dc20   94–6016

Printed in the United States of America
Set in Bodoni Old Face
Designed by Francesca Belanger

Dedicated fondly to the memory of

Leo M. Bluestein & Weyman F. Morrissey

*Kindred spirits worlds apart who both taught their sons
the true meaning of home and happiness. Thank you,
each of you, for your intellectual curiosity, your love
of life, your sense of self, and your boundless
respect for others.*

Acknowledgments

We gratefully acknowledge the support of Susan Ramer, our literary agent, whose unstinting belief in us and in this book made it a reality.

Thanks are due Michael Fragnito and Cathy Hemming, whose clear vision provided editorial direction for *Home Made in the Kitchen,* and all the other folks at Viking Studio Books who helped our concept take shape. Martha Schueneman, our talented hands-on editor, deserves special thanks for so many long hours, so much encouragement.

For knowledge and assistance graciously shared, we acknowledge Elaine Barlas, Elaine Brooks, Ann E. Bloomstrand, Eleanor Bluestein, Cheryl Blumenthal, Ricki Carroll of New England Cheesemaking Supply Co., Lisa & Lou Ekus, Claudia Clark Potter, Colin Reeves, William Rice, Greg Snider, Doris and Jim Stockwell of Spiceland, Inc., and Jill Van Cleave.

Lastly, we thank Sara F. Bluestein for giving her son the courage to tackle any culinary or craft challenge, and Elizabeth A. Morrissey for instilling in her son an enthusiastic appreciation of good food and good times with friends.

Contents

Introduction

Many aspects of domestic life enjoyed by our great-grandparents at the last turn of the century reflected a simple elegance that was lost when subsequent generations embraced mass-produced goods. Foodstuffs were fresh and wholesome, often homegrown and preserved for the months to come. Pantries and sideboards overflowed; homes were filled with functional and decorative household items lovingly crafted by hand.

By the time our parents settled into the suburban landscape at mid-century, we had become willing and eager consumers, lured by the commercial marketplace's promises of convenience and abundance. Pickling, preserving, smoking, and cheese making were consigned to the realm of the quaint; even baking bread and making candy were something one's grandmother did.

But ever so slowly, the pendulum has begun to swing back. As the appeal of the mass-produced, the prepackaged, and the disposable fades, the homegrown, the home-cooked, and the handcrafted are once again coming into favor. We've noticed that, one by one, our thirty- and forty-something acquaintances have resurrected many of the culinary and household arts that haven't been widely practiced in decades.

Perhaps this is a direct response to the bland uniformity of the commercial overabundance that has surrounded us for so long. Perhaps it's a result of the fact that modern technology has drastically reduced the time and effort entailed. Perhaps it's just part of an attempt to regain a sense of fulfillment and accomplishment. For whatever reason, activities once undertaken out of necessity are now leisure pursuits.

For many of us, now returning to the home to raise families after years of careers propped up by "hire-out, take-out, and order-in," the attempt to define our future involves relearning the traditions of a more domestically rooted past.

We wrote *Home Made in the Kitchen* as a sourcebook for modern families rediscovering the forgotten arts of past generations and reinterpreting them as they pass these arts along to the next. Loosely organized around the kitchen arts that were common in the Victorian era, it bridges the years to reflect the more cultivated tastes and limited time constraints that characterize life at this turn of the century.

Having often been frustrated ourselves by laborious how-to books that told quite a bit more than we actually wanted to know, we set out to simplify things. Our goal is for you to be able to start from scratch and master the basics within a few odd hours carved out of a busy schedule, and we further this goal by writing recipes that produce smaller than traditional quantities and fully utilize modern technology.

Thus, *Home Made* recipes show you how to pickle by the jar, churn butter or knead bread dough in a food processor or stationary electric mixer, smoke sausage in a kettle grill or in a wok, and grow herbs in pots and dry them in a microwave.

From fashioning elegant candies by hand to flavoring vinegars and infusing oils, from steeping delicate cordials to making creamy, flavorful soft cheeses, we offer streamlined instructions, interspersed with Victorian lore and anecdotes from household encyclopedias of the era.

Home Made projects are designed as building blocks; you can pursue one or several progressive activities according to personal taste.

You can start an indoor herb garden to supply fresh herbs for pickling, for flavoring vinegar, cheese, mayonnaise, or butter, or for scenting candles . . . dry the herbs for seasonings, herbal teas, or recycled blender paper . . . and use the blender paper to make custom labels for pickle and preserve jars.

Add the flavored vinegars or liqueurs to preserves to make sauces, serve the breads in a saltbread basket, the candies in an edible chocolate centerpiece or gingerbread bowl, and the ice creams in chocolate serving cups. Combine sausages and smoked cheeses with pickles to create a stunning antipasto platter or layer with mozzarella on bread dough for a hearty pizza.

We include several ideas that allow you to package *Home Made* goods attractively for display or giving. You'll find projects for painting jelly pots and preserve jars, decorating fabric Mason jar covers and gift cards, fashioning individual decanter labels from oven-baked clay, and forming edible chocolate gift boxes.

In an era of dissatisfaction with the manufactured and the mundane, *Home Made in the Kitchen* offers simple, quick, and inexpensive ideas for entertaining with grace, creating unique gifts, and adding elegant personal touches to the dinner table and buffet. Through it, we hope to rekindle some of the spirit and style of the late nineteenth century as we rapidly approach the twenty-first.

Home Made
in the Kitchen

Pickles & Preserves

O nce basic pantry staples for nourishment year-round, homemade pickles and preserves now seem quaint and somewhat curious undertakings. We can, after all, choose from row upon row of ready-made pickles and preserves lining the aisles of our neighborhood supermarket. Yet pickling and preserving are staging a surprising comeback.

Home Made pickling and preserving allow you to select ingredients personally, to create a finished product from scratch, and to fashion it into a very special gift. They afford opportunities for family pursuits that will long be remembered, from scouring farmers' markets for produce to hand-decorating jars, labels, and gift cards, and spending quiet evenings by the fire assembling holiday gift baskets.

Before proceeding, be forewarned that the sights, smells, and tastes of a kitchen given over to pickling and preserving issue a sensory call to another time and place. Close your eyes and let yourself be transported to a Victorian house, its garden sprawling with vines and bushes from which the bounty will be reaped. As the harvest season nears, bushel baskets overflow with ripe produce to be "put by" for the long winter to come. Crocks are filled and carted to the cellar, while in the hearth a fire burns bright beneath myriad bubbling kettles. Pantry shelves creak and shift under the growing weight of colorful jars of all sizes, each containing a bit of the spirit of the harvest that will be rekindled and shared during the months ahead.

INGREDIENTS

Freshness of ingredients is key to successful pickling and preserving. Nothing equals produce that has been allowed to linger on the vine until ripe, has been picked at just the right time, and has made its way into your kitchen within the first crucial day or two.

Finding the freshest ingredients is easy, thanks to the growing popularity of farmers' markets that abound in and around most metropolitan areas. A typical market day starts early, with the air still crisp and many a shopper bearing a steaming cup of coffee. The mood is congenial, for you are among kindred spirits who share a passion. We have been here before, most of us, and we'll all be back. Shopping the markets, many of which we visited around the country while writing this book, is an easy addiction, one that we've given ourselves over to entirely.

One weekend, we found vibrant cherry tomatoes in a rainbow of colors and rare black currants on the dew-covered statehouse grounds beneath the capitol dome in Madison, Wisconsin. On another, we weathered a sudden squall selecting bushels of pickling cucumbers on one of the narrow covered walkways of the old Minneapolis market, flanked on both sides by overflowing truckbeds.

At home in Chicago, where one of the most popular markets is held on a weekday morning in the heart of the Loop, we routinely jostle for produce with prominent chefs and office workers on their coffee breaks.

From Manhattan's Union Square, where rows of produce stalls give way to trucks spilling onto adjoining streets from which game birds, fresh sausages, and farmhouse cheeses are sold, to Seattle's cacophonous Pike Street Market, where vendors hawk salmon and souvenirs amidst the Northwest bounty, each market has its own unique personality with special finds for the *Home Made* kitchen.

Equipment

Since we've adapted *Home Made* pickling and preserving recipes to yield smaller quantities for smaller families and, all too often, smaller kitchens, you won't need much in the way of special equipment.

Replace the pickling crock in the cellar with a niche on your refrigerator shelf, and dispense with the cauldrons of yore—any good-sized soup kettle or stockpot will suffice for *Home Made* pickling. Recipes that necessitate cumbersome pressure sealers are banished from our repertoire.

Preserving in Victorian households started with boiling fruit and syrup in huge porcelain vats and often ended with a hot-water bath in a converted tin washbasin fitted with a grid of wooden slats. We require only the common 4½- to 5-quart *Dutch oven,* or its oval-shaped cousin, the *French oven.* The key characteristic of this pot is its width, which allows the contents to be evenly distributed over the cooking surface, enabling rapid boiling at a high temperature. For our recipes, you won't need a special jelly thermometer.

Home Made pickles and preserves are made by the jar, and your primary need is a ready supply of *Ball or Kerr self-sealing Mason jars,* available at almost any supermarket in ½-pint, 1-pint, and 1-quart sizes. While the jars and their rings are reusable, the flat metal seals that go atop the jar before the ring is screwed on are not. *Replacement seals* are stocked alongside the Mason jars in most stores.

Long-handled, jar-lifting tongs will enable you to safely submerge and retrieve jars and seals from boiling water. Designed specifically for this purpose, jar-lifting tongs are available from kitchenware stores.

A *widemouthed canning funnel,* also available from kitchenware stores, enables you to fill jars with boiling ingredients easily. A canning funnel also will prove helpful with recipes in which solid ingredients are cooked in the pickling brine before the liquid is poured into jars.

In many recipes, we call for *nonreactive containers or pots.* Glass, enamel, stainless steel, or anodized aluminum (such as Calphalon or Magnalite) will do fine, but copper, plain aluminum, and cast-iron receptacles combine with some ingredients to cause an unwanted chemical reaction. Enameled cast iron is nonreactive, but we caution against using it for preserving, as the fruit could stain the enamel coating.

TECHNIQUES

Many recipes call for *hot sealing* pickles or preserves. The key to proper sealing is to keep all components as hot as possible right up until the seal is secured. While ingredients are prepared, Mason jars and their flat metal seals (it's not necessary to boil the rings) are sterilized and kept in boiling water, then removed, filled, and immediately sealed one by one.

In recipes that do not call for hot sealing, *sterilization* can be done in advance, either by submerging jars and seals for 5 to 6 minutes into a pot of boiling water sufficient to cover the top of the jars by 1 to 2 inches, or simply by running them through a hot dishwasher.

A few recipes require you to put the sealed jars through a *hot-water bath*. Choose a stockpot tall enough to allow at least 3½ inches above the top of the jars—we've found that an 8-quart pot is big enough. Place a metal cooling rack in the pot to prevent the glass jars from coming into direct contact with the bottom, which will become very hot.

Fill the pot with water to cover the jars by 2 inches (the extra 1½ inches allows the water to boil without spilling over). Bring to a boil. Using tongs, carefully submerge the jars into the water and boil as directed in the recipes.

To *check the seals,* run your finger across the top to ensure that the surface is concave, and press down on the center of the seal. If you hear a pop, the jar did not seal properly. You can also test by unscrewing the ring, grasping the edges of the seal, and gently trying to pull it off (without actually prying). If it comes off, the jar did not seal properly.

Improper sealing happens when one of the components is not hot enough, or the jar is not sealed fast enough. Should this happen, store the pickles or preserves in the refrigerator and use within 3 months.

Unless otherwise specified, *store* pickles and preserves just about anywhere out of direct sunlight or away from a heat source such as a stove or radiator. When we call for storage in a cool, dark place, a kitchen cabinet or pantry shelf works well in most cases; if your kitchen is particularly warm or unventilated, use the refrigerator. Always refrigerate pickles and preserves after opening.

Standard Precautions: As with any handling of raw foodstuffs, use caution in pickling and preserving. Always refrigerate pickles and preserves once the seal has been opened and use within a reasonable amount of time. If you suspect at any time that the seal of an unopened jar has popped, is seeping, or has an abnormal smell, discoloration, or mold, do not consume the contents.

❖ ❖ ❖

Pickles

Most of us are intrigued by the very notion of pickling, raised as we were in households where the "larder" was stocked, more often than not, with goods harvested from supermarket shelves. For those whose grandmothers dwell not in farmhouses but in condominiums, the exotic smells of brines and spices in the pickling kitchen exert a subliminal pull and spark an awakening of long-dormant senses.

THE BASICS

Pickling is essentially a process of preserving foods in a brine, usually of spiced vinegar. Most commonly, the ingredient preserved is a cucumber, yielding a "pickle," but green beans or okra, tomatoes or sour cherries can be pickled with savory results.

Home Made recipes use either of two methods of pickling: hot sealing, in which ingredients are packed in a boiling brine, or our updated version of crock fermenting, which uses a refrigerator instead. In both versions, we've eliminated time-consuming steps associated with old-fashioned pickling to reduce delay in gratification. All *Home Made* pickles will be ready to eat within 10 days.

Refrigerator pickles, which include Sour Tomatoes, Kosher Dills, and Sour Gherkins, are remarkably easy to make. Recipes require neither packing ingredients in boiling liquid nor putting the sealed jars through a hot-water bath. Cucumbers pickled in the refrigerator tend to be crunchier than their hot-sealed counterparts, since they aren't softened by cooking.

Refrigerator pickles, however, must be kept in the refrigerator for safe storage; they cannot be stored in the pantry or shipped. Shelf life for the refrigerator recipes tends to be shorter, from 3 to 6 months, as compared to a year or more for hot-sealed pickles.

Our hot-sealing recipes require a bit more effort, but are much simpler than traditional pickling recipes, since we reduce the volume to small, easily manageable quantities. You'll be pickling by the jar, not by the vat.

Recipes for Peppered Okra, Dilled Beans, and Spicy Sugar Peas call for processing the sealed jars in a hot-water bath. The Zucchini

The prime season for the pickling cucumbers is summer to fall. Shop for tomatoes during the summer, and for green tomatoes in the fall. Sour cherries are in season only in early to midsummer, as are sugar peas. Okra starts to come to market in late summer, while beans and zucchini are often available all year around.

Bread and Butter Pickles, the Basil Tomatoes, and the Sour Cherries call for cooking the ingredients in brine, which should generate enough heat so that the seal will take readily without a hot-water bath. However, we recommend hot-water baths if you intend to ship the Bread and Butter Pickles or Sour Cherries.

Schedule your pickling around seasonal availability. In this era of rapid transport from fair-weather climates and the proliferation of hothouse produce, it is easy to forget that there was a reason why our ancestors pickled at harvest time. Make every effort to select ingredients from local farmers, picked at their prime.

Select pickling ingredients that are blemish-free and uniform in color, shape, and size. You'll be putting them on display, so choose the best. This is the same rationale that dictates shopping the farmers' markets. In a pinch, you might make bread and butter pickles using a zucchini purchased from a grocer whom you know stocks only the freshest of produce. But why bother pickling a hothouse tomato?

The best source for the fresh herbs is your own indoor kitchen herb garden (see chapter 8), but fresh herbs are readily available in most supermarkets these days.

As always, vegetables and fruits should be thoroughly rinsed and dried before pickling. This is especially important with cucumbers, which can harbor a lot of residual grit.

Mark jars by contents and date with a grease pencil or peel-off label as you seal them so that you can affix a decorative label if you choose later.

Personalized Mason Jar Labels on Citrus Paper

Home Made pickles and preserves are a gift of love that should bear your label proudly. And what better canvas for your signature label than a delightfully aromatic citrus paper you've made yourself? It's a lot easier to do than you might think, and adds a warm, homey touch that will long be remembered.

Follow the directions on page 186 for making Recycled Blender Paper, using the option that calls for thin strips of lemon or orange zest.

Unscrew the ring of the filled and sealed Mason jar and place the ring upside down on the paper. Trace the inner circle in pencil and cut out the circle. Don't worry if the paper frays slightly around the edge, as this will only add to the rustic feel.

Pick the household member with the best printing to inscribe in felt-tip pen the contents of the jar and a message like "Made expressly for (recipient) by (your name)."

Rub the back of the label with a glue stick, press it firmly on the metal seal and rub smooth, and screw the ring back on.

Kosher Dills

Legend has it that an 1890s debutante once substituted a pail of pickles for the basket of cookies young ladies customarily lowered from their window to reward serenaders, only to find a pickle impaled on each picket of the front fence the next morning.

We think your household will prove more appreciative of this quintessential deli pickle—here in the quickest version ever! The refrigerator process not only adds ease, but produces a crisp pickle that holds its taste over the crunch of time.

❖ ❖ ❖ **F**or any of the cucumber recipes, a grape leaf or two may be added to each jar if extra crispness is desired. ❖ ❖ ❖

> 2 dill flowers
> 2 garlic cloves, peeled and halved lengthwise
> 1 small, dried hot chili
> 1¼ pounds (8–10) pickling cucumbers
> 6 long sprigs fresh dill
> 1 tablespoon coarse kosher salt

Put a dill flower, 2 half cloves of garlic, and the dried chili on the bottom of a sterilized 1-quart Mason jar. Add the cucumbers upright, leaving a small hole in the center. Fill the hole with the sprigs of dill. If using shorter cucumbers (3 to 4 inches long), add a few more on top to fill the jar to the shoulder. Add the remaining dill flower and half cloves of garlic. Top with the salt.

Fill the jar with cold water to within ⅛ inch of the top. Place a sterilized seal firmly on top and screw on the ring. Shake the jar a few times to dissolve the salt.

❖ ❖ ❖ **V**ariation: For "Half-Sour" Dills, which are milder and crunchier, refrigerate the pickles after the first 4 to 5 days; do not let them sit for the additional 2 days. ❖ ❖ ❖

Place the jar upside down on a counter, out of direct sunlight and away from heat. Leave the jar for 4 to 5 days, alternately flipping it right side up one day and upside down the next, until the liquid inside becomes murky. Let sit right side up for 2 more days, then refrigerate.

The pickles should be ready to eat as soon as chilled, with a refrigerator shelf life of about 6 months. However, if you don't like hot pickles, remove the chili pepper after 1 month.

Yield = 1 quart

Dilled Beans

Try this recipe in both the traditional version that has graced farmhouse dinner tables for generations, and in our updated variation, which substitutes sugar peas for beans and adds an undertone of pepper. Either version makes a great gift, so you can target the culinary conservatives and those with reform-minded taste buds on your list. Both can do double duty as an easy, light side dish or as an hors d'oeuvre.

⅔ cup distilled white vinegar
⅔ cup water
1 tablespoon coarse kosher salt
1 dill flower
2 garlic cloves, peeled and halved lengthwise
1 fresh serrano pepper
⅛ teaspoon celery seed
¼ teaspoon mustard seed
¼ teaspoon whole white peppercorns
1 pound mixed green and wax beans, trimmed
5 sprigs fresh dill

Bring a pot of water, sufficient to cover an inch or 2 over the top of a 1-pint Mason jar, to a boil. Using tongs, submerge the jar into the water and boil for at least 5 to 6 minutes, adding the seal toward the end. Keep the water at a boil.

Meanwhile, combine the vinegar, water, and salt in a large glass measuring cup or other microwave-safe container and bring to a boil in a microwave oven (about 3 minutes at full power) or over high heat in a small, nonreactive saucepan.

Carefully remove the jar from the boiling water. Put the dill flower, garlic, pepper, and spices on the bottom. Pack the beans upright, interspersed with the dill sprigs, and fill with the boiling vinegar mixture to within ¼ inch of the top of the jar. Wipe the mouth of the jar clean.

Remove the seal from the boiling water and place firmly on top of the jar. Screw the ring on immediately.

Put the jar through a 15-minute hot-water bath (see page 6). Remove the jar from the hot-water bath with tongs, flip it upside down, let it sit overnight, and check the seal.

The beans should be ready to eat in 3 to 4 days, with a shelf life of at least 1 year.

Yield = 1 pint

✧ ✧ ✧ **Variation: For an interesting twist, substitute sugar peas for beans. Given their larger size, you'll need only about 6 ounces for a 1-pint yield.**

We like them on the spicy side, so we double the amount of white peppercorns and add ¼ teaspoon red pepper flakes, omitting the serrano pepper, celery seed, and mustard seed. Leave the stem on the sugar peas. Otherwise, follow directions as given for dilled beans.

To eat, grab the stem, peel the pod open, and remove the tender peas. ✧ ✧ ✧

Peppered Okra

Long a staple of rural Southern kitchens, okra is shedding its down-home image as urban cooks put it to new uses. This version, with its distinctive pepper flavor, serves equally well as cocktail fare or as an accent to blander foods.

1¼ cups distilled white vinegar
1 cup water
2 tablespoons coarse kosher salt
4 garlic cloves, peeled and slightly crushed
4 fresh cayenne chili peppers
2 teaspoons mustard seed
2 pounds (48–50 2- to 3-inch-long pods) okra
4 sprigs fresh dill

Fill a large pot with enough water to cover the Mason jars by an inch or 2. Bring to a boil, then submerge jars into the water, using tongs. Boil for 5 to 6 minutes, adding the seals after 3 to 4 minutes. Keep the water at a boil until all the jars are filled and sealed.

Meanwhile, combine the vinegar, water, and salt in a microwave-safe container and bring to a boil in a microwave oven (about 3 minutes at full power). This may also be done on the stove in a small, nonreactive saucepan over high heat.

Remove a jar from the boiling water. Put a garlic clove, a chili pepper, and ½ teaspoon of the mustard seed on the bottom. Stand the okra in the jar upright, alternating thick and thin ends of the pods, along with a sprig of dill. Make sure the pods are wedged in tightly.

Pour in the vinegar mixture to cover the okra, filling to within ½ inch of the top of the jar. Wipe the mouth of the jar clean. Using tongs, remove a seal from the boiling water and place firmly atop the jar. Screw the ring on immediately and set aside. Repeat this process until all the jars are filled and sealed.

Put the jars through a 15-minute hot-water bath (see page 6).

Carefully remove the jars from the hot-water bath with tongs, flip upside down, let sit overnight on a dish towel placed atop the counter, and check seals.

The okra should be ready to eat in 1 week, with a shelf life of at least 1 year.

Yield = Four ½-pints

❖ ❖ ❖ **To yield two 1-pint jars of peppered okra, reduce the total amount of garlic, chili peppers, mustard seed, and dill sprigs by half, and use 24 to 25 okra pods 3 to 4 inches long.** ❖ ❖ ❖

Sour Cherries

We think this is the most elegant of our pickling recipes. It starts with a patrician among seasonal fruits, the sour cherry, available for only a brief time in midsummer. The end result is definitely an adult pickle—a sophisticated medley of sweet and savory flavors that produces a pronounced pucker.

1 cup balsamic vinegar
⅔ cup water
¼ cup dark brown sugar, firmly packed
1 strip lemon zest, 3 to 4 inches long and about 1 inch wide
6 whole cloves
6 allspice berries
1 cinnammon stick
¾ pound (about 2 cups) firm, ripe, unpitted sour cherries

Combine the vinegar, water, brown sugar, lemon zest, cloves, allspice, and cinnamon in a medium nonreactive saucepan. Stir and bring to a boil over medium heat. Reduce the heat and maintain a gently rolling boil for 15 minutes.

Meanwhile, fill a kettle with water to cover an inch or 2 over the top of a 1-pint Mason jar and bring to a boil. Using tongs, submerge the jar into the water and boil for 5 to 6 minutes. Add the seal and allow to keep boiling.

Add the cherries to the vinegar mixture. Raise the heat to high, bring back to a boil, and boil an additional 2 minutes.

Ladle the cherry mixture into a sterilized Mason jar, or pour it in with a widemouthed canning funnel. Fill the jar to within ⅛ inch of the top, making sure to use as many of the whole ingredients as possible, including the cloves and allspice berries. Don't worry if you have some extra liquid left.

Wipe the mouth of the jar clean. Place a seal on top firmly, and screw the ring on.

Quick Corned Beef

There's no need to wait for Saint Patrick's Day when you can "corn" the beef yourself while it cooks. This recipe utilizes Sour Gherkins and a bit of their pickling brine to achieve a subtle, old-fashioned brisket taste, less salty and spicy than the deli variety.

> 3-pound Boston-cut beef chuck roast
> 2 Sour Gherkins, quartered lengthwise
> ¼ cup Sour Gherkin pickling brine
> ¼ teaspoon pickling spice

Preheat the oven to 325° F.

Using a sharp paring knife, make 8 evenly spaced, 2-inch-deep incisions into the side of the roast, twisting the knife to create a cavity. Insert a pickle quarter into each space.

Line a baking pan with a doubled sheet of aluminum foil about 2½ times the length of the roast, making sure to fold the foil up the sides of the pan. Place the roast in the pan, pour the brine over, and sprinkle the pickling spice on top. Bring the long ends of the foil together and roll to secure, then fold up the sides to enclose the roast.

Bake for 1½ hours (or 30 minutes per pound). Remove from the oven, slit open the foil, and let the roast sit for 10 minutes before slicing thinly across the grain, starting with the smaller end. Garnish, of course, with Sour Gherkins and *Home Made Dijon-Style Mustard* (page 59).

Yield = 4–6 servings

Put the jar through a 15-minute hot-water bath (see page 6) if you intend to ship the cherries.

Set the jar upside down overnight, then check the seal. Store in a cool, dark place.

The cherries should be ready to eat in a week to 10 days, with a shelf life of at least 1 year.

Yield = 1 pint

Sour Gherkins

Gherkins are the traditional accompaniment to cold meats and sausages. We like them on the sour side, with lots of character. This recipe yields a quart, which should keep your larder stocked through the winter.

> 4 cups water
> 7 teaspoons pickling salt
> 1½ teaspoons pickling spice
> 6 sprigs fresh dill
> 2 dill flowers
> 2 garlic cloves, peeled and slightly crushed
> 1 pound (16 to 20 2-inch-long) pickling cucumbers

In a medium, nonreactive saucepan, combine the water, pickling salt, and pickling spice and bring to a boil over high heat. Reduce the heat to low and simmer, covered, for 5 minutes. Remove from the heat, uncover, and let cool. (To speed cooling, set the pan in a sink filled with 2 inches of cold water and some ice cubes.)

Place all 6 dill sprigs, 1 of the dill flowers, and 1 garlic clove on the bottom of a sterilized 1-quart Mason jar. Add the cucumbers. Top with the remaining dill flower and garlic clove, leaving about 1 inch at the top of the jar.

Pour the cooled brine into the jar to within ⅛ inch of the top. Don't be concerned if you have a little excess liquid, but do make sure all the spices get into the jar. Place a sterilized seal firmly on top and screw the ring on.

Place the jar upside down on a counter overnight, out of direct sunlight and away from heat, then refrigerate.

The gherkins should be ready to eat 10 days after refrigerating, with a refrigerator shelf life of about 6 months.

Yield = 1 quart

Zucchini Bread & Butter Pickles

This version of the classic bread and butter pickle is more savory than the mass-produced variety, with no telltale commercial crinkle. Because zucchini is readily available, you can make this year-round. Use either two 1-pint Mason jars or a 1-quart jar.

> 1½ pounds (about 6 1-inch-thick) zucchini
> 4 small white onions, peeled and quartered
> 3 tablespoons coarse kosher salt
> 2½ cups water
> 1¼ cups distilled white vinegar
> ½ teaspoon celery seed
> 1¼ teaspoons mustard seed
> ⅜ teaspoon ground turmeric
> ⅜ teaspoon dry mustard
> 1¼ cups sugar

Trim and cut the zucchini into ¼- to ⅜-inch-thick slices. Combine the zucchini slices, onion, salt, and water in a bowl, mix well, and let sit for 2 hours. Transfer to a colander and rinse under cold running water. Drain and set aside.

In a large kettle, put enough water to cover an inch or 2 above the top of the Mason jars. Bring to a boil, then submerge jars into the water, using tongs. Boil for 5 to 6 minutes, adding the seals after 3 to 4 minutes. Keep at a boil.

Combine the vinegar, celery seed, mustard seed, turmeric, dry mustard, and sugar in a small, nonreactive saucepan and bring to a boil over high heat. Throw in the zucchini and onion, turn the heat off, and let sit for 10 minutes, then bring back to a boil over high heat.

Remove a jar from the boiling water with tongs. Taking care to retrieve zucchini, onion, and spices, ladle the mixture into the jar, filling to within ¼ inch of the top. (A widemouthed canning funnel will prove particularly helpful.)

Wipe the mouth of the jar clean. Using tongs, remove a seal from the boiling water and place firmly atop the jar. Screw on the ring and set aside.

If using pint jars, repeat the process for the second jar.

Put the jars through a 15-minute hot-water bath (see page 6) if you intend to ship them.

Turn the jars upside down and let sit overnight on a dish towel

Antipasto Grazing

One of our favorite ways to show off pickles is to arrange a selection of antipasti plates featuring various other *Home Made* creations. This makes a stylish spread for 4, which can serve either as an indulgent first course or as a light late-evening supper.

FOR THE CENTERPIECE DISH:
Place a small bowl or ramekin in the center of a large plate and fill with about ½ cup Zucchini Bread and Butter Pickles. Ring the bowl with 5 or 6 Sour Tomato wedges. Arrange ½ pint Peppered Okra around the plate, radiating from the ring of Sour Tomatoes. Intersperse 12 Kosher Dill spears (3 pickles quartered lengthwise) amid the okra. Scatter Basil Tomatoes over the entire plate.

FOR ANTIPASTI #1:
Cut 8 slices from a baguette of Classic French Bread (page 156) and toast them lightly. Spread Herbed Chèvre (page 87) over each slice. Top each with 2 thin strips of "Sun-Dried" Tomatoes (page 194) that have been reconstituted in Garlic Oil (page 38).

FOR ANTIPASTI #2:
Spread a thin layer of Crème Fraîche (page 88) on 8 crackers. Top each with 2 slices of Smoked Salmon (page 109) and garnish with a sprig of fresh dill.

FOR ANTIPASTI #3:
Spread a little Honey Mustard (page 57) on 8 slices Honey-

Basted, Hickory-Smoked Ham (page 108). Place a Sour Gherkin spear (2 gherkins quartered lengthwise) on each slice, and roll the ham around the pickle.

FOR ANTIPASTI #4:

Top each of 8 cooked Chicken Sausage patties (page 124) with about ½ teaspoon Red Pepper Jelly (page 60).

Scatter the antipasti plates on the table around the pickle centerpiece. Finish the arrangement with a second small bowl filled with about ½ cup Sour Cherries.

on a counter. Check the seals, then store in a cool, dark place.

The pickles should be ready to eat in 2 to 3 days, with a shelf life of at least 1 year.

Yield = 2 pints or 1 quart

Sour Tomatoes

Here we use one of fall's most treasured harvests—green tomatoes. Green tomatoes can actually be had earlier in the year by picking tomatoes before they ripen; in autumn you will find green tomatoes in ready abundance.

> ¼ cup distilled white vinegar
> 4 cups hot water
> 3 tablespoons coarse kosher salt
> 2 garlic cloves, peeled and halved lengthwise
> 2 dill flowers
> 4 sprigs fresh dill
> 4 green tomatoes, quartered
> 1 tablespoon pickling spice

Combine the vinegar and water in a medium, nonreactive saucepan over high heat. Stir in the salt until it dissolves. Bring to a boil and continue to boil for 5 minutes. Remove from the heat and allow to cool thoroughly.

Place 2 garlic halves and a dill flower in a sterilized 1-quart Mason jar. Stack the tomato quarters loosely in the jar, interspersing with the sprigs of dill. Top with the remaining garlic and dill flower. The contents should reach only to the shoulder of the jar.

Add the cooled vinegar mixture to within ¼ inch of the top. Put a sterilized seal firmly on top, making sure the mouth of the jar is clean and dry, and screw on the ring.

Place the jar upside down on a counter, out of direct sunlight and away from heat. Leave the jar for 4 to 5 days, alternately flipping it right side up one day and upside down the next, until the liquid inside becomes murky. Store in the refrigerator.

The tomatoes should be ready to eat within 2 days after refrigerating, with a refrigerator shelf life of about 6 months. Don't be alarmed if the garlic turns purple or blue; this occurs because of a harmless acid reaction.

Yield = 1 quart

Basil Tomatoes

Farmers' market stalls brimming with fresh cherry tomatoes in vibrant yellows, oranges, and reds inspired this colorful rendition. Most pickles fall into the workhorse category of the food world, but this recipe could coast on its looks alone. Serve as an appetizer or as an attractive change from the traditional green salad.

⅔ cup distilled white vinegar
⅔ cup water
1 tablespoon coarse kosher salt
3 thin lemon slices
1 garlic clove, peeled and halved lengthwise
1 pound cherry tomatoes of mixed colors
4 fresh basil leaves

Combine the vinegar, water, and salt in a large glass measuring cup or other microwave-safe container and bring to a boil in a microwave oven (about 3 minutes at full power), or bring to a boil over high heat on the stove in a small, nonreactive saucepan. Set aside to cool.

Put a lemon slice and the garlic on the bottom of a sterilized 1-pint Mason jar. Add half of the tomatoes and 2 basil leaves, then another lemon slice. Add the remaining tomatoes and basil leaves, filling only to the shoulder of the jar. Top with the last lemon slice.

Add the cooled vinegar mixture to within ⅛ inch of the top. Place a sterilized seal firmly on top and screw the ring on.

Turn upside down and let sit overnight, then refrigerate.

The tomatoes should be ready to eat 5 to 7 days after refrigerating, with a refrigerator shelf life of about 3 months.

Yield = 1 pint

Spicy Cornichons

No pickling treatise would be complete without an old-fashioned pickle-barrel-variety recipe. This is the barrel-type pickle in our kitchen, packed, if not in a barrel, in a gallon jug. It's dipped into constantly for a quick nibble, to dress up humble cold meats or bring a tony pâté down to earth, or to add life to tartar sauce or Russian dressing.

This recipe calls for neither hot sealing nor refrigeration. However, it contains enough vinegar to keep for about 3 months if stored in a cool, dark place, out of direct sun and bright light.

> 5 pounds (about 160 1-inch-long) pickling cucumbers
> 1 cup pickling salt
> 4 sprigs fresh tarragon
> 1 small white onion, peeled and sliced ¼ inch thick
> 2 large bay leaves
> 1 teaspoon whole black peppercorns
> 3½ teaspoons mustard seed
> 2 teaspoons allspice berries
> 1 teaspoon whole cloves
> 2 cups white wine vinegar
> 1 cup tarragon vinegar

In a very large (at least 6-quart) nonreactive container, combine the cucumbers and salt. Shake the container to mix well; you want to coat the cucumbers thoroughly with salt. Cover the container with a cloth and set aside for 24 hours, shaking it occasionally when you pass by.

Transfer the cucumbers to a colander and rinse well under cold running water.

Place the tarragon sprigs on the bottom of a 1-gallon clamp jar with a tight-sealing lid. Layer the cucumbers and onion rings. Add the spices, pour in the vinegars, and clamp shut. Store in a cool, dark place.

The cornichons should be ready to eat in a week to 10 days, with a shelf life of about 3 months.

Yield = 1 gallon

Preserves

Like pickling, salting, and drying, preserving was once an important means of keeping foods beyond their season.

Victorians embraced this undertaking with considerable ardor—which is fortunate in light of the quantities they preserved, as well as the rather rudimentary equipment sometimes involved. (One 1908 household encyclopedia tells how to take a hammer and chisel to an old wash boiler to adapt it for preserving.)

The relative economy of home preserving was often stressed, for as one period source noted: "Prices ranging from 75 cents to $1.50 per quart at retail for a high grade article are not infrequent."

THE BASICS

Classic preserving involves boiling fruits in sugar syrup to produce jellies and jams, which use the juice of the fruit; preserves and marmalades, in which pieces of fruit are added; and fruit butters, using mashed fruit from which the juice has boiled off.

"Freezer" preserves are a twentieth-century invention where the fruit and sugar are preserved by freezing rather than cooking. Although they have just about the same shelf life in the freezer as cooked preserves have in the pantry, freezer preserves can't be shipped and are really best used as a quick way to supply your own household.

We've also included recipes for mincemeat and chutneys, which are actually hybrids of preserving and pickling in that both sugar and vinegar are preservatives.

Most recipes yield from three to five ½-pint jars, which we've found to be a manageable volume, yet one that produces enough of a supply for home use and gift giving to make the endeavor worthwhile.

Most recipes involve hot sealing. Be sure to heat both the containers and the contents according to directions, and to fill and seal each jar before going on to the next, as degree of heat and speed of sealing are important. Any preserves that you decide not to store can be eaten as soon as they've cooled a bit.

For home use, hot-water baths are called for only in Strawberry

Painting Jelly Pots & Mason Jars

Hand painting colorful jelly pots to hold your gifts is simple and will leave an impression of thoughtfulness long after the last bit of preserves has been consumed. Just slip the sealed Mason jar into the decorated jelly pot and pack with color-coordinated tissue paper or bubble wrap for shipping.

We also offer suggestions for decorating the Mason jars themselves, but note that one option is best executed before the jar is filled.

More is definitely merrier with these projects. Even younger children can participate with careful supervision and some patient guidance.

You will need:

· Solid white ceramic jelly pots, large enough to hold ½-pint Mason jars (available from crafts shops, housewares stores, and kitchenware stores, or see the Source Guide)
· ½-inch masking tape
· Small, soft-bristle paintbrushes
· Acrylic ceramic paint (This is water-soluble while wet, but indelible when totally dry and oven-baked. It's available in most crafts shops, or see Source Guide.)
· Optional: a small, unused sponge (a narrow strip cut off the end of a kitchen sponge will do fine)
· Optional: indelible, nontoxic acrylic glass paint

Cut 4 strips of masking tape about 5 to 6 inches long, depending on the size of the pot. Leaving a triangular "tip" of masking tape at the top exposed (this will make removing easier), press the first strip onto the pot, starting at the top rim (or directly under the lip if the pot has one) and running at a 45-degree angle down and to the left. Tuck the bottom tip under the pot.

Apply the remaining strips the same way at equal intervals around the pot. This pattern will produce 4 bold, thick stripes, or use your imagination and vary the pattern, changing the number and thickness of the tape strips.

Grasping the pot at the top and bottom, or on the tape, paint between the strips of masking tape. Apply the paint evenly, taking care not to leave globs, especially along the tape. You may want to paint the knob or handle on the pot's cover as well.

Let the paint dry for at least an hour, until the edges along the tape begin to look dry. Carefully peel off the tape; the paint should still be soluble enough at this point that you can dab any excess off with a damp cloth if need be.

Set the pot aside and let dry for 3 to 4 days. When thoroughly dry, place on the center rack of a cold oven, turn the heat on to 375° F., and "bake" for 1 hour. Turn off the heat and allow the pot to cool inside the closed oven, about 2 hours. When cool, the pot will be waterproof, heat-resistant, and ready to use.

Rhubarb Preserves and Meatless Mincemeat. We haven't found the additional step necessary in the other recipes, which we have made numerous times without ever having a seal not take. However, if you are going to ship, we recommend putting the Cooked Berry Preserves, Apricot Orange Marmalade, Apple Butter, and chutneys through a hot-water bath as well.

Lastly, we include a novel twist in two recipes where fruit is preserved in alcohol. These treats do not require hot sealing since the alcohol is sufficient to preserve the fruit, but are best if left to age for a few weeks.

As with pickling, fresh ingredients are crucial to successful preserving. Although many fruits are available year-round, the cost skyrockets in the winter and the degree of freshness is never as certain. We prefer to buy locally grown fruit that's in season from farmers' markets and roadside fruit stands. Another enticing option is to take a field trip to a "you-pick-it" farm or orchard (see page 27).

Always remove leaves and stems, rinse fruit thoroughly under running water, and allow it to warm to room temperature before beginning the recipe. Don't forget to mark the contents and date on each jar after sealing (using a grease pencil or peel-off label will leave the surface clean for painting and decorating).

Cooked Berry Preserves

"Preserved fruit," according to one "book of receipts" from the last turn of the century, "is perhaps most often classified with candy and other sweet-meats as a luxury."

We think you'll agree! The sweetness and smooth texture of these pre-serves derive solely from the fruit and sugar, with no pectin. Leave whole chunks of fruit intact to lend a rustic, old-fashioned feel.

> 2 pints blueberries
> 4 cups sugar
> 2 tablespoons freshly squeezed lemon juice
> 1 teaspoon grated lemon zest

Combine the blueberries and sugar in a nonreactive Dutch oven. Mash about ⅔ of the berries to release their juice, leaving the remaining fruit whole. Bring to a boil over medium heat, stirring with a wooden spoon to dissolve the sugar completely. Reduce the heat to maintain a constant low boil and cook for 15 minutes; gently scrape the sides and bottom of the pot every 5 minutes or so with a wooden spoon to incorporate any sugar crystals into the boiling mixture. At the last moment, stir in the lemon juice and zest, which keep the preserves from darkening.

Meanwhile, fill a large stockpot with sufficient water to cover ½-pint Mason jars, allowing an inch or 2 extra depth since some water will boil off. Bring to a boil. Using tongs, submerge 4 jars into the water and boil for 5 to 6 minutes. Add the seals toward the end. Allow to continue boiling.

One by one, carefully remove each jar from the boiling water, fit with a canning funnel and ladle in the preserves to within ¼ inch of the top. Wipe the mouth of the jar clean. Remove a seal from the boiling water and place atop the jar, then screw on the ring.

Put the jars through a 15-minute hot-water bath (see page 6) if shipping.

Let the jars sit overnight, turned upside down on a dish towel. Check the seals.

The preserves should be ready to eat immediately, with a shelf life of at least 1 year.

Yield = Four ½-pints

PAINTING THE MASON JAR

If you're using "quilted" jars, which have a raised cross-hatch pattern through the glass, you might want to paint the jar to match the stripes on the jelly pot.

Use the same acrylic ceramic paint you used to paint the jelly pot. Dip an end of the sponge into the paint, and apply a light coat over the jar, making sure that the paint gets into the crevices between the crosshatches. Using the clean, long edge of sponge, rub the entire surface of the jar lightly, so you remove the paint from the raised pattern only. Wipe the raised surface again lightly with a dry paper towel. This will leave a clear, shiny quilted pattern over the raised surface of the glass, with satiny color in the crevices. Allow the paint to dry for 2 hours.

Many quilted jars have a flat oval set into the crosshatch pattern, where you can paint the name of the recipient or contents.

Another popular line of ½-pint Mason jars has an embossed fruit arrangement on the glass that can be colorfully painted. This is much easier to do with an empty jar that can be held up to the light: Use indelible acrylic glass paints, which are heat-resistant and will withstand sterilization or a hot-water bath. Make sure that the paint you buy is nontoxic (lead-free). Allow to dry completely, according to manufacturer's instructions, before using the jar.

Freezer Fruit Preserves

The fruit in this recipe is actually preserved by freezing, which dispenses with lengthy cooking and hot sealing. The resulting preserves have an intense color and fresh fruit taste. Talk about easy!

> ✧ ✧ ✧ *W*e use Mason jars for Freezer Fruit Preserves because they are so convenient and make it easy to keep a store on hand. You can also use clamp jars, plastic storage containers, or any other receptacle that seals tightly enough to prevent freezer burn. ✧ ✧ ✧

½ pint raspberries
½ pint blackberries
2½ cups plus 2 tablespoons sugar
2½ tablespoons fruit pectin
6 tablespoons water

Combine the raspberries and blackberries in a large, nonreactive bowl. Coarsely mash with a potato masher or a fork, leaving some fruit whole. You should have about 1½ cups of crushed fruit.

Add the sugar and stir until most of it has been absorbed into the berry juice; the consistency should be thick and soupy. Set aside for 10 to 15 minutes, or until the mixture no longer appears or tastes granular.

Put the pectin into a small saucepan and add the water, stirring until the pectin is dissolved. Stirring constantly, bring to a boil over high heat and boil for 1 minute. Remove from the heat, dump into the berry mixture, and stir vigorously until thoroughly mixed, about 3 minutes.

Transfer the mixture into 3 sterilized and thoroughly dried ½-pint containers, leaving about ½ inch at the top for the preserves to expand when frozen, and seal.

Let sit at room temperature for 24 hours, then freeze for at least 24 hours.

The preserves have a shelf life of at least 1 year in the freezer, or 4 to 6 weeks in the refrigerator after thawing. (Thaw for a few minutes at room temperature before using.)

Yield = Three ½-pints

> ✧ ✧ ✧ *I*n the Cooked Berry Preserves and Freezer Fruit Preserves recipes, feel free to use other fruits than the ones we call for. Substitute an equal amount of raspberries, blackberries, hulled strawberries, stemmed gooseberries or fresh currants, or any creative combination for the blueberries in Cooked Berry Preserves. A pint of blueberries or hulled strawberries, or a full pint of raspberries or blackberries by itself will yield delicious Freezer Fruit Preserves as well. ✧ ✧ ✧

Strawberry Rhubarb Preserves

Let the kids have the other preserves and save this for your own breakfast—rhubarb is a singularly adult taste treat. Here, its natural tartness is tempered with strawberries. Try it on Home Made *Semolina Challah (page 151) fresh out of the oven.*

> 1 pound rhubarb, trimmed and cut into 1-inch slices
> (about 2 cups)
> 4 cups sugar
> 2 pints strawberries
> 2 tablespoons freshly squeezed lemon juice
> 1 tablespoon coarsely grated orange zest

In a large bowl, combine the rhubarb and sugar, mixing well. Set aside at room temperature, uncovered, for at least 8 hours. The rhubarb should appear "cooked"—mushy and juicy.

Hull the strawberries and cut each into 3 to 4 slices. Add to the rhubarb and stir thoroughly, making sure that no sugar residue remains on the bottom of the bowl. Mash with a potato masher, leaving about a third of the sliced strawberries intact.

Transfer the mixture to a nonreactive Dutch oven and bring to a boil over medium heat. Adjust the heat to maintain a low boil and cook for a total of 25 minutes. After the first 5 minutes, gently scrape any sugar from the sides and bottom of the pan with a wooden spoon. Repeat in another 5 minutes.

◊ ◊ ◊ **After the Strawberry Rhubarb Preserves have cooked about 15 minutes, skim the foam off the top, put into a glass container, cover, and refrigerate. When chilled, it makes a "strawberry fluff" that children—and more than a few grownups—find irresistible on toast.**
◊ ◊ ◊

Versatile Preserve Sauces

In addition to their obvious uses, *Home Made* preserves are wonderful bases for sauces, glazes, and relishes. Here are a few suggestions, but have fun creating your own recipes using *Home Made* preserves.

FRUIT SAUCES FOR POULTRY, PORK, OR GAME (SERVE WARM ON THE SIDE)

For every ½ cup Raspberry or Blueberry Preserves (cooked or freezer preserves work equally well), add ¼ cup chicken stock or bouillon and 2 tablespoons Raspberry Vinegar (page 45) or Blueberry Vinegar (page 44).

APRICOT ORANGE GLAZE AND SAUCE FOR CHICKEN, ROCK CORNISH HENS, OR CAPON

For a glaze (brush on the bird before putting it in the oven or use to baste while roasting), mix ¼ cup Apricot Orange Marmalade with 2 tablespoons Coffee Liqueur (page 71).

For a sauce (serve warm on the side), heat ½ cup Apricot Orange Marmalade with ¼ cup chicken stock or bouillon. If desired, spike with 2 teaspoons Orange Brandy Cordial (page 68) or Coffee Liqueur (page 71).

STRAWBERRY RHUBARB RELISH

For a refreshing change from the all too common cranberry relish on your holiday buffet, quarter an unpeeled orange and remove the seeds. Coarsely chop in a food processor. Add

When the fruit has cooked for 20 minutes, stir in the lemon juice and orange zest.

Meanwhile, bring a large pot of water to a boil, sufficient to cover an inch or 2 above the top of ½-pint Mason jars. Place 5 jars into the boiling water, using tongs. Boil for 5 to 6 minutes, adding the seals toward the end, and leave at a boil.

Carefully remove the first jar, fit with a canning funnel, and ladle in the preserves to within ¼ inch of the top. Wipe the mouth of the jar clean and top with a seal. Screw the ring on immediately. Repeat for the remaining 4 jars.

Put the sealed jars through a hot-water bath for 15 minutes (see page 6).

Flip the jars upside down, set on a dish towel, and let sit overnight. Check the seals.

The preserves should be ready to eat immediately, with a shelf life of at least 1 year.

Yield = Five ½-pints

Apricot Orange Marmalade

Apricots make this classic more appealing to "sweet tooths" without sacrificing its distinct, tart bite. There's something about marmalade that conjures up hearth and home, for as an old Farm Journal *cookbook advises: "Bring out a jar of marmalade for breakfast the first winter morning a snowstorm strikes with fury."*

> 2 medium navel oranges
> 4½ cups pitted, sliced apricots (unpeeled)
> 3 cups sugar

Coarsely grate and reserve the zest from the oranges and peel off the white pith underneath. Separate the orange segments, cutting away the membranes and removing any seeds.

Combine the orange segments and zest, apricot slices, and sugar in a nonreactive Dutch oven and bring to a boil over medium heat. When the mixture begins to boil, mash the fruit coarsely with a long-handled wooden spoon, being careful not to let it spatter.

Reduce the heat enough to maintain a low boil, and cook for an additional 15 minutes. Every few minutes, gently scrape the bottom and sides of the pot with a wooden spoon and incorporate any sugar that may have crystallized.

Meanwhile, fill a large pot with sufficient water to cover an inch or 2 above the top of ½-pint Mason jars and bring to a boil. Submerge 4 jars into the water, using tongs. Boil for 5 to 6 minutes, adding the seals toward the end, and leave boiling.

One by one, extract the jars from the boiling water, fit with a canning funnel, and ladle in the fruit to within ¼ inch of the top. Wipe the mouth of the jar clean if needed, extract the seal and place firmly on top, and screw on the ring.

Put the jars through a 15-minute hot-water bath (see page 6) if shipping.

Let the jars sit upside down on a dish towel overnight. Check the seals.

The marmalade should be ready to eat immediately, with a shelf life of at least 1 year.

Yield = Four ½-pints

1½ cups whole fresh cranberries and ¼ cup Strawberry Rhubarb Preserves. Process until all the ingredients are finely chopped. Transfer to a bowl and garnish with 2 tablespoons blanched chopped almonds. Refrigerate at least 3 hours before serving.

Apple Butter

Rich, creamy, and slightly pungent, Apple Butter makes a nice change of pace for breakfast or as a thoroughly satisfying snack—it holds its own with hearty Home Made *Multigrain Bread (page 166).*

Don't peel the apples—the skin keeps the apples intact while cooking, and comes off easily afterward in a food mill.

> 4 pounds McIntosh apples, stems removed and cut into quarters
> 2 cups water
> 1 cup granulated sugar
> 1 cup dark brown sugar, firmly packed
> 1 teaspoon ground cinnamon
> ¾ teaspoon ground cloves
> ¼ cup freshly squeezed lemon juice
> 1 teaspoon finely grated lemon zest

Put the apples and water into a nonreactive Dutch oven. Cover and cook over medium heat until the apples are fork-tender, about 15 minutes. Remove from the heat.

Hand-Decorated Mason Jar Covers & Gift Cards

An easy way to package your preserves with panache, this project is also guaranteed to delight the younger members of your household!

You will need:

- Plain paper or tracing paper
- Scissors
- Small red potatoes, cut in half
- Paring knife
- 12-inch squares of solid, light-color cotton muslin (Each square will make four ½-pint Mason jar covers.)
- Opaque fabric paints (try a crafts shop or see the Source Guide)
- Felt tip pens
- Optional: pinking shears
- Inked stamp pads in colors similar to the fabric paints
- Unlined 3 x 5-inch index cards or sheets of light-color cardboard
- Paper punch
- Curling ribbon, decorative elastic ties, or strips of raffia

Choose a fruit that echoes the contents of the Mason jar (i.e., blueberries to decorate a jar of blueberry preserves, etc.). Draw your own artwork, about 1 inch in size, on a plain piece of paper, or trace a strawberry from the drawing on page 22.

Cut out the drawing and tape it onto the flat side of a potato half. Cut the outline of the fruit ⅛- to ¼-inch deep into the sur-

Using a slotted spoon, transfer the apples in batches into a food mill placed over a large bowl. Work the apples through the mill until all are pureed, periodically discarding the skin that accumulates.

Rinse out the Dutch oven. Add the apple pulp, sugars, and spices, mixing well. Stir in the lemon juice and zest. Cook over low heat for about 15 minutes, stirring occasionally, until the apple butter is thick enough to coat the back of a spoon, or no ring of water forms around the edge of a small amount spooned onto a saucer.

Meanwhile, bring to a boil a large pot filled with water enough to cover an inch or 2 over the top of ½-pint Mason jars. Using tongs, submerge 5 jars into the boiling water and boil for 3 to 4 minutes. Add the seals and boil another 2 minutes. Leave at a boil.

Remove the first jar from the boiling water with tongs. Fit with a canning funnel and ladle in the hot apple butter to within ¼ inch of the top. Carefully extract a seal from the boiling water and place firmly on top, making sure the mouth of the jar is free of residue. Screw the ring on. Repeat the process until all jars are filled and sealed.

Put the jars through a 15-minute hot-water bath (see page 6) if shipping.

Place the jars upside down on a dish towel and let sit out overnight. Check the seals.

The Apple Butter should be ready immediately, with a shelf life of at least 1 year.

Yield = Five ½-pints

Apple Chutney

We find Apple Chutney a pleasant, versatile change from the mango chutneys most frequently encountered in restaurants or in ready-made form. It brings out the best in a wide variety of meats and fish, and is the perfect accompaniment for any kind of mixed grill.

1½ pounds Jonathan apples (or another firm variety that will hold its shape when cooked), peeled, cored, and finely chopped (about 3½ cups)

1½ pounds McIntosh apples (or another soft variety that will fall apart in cooking), peeled, cored, and finely chopped (about 3½ cups)

¼ cup cider vinegar

2 cups distilled white vinegar

2 cups dark brown sugar, firmly packed

2 cups golden raisins

2 tablespoons finely minced crystallized ginger

1 teaspoon ground turmeric

½ teaspoon ground ginger

¼ teaspoon crushed red pepper flakes

⅛ teaspoon cayenne pepper

2 teaspoons finely minced garlic

1¼ teaspoons salt

2 tablespoons freshly squeezed orange juice

1 teaspoon dried tarragon

Combine all the ingredients in a nonreactive Dutch oven and bring to a boil over high heat. Lower the heat to medium-low and simmer, stirring occasionally, for about 20 minutes or until all the liquid has evaporated and the mixture has thickened.

While the chutney is simmering, bring to a boil a large pot of water (sufficient to cover an inch or 2 over the top of ½-pint Mason jars). Place 5 jars into the boiling water, using tongs. Boil for 3 to 4 minutes, add the seals, and boil another 2 minutes. Allow to continue boiling.

Carefully remove the first jar from the boiling water. Fit with a canning funnel and ladle the chutney to within ¼ inch of the top of the jar. Remove a seal and place firmly on top, making sure the mouth of the jar is clean. Screw the ring on. Repeat for the remaining 4 jars.

face of the potato and remove the paper. Using a paring knife, carefully cut off the outer part of the potato, leaving a raised impression of the fruit.

Bring on the aspiring artists! Firmly grasp the potato half, lightly dip the side with the fruit impression into the fabric paint, and stamp the design onto the muslin square. Let dry until the paint is no longer tacky, about 2 hours. Use felt-tip pens to finish the artwork (i.e., draw in the seeds and cap on strawberries or a stem and leaf on blueberries).

While the cloth dries, make gift cards by folding index cards in half, or by cutting 3-inch or 4-inch squares out of a sheet of cardboard paper and folding them in half. Rinse the paint from the potato and let it dry, moisten the surface on the stamp pad, and stamp a single fruit impression onto the outside of the card. Let dry and finish with a felt-tip pen as you did the cloth. On the inside, write the contents of the jar or a personal message. Punch a small hole in the upper left-hand corner of the card.

After the cloth is completely dry, cut it into four 6-inch squares. For a rustic touch, use pinking shears, cutting around the outside border before cutting into squares. Drape a square over the top of each jar.

Thread the gift card onto a strip of raffia, curling ribbon, or a decorative elastic tie, and fasten around the square of cloth.

Put the jars through a 15-minute hot-water bath (see page 6) if shipping.

Spread a clean dish towel on a countertop. Flip the jars upside down on the towel and let stand overnight. Check the seals.

The chutney should be ready to eat immediately, with a shelf life of at least 1 year.

Yield = Five ½-pints

Green Tomato Chutney

Here's another use for green tomatoes, our favorite autumn treat. A little tangier than the apple version, this chutney works best with cold meats and cheeses. Complete the charcuterie plate with some Home Made *Sour Gherkins (page 13).*

2¼ pounds green tomatoes, peeled, cored, and
    chopped into ¼- to ½-inch chunks (about 6 cups)
½ cup white tarragon vinegar
1 cup cider vinegar
1½ cups dark brown sugar, firmly packed
½ cup granulated sugar
1 teaspoon coarse kosher salt
2 tablespoons finely chopped crystallized ginger
1 cup golden raisins
1½ teaspoons ground coriander
2 teaspoons curry powder
1 tablespoon grated lemon zest
2 tablespoons freshly squeezed lemon juice
2 teaspoons finely chopped garlic

Put the tomatoes into a nonreactive Dutch oven. Add the remaining ingredients and bring to a boil over high heat. Reduce the heat to medium-low and simmer about 40 minutes, stirring occasionally, until most of the liquid has evaporated and the mixture has thickened.

When the chutney is close to done, fill a large pot with water sufficient to cover ½-pint Mason jars by an inch or 2 and bring it to a boil. Using tongs, submerge 3 jars into the boiling water and boil for 5 to 6 minutes, adding the seals toward the end. Leave at a boil.

Carefully remove a jar. Fit with a canning funnel and ladle in the chutney to within ¼ inch of the top. Clean the mouth of the jar, re-

If you're going to make something from scratch, why not start at the source? A burgeoning array of "you-pick-it" farms and orchards within a drive of an hour or two from many cities offers the opportunity for fun-filled excursions. Kids of all ages will enjoy the outing—from small children, who will love going on a quest to find the smallest (or reddest, or whatever) apple, to seniors, who may be more comfortable in the cooler hours of early morning or late afternoon.

Many you-pick-it devotees develop rituals around their fruit farm treks. One woman we know, who prefers not to bend over to pick fruit from low-lying bushes, keeps a pair of knee pads in the trunk of her car. To guard against telltale berry stains, she always wears blouses in the shade of the fruit she intends to pick.

Another friend and her infant daughter, neither of whom has the time or patience for more sedentary sun worshipping, regularly don bathing suits and go picking at high noon.

move a seal and place firmly on top, and screw the ring on. Repeat with the other two jars.

Put the jars through a 20-minute hot-water bath (see page 6) if shipping.

Let the jars sit out overnight, turned upside down on a kitchen towel. Check the seals.

The chutney should be ready to eat immediately, with a shelf life of at least 1 year.

Yield = Three ½-pints

Meatless Mincemeat

This is a light rendition of the Yuletide classic. Because we dispense with the meat, the mincemeat can be easily and safely sealed in Mason jars for gift giving or storing until you just "need a little Christmas."

> 2 pounds green tomatoes, cored and coarsely chopped (about 5 cups)
> ¾ pound Jonathan or other firm, tart apples, cored and coarsely chopped (about 1½ cups)
> ½ pound firm Bartlett pears, cored and coarsely chopped (about ¾ cup)

Personal quirks notwithstanding, you won't need to make a lot of special preparations before setting out. Wear durable, comfortable clothes and shoes, and a hat if you prefer a bit of shade. A pair of gardening gloves will protect sensitive skin. If you will be picking fruit that grows on low bushes (as opposed, for example, to apples from trees) and don't stoop easily, throw an old towel to kneel on into the car.

A Styrofoam cooler or insulated picnic bag is a good idea for transporting more delicate fruit, such as raspberries or currants, especially if you will be on the road for a while. Or bring along some towels to lay over bags of fruit in the car to keep them out of direct sunlight.

Seasonal availability of fruit differs according to geographic region, but, in general, cherries and apricots are ripe for picking in early summer, berries through the summer, and apples in later summer to fall.

In planning your excursion, allow 2 to 3 hours for picking. For an added treat, pack a basket of *Home Made* goodies for a picnic en route.

◈◈◈ **I**n addition to its use as a relish, mincemeat makes a great pie filling. If you're making the pies within a few days, dispense with sealing and store the mincemeat in the refrigerator.

To make two Mincemeat Pies, preheat the oven to 450° F.

Remove the mincemeat from the refrigerator and bring to room temperature. Mix in a little more rum and ½ cup chopped walnuts, if desired. Divide the mincemeat between two 9-inch pastry-lined pie plates, top each with a second crust, and crimp the edges of the crusts together. Prick the top crusts in 4 spots with the tines of a fork.

Bake for 10 minutes, then lower the oven temperature to 350° F. and bake about 20 minutes longer, or until the crust is golden. Remove the pies and cool on a rack. ◈◈◈

2 tablespoons freshly squeezed lemon juice
½ cup raisins
⅜ cup finely diced dried apricots
½ teaspoon finely grated lemon zest
½ tablespoon finely grated orange zest
½ teaspoon ground allspice
⅜ teaspoon ground nutmeg
⅜ teaspoon ground cloves
⅛ teaspoon ground ginger
¾ teaspoon ground cinnamon
1½ cups dark brown sugar, firmly packed
¼ cup white wine vinegar
¼ cup dark rum

Combine the tomatoes, apples, and pears in a nonreactive Dutch oven. Add the lemon juice and stir to coat.

Add all the remaining ingredients except the rum, mixing thoroughly. Bring to a boil over medium heat. Lower the heat and simmer, uncovered, for about 1¼ hours or until all the liquid has been absorbed and the mixture has thickened, stirring occasionally to make sure it doesn't stick to the bottom. Stir in the rum in the last few minutes of cooking.

When the mincemeat is almost done, fill a large pot with water sufficient to cover an inch or 2 over the top of the size Mason jars you will be using. Bring to a boil. Using tongs, place either a 1-quart Mason jar or two 1-pint jars into the boiling water. Boil for 3 to 4 minutes, add the seal or seals, and boil another 2 minutes. Leave at a boil.

Carefully remove a jar from the boiling water with tongs and fit with a canning funnel. Ladle in the boiling mincemeat to within ¼ inch of the top of the jar. Remove a seal from the boiling water and place firmly on top, making sure the mouth of the jar is clean. Screw the ring on immediately.

Repeat with the second jar if using the pints.

Process for 20 minutes in a hot-water bath (see page 6).

Turn the jars upside down on a dish cloth and allow to cool for at least 2 hours. Check the seals.

The mincemeat should be ready to eat the next day, with a shelf life of at least 1 year.

Yield = 1 quart or 2 pints, or enough to make two 9-inch pies

Brandied Fruit

In olden days, fruit preserved in alcohol was referred to as "bachelor's preserves"—whether because of the slightly wicked inclusion of spirits or because it was thought to provide a bachelor's only ration of fruit, we're not sure.

Of the single gentlemen so in demand by Victorian hostesses, few seemed to make it to a ripe old age, prompting one observer to speculate that "late hours and a confusion of sauces must have accounted for their early departure from the scene."

> 1 pint black currants, stemmed
> 1 pint red currants, stemmed
> 1 pint gooseberries, stemmed
> 1 pint black raspberries
> 4 cups sugar
> 4 cups brandy or cognac
> 4 cinnamon sticks
> 2 vanilla beans, cut in half crosswise

In a very large bowl, combine the currants, berries, and sugar, tossing gently to coat. Be careful not to crush the fruit.

Put 2 cups of the mixture in each of four 18-ounce clamp jars. Slowly pour 1 cup of brandy over the fruit. Put a cinnamon stick and half a vanilla bean in the center of each jar. Seal and store in a cool, dark place.

The fruit should be ready to eat in about 4 weeks, with a shelf life of 6 months.

Yield = Four 18-ounce jars

◇ ◇ ◇ **U**se black raspberries, which are firmer and will hold their shape better than the red variety. Gooseberries may vary in color from light green to purple; any shade will do.

We love the tartness that currants lend and the novelty of whole preserved gooseberries, but encourage experimenting— substitute any combination of blackberries, blueberries, or pitted cherries.

For an unusual but hardy variation, replace the brandy with a good-quality sipping bourbon or sour mash whiskey. ◇ ◇ ◇

Brandied Sour Cherry Sauce

In this two-step recipe, the delectable midsummer fruit is first preserved in alcohol and sugar, then made into a sauce a few weeks later. Of course, who's to tell if a few of the potent cherries are diverted for sampling on the way? The resulting sauce is rich, chock-full of cherries, and versatile, making an elegant topping for ice cream or cake.

For the cherry preserves:

    1 pound sour cherries, pitted (about 2 cups)
    1¼ cups sugar
    1 cinnamon stick
    2 cups brandy

For the sauce:

    ⅓ cup sugar
    2 tablespoons water
    ½ teaspoon glycerin

Put a third of the cherries (about ⅔ cup) in the bottom of a sterilized and thoroughly dried 1-quart Mason jar. Add ¼ cup of the sugar, layering the ingredients as you add them; do *not* mix. Add another third of the cherries, then ½ cup of the sugar. Top with the remaining cherries, then the last ½ cup sugar.

Push the cinnamon stick through the center of the jar. Pour the brandy over the cherries and sugar, leaving ⅛ inch at the top of the jar. Clean the mouth of the jar if necessary, place a seal firmly on top, and screw the ring on. Store in a cool, dark place for 4 weeks.

To make the sauce, strain the cherry liquor through a fine sieve into a 4-cup glass measuring cup. Divide the cherries equally among three 12-ounce clamp jars.

Rinse the sieve and line with a flat-bottomed coffee filter. Fit over a clean Mason jar or a bowl that has a cover and gradually pour the cherry liquor through, allowing it to drip into the bowl. If the liquid is not yet clarified—if it still is milky and contains sediment—strain a second time, using a damp filter.

Combine the sugar and water in a small saucepan. Stir and simmer over medium-low heat for 5 minutes, until the sugar has totally dissolved, leaving a thin, clear syrup. Remove from the heat and stir in 2 tablespoons of the cherry liquor, dislodging any sugar crystals that may have clung to the pan. Let the syrup cool to room temperature, then stir in the glycerin.

When cool, pour the syrup into the cherry liquor, cover, and shake to blend. Divide evenly among the clamp jars and seal. Store in a cool, dark place.

The sauce should be ready to eat within 10 to 14 days, with a shelf life of about 6 months.

Yield = Three 12-ounce jars

Oils, Vinegars, & Condiments

Picture a cheesecloth-covered crock on a pantry shelf, its contents a vinegar culture steeping in wine. Close by sit an assortment of fruit and vegetable catsups. The aroma of just-picked apples cooking down into fresh applesauce emanates from the adjoining kitchen.

This image is classic, suspended in time and place; the setting could easily be the cluttered, subterranean kitchen of a town house in the 1890s.

Then picture a shelf of bottled oils, each infused with the intense flavor of horseradish, or garlic, or chili. Beside them are brightly colored flasks of fruit-flavored vinegars—peach, cranberry, raspberry—some festively finished with a sprig of lemon thyme or sage.

This image conjures up a kitchen of the 1990s, ready to dispense concoctions that would be alien to the subdued taste buds of our Victorian ancestors, in flavor combinations that they could barely have imagined in uses they would not have considered.

Perhaps more than any other chapter of *Home Made in the Kitchen*, this far-ranging collection of robust substances for cooking, dressing, and garnishing contemporary meals represents the essence of *Home Made*—the marriage of classic kitchen crafts to contemporary tastes.

In the spirit of the union, we present not only something old—actually, some things old—and some things new, but also something borrowed (our rendition of a horseradish-infused potato dish made popular by a Chicago restaurant) and something blue (the blueberry vinegar so favored by the chef-practitioners of California cuisine).

❁ ❁ ❁

INGREDIENTS

In making mayonnaise, in which eggs are lightly cooked, we like to play it safe and use *Nest Eggs®* brand eggs (see Source Guide), or another brand of eggs from "uncaged" hens, raised in much more sanitary conditions than those that produce most commercial eggs, and fed drug-free diets. Nest Eggs® are also produced under a salmonella control program.

EQUIPMENT

The limited equipment requirements for *Home Made* oils, vinegars, and condiments are similar to those for pickling and preserving.

Start with a supply of *Ball or Kerr self-sealing Mason jars,* available at almost any supermarket in ½-pint, 1-pint, and 1-quart sizes. The jars and their rings are reusable, but the flat metal seals are not. *Replacement seals* are stocked alongside the Mason jars in most stores.

A sturdy pair of *long-handled, jar-lifting tongs* will enable you to safely submerge and retrieve jars and seals from boiling water. Designed specifically for this purpose, jar-lifting tongs are available from kitchenware stores.

A *widemouthed canning funnel,* also available from kitchenware stores, is useful in preparing catsups and savory jellies; jars can easily be filled with hot ingredients.

Many oil and vinegar recipes call for straining ingredients through *fine mesh sieves* into *glass measuring cups.* A small sieve fitted atop a 1-cup measuring cup is the best combination for smaller-yield recipes. For vinegars made in larger quantities and for those that require straining through *flat-bottom coffee filters,* use a medium sieve with a 2- or 4-cup measuring cup.

Mustard seed is put through a *grinder* in the preparation of *Home Made* mustards. Electric spice grinders are designed specifically for such tasks, although an electric coffee grinder or a manual nutmeg grinder will also serve the purpose. A *mortar and pestle* can be used in a pinch, but entails somewhat more effort in recipes that call for grinding mustard seed to a fine consistency.

We sometimes call for *nonreactive containers or pots.* Glass,

---

Paint-Drip Bottles with Hand-Painted Stoppers

For dramatic dinner table presentation, serve *Home Made* oils and vinegars in bottles, cruets, or flasks that have been painted in vivid free-form patterns in colors that match the table settings.

You will need:
· Acrylic paints in squirt bottles (available at crafts shops or see Source Guide)
· Optional: small, soft-bristle paintbrushes

To paint flasks, lay the flask flat on a layer of newspaper. Hold the bottle of paint a few inches above the flask and squirt the paint onto the flask in a free-form pattern. We usually start with some variation of an X and proceed as the muse inspires. Cover as little or as much of the flask as you wish, allowing the paint to run freely over the surface. Dry for about 12 hours and add a second color if desired. Repeat the process to paint the back side of the flask, or leave it plain.

To paint bottles or cruets, hold the container by its neck slanted downward at a 45-degree angle, suspended over newspaper. Squirt the paint on in a free-form pattern while rotating the bottle. Allow the paint to dry for about 12 hours, then add a second color if desired.

The effect can be carried onto the bottle or cruet stopper

if it is attached to a glass knob, or to the ceramic clamp stoppers affixed to flasks. Use the paint to cover the whole stopper, create a pattern of concentric circles, or dot the small circular indentation left at the top of the glass knob from the rod that was used to blow the glass.

enamel, stainless steel, or anodized aluminum (such as Calphalon or Magnalite) will do fine, but copper, plain aluminum, and cast iron combine with some ingredients to cause an unwanted chemical reaction. Enameled cast iron is nonreactive, but the enamel coating may stain.

With the exception of catsups and savory jellies, which are usually hot sealed in Mason jars, *Home Made* oils, vinegars, and condiments can be put into a variety of decorative bottles, cruets, flasks, and clamp jars.

We often store oils in the Mason jars used during preparation because it's so easy to identify the contents and the quantity on hand at any time, but use *paint-drip bottles* for a dramatic dinner table presentation or hostess gift.

Once steeped in Mason jars, vinegars can be transferred to *flasks fitted with clamp stoppers* or to *decorative bottles or cruets with corks,* which come in a variety of shapes and sizes. For the one-step herb vinegars, we keep a supply of old *wine bottles* on hand.

Glass clamp jars in a variety of sizes are handy containers for mustards, as well as for refrigerator storage of catsup or savory jelly that has not been hot sealed.

While glass receptacles are readily reusable, it's best to replace *corks* and the *rubber rings* with each use. Look for replacements in the housewares section of larger hardware stores or see the Source Guide.

TECHNIQUES

A few recipes in this chapter call for *hot sealing.* The key to proper sealing is to keep all components as hot as possible right up until the seal is secured. Thus the Mason jars and their flat metal seals are sterilized and kept in boiling water while ingredients are prepared, then removed, filled, and immediately sealed—one by one in those recipes that yield more than one jar. It is not necessary to boil the rings that are screwed on to keep the seal intact.

Sterilizing the jars and seals used in steeping vinegars or the wine bottles for herb vinegars can be done in advance, either by boiling for 5 to 6 minutes in a deep pot of water sufficient to cover the jars or bottles by 1 to 2 inches, or simply by running them through a hot dishwasher.

If you'll be shipping catsups, savory jellies, or applesauce, put the sealed jars through a *hot-water bath:* Choose a stockpot at least 3½ inches taller than the jars; we usually use a shallow 8-quart pot for ½-pint and pint jars. Place a metal cooling rack in the pot to prevent the glass jars from coming into contact with the bottom, which will become very hot.

Fill the pot with water to cover the jars by 2 inches (the extra 1½ inches is to allow the water to boil without spilling over). Bring to a boil. Using tongs, submerge the jars into the water and boil for the time specified in individual recipes.

To *check seals,* run your finger across the seal to ensure that the surface is concave, and press down in the center. If you hear a pop, the jar did not seal properly. You can also test by unscrewing the ring and gently trying to pull the seal off (without actually prying). If it comes off, the jar did not seal properly.

Improper sealing usually happens when one of the components isn't hot enough, or if the jar isn't sealed fast enough. Should this happen, store the jar in the refrigerator and use within 6 months.

Unless otherwise specified in individual recipes, *store* vinegars and condiments just about anywhere other than in direct sunlight or close to heat. When we call for storage in a cool, dark place, a kitchen cabinet or pantry shelf works well in most cases; if your kitchen is particularly warm or unventilated, store in the refrigerator. Some oils may be kept in any cool, dark place; others must be refrigerated.

Oils

"Many people have the idea that a finely-flavored dish must cost a great deal," advises a cyclopedia of practical hints for modern homes, circa 1886. "That is a mistake. If you have un-tainted meat, or sound vegetables, or even Indian meal, to begin with, you can make it delicious with proper seasoning. One reason why French cooking is much nicer than any other is that it is sea-soned with a great variety of herbs and spices."

One of the most exciting culinary trends applies this age-old wisdom in a way that is transforming the once-humble bottle of oil on pantry shelves. Cooks across the country who have made and

Home Made *Mayonnaise*

The difference between freshly made mayonnaise and the bottled variety is unforgettable. Home Made *mayo is not only easy, requiring only a little stamina for whisking, it's also safe. Whereas most mayonnaise recipes call for raw egg, which can harbor bacteria, we use cooked.*

> 2 large egg yolks
> 2 teaspoons freshly
>   squeezed lemon juice
> ½ teaspoon salt
> 1 cup extra virgin olive oil
> 4 teaspoons boiling water

Fill the bottom of a double boiler about halfway with water and bring to a boil over medium heat. Reduce the heat to low and put the egg yolks in the top of the double boiler. Cook for 2 to 3 minutes, whisking constantly, until the yolk thickens and begins to bubble around the edge. (This can also be done with the egg yolk in a bowl suspended over a saucepan; be sure the boiling water in the saucepan does not touch the bottom of the bowl.)

Beat in the lemon juice and salt and cook for about 30 sec-onds more, whisking, until the juice is completely incorporated.

While continuing to whisk, remove the pan from the heat. Slowly add the oil in a thin stream, about a teaspoonful at a time, whisking until each teaspoonful is absorbed before adding the next.

Continue until about half the oil has been added and the mixture has thickened to the consistency of cream. It is vital to whisk constantly from the time you first put the egg yolk over the boiling water until this stage is reached; now is the time to give your wrist a little rest.

Whisk in the remaining oil a tablespoonful at a time, until completely incorporated into the mixture, then whisk in the boiling water.

The mayonnaise should be ready to use immediately and can be kept in the refrigerator for about 3 days.

Variation: Make delightful flavored mayonnaises by substituting 1 cup of any *Home Made* oil for the olive oil, or by substituting 2 teaspoons of any *Home Made* vinegar for the lemon juice.

For Herb Mayonnaise, put 3 tablespoons *Home Made* fresh Fines Herbes (page 51) into a fine sieve and blanch by pouring 1 cup boiling water over. Drain and whisk into the mayonnaise after the boiling water has been added.

Yield = About ¾ cup

used flavored vinegars for years are now discovering the delights of oils flavored with herbs, spices, and other seasonings. Easily prepared, these oils are also highly versatile, providing a quick and economical way to add flair to home cooking.

Flavored oils are drizzled over vegetables or fish, or tossed with pastas. They stand alone with crusty bread for dipping or as marinades for red meat, poultry, and seafood. They're sautéed in, used in salad dressings, and incorporated into wonderful *Home Made* mayonnaises.

"It is not so many years ago," another turn-of-the-century treatise advises, "that salads were considered a luxury only to be found on the tables of the wealthy. Today a wider knowledge of cookery has taught the housewife who has to set a table with a small income that there is no more economical, wholesome dish than a well-made salad. She is beginning to realize, as the French do, that almost anything can be put into a salad, and that even cheap materials . . . make a palatable and most sightly dish."

While the uses for flavored oils go well beyond the realm of salads, they *do* make terrific vinaigrette salad dressings—either in combination with red or white wine vinegar or with *Home Made* vinegars. Mix to taste, starting with 2 parts oil to 1 part vinegar, adding more oil as desired.

The Basics

The incentives for flavoring your own oils at home are great—commercial flavored oils are seldom available, what is on the market is expensive, and flavored oils have a relatively short shelf life.

Besides, flavored oils are incredibly easy to make. Start either with an olive oil or with canola oil, which is flavorless and doesn't compete with mild-flavored additions. The entire process consists of adding the flavoring to the oil, letting the mixture steep for from 1 hour to 2 days, and straining.

Home Made flavored oils fall into two categories—those made with dried herbs and spices (Curry Oil and Rosemary Oil) and those made with fresh ingredients (Basil Oil, Garlic Oil, or Horseradish Oil).

Curry Oil and Rosemary Oil can be stored in any cool, dark place (a kitchen cabinet away from the stove or a pantry shelf is ideal) for up to 2 months with little fear of spoilage. These recipes are easily doubled if you think you will use the greater quantity during that period of time.

The water content of fresh flavorings, when added to oil, yields a mixture of limited longevity. We recommend making Basil Oil, Garlic Oil, and Horseradish Oil in small quantities for quick use. They must be stored in the refrigerator and should be used within a week. Oils may solidify when refrigerated and should be brought back to room temperature before use.

Garlic Oil

Those of us who consider garlic the ultimate gift of the gods rely heavily on this oil, using it on almost any culinary occasion that calls for oil and would benefit from the divine addition of a tinge of garlic.

Dip Italian bread in Garlic Oil as an hors d'oeuvre or marinate steaks in it. Mixed with white wine vinegar, it's terrific on salads. Warmed Garlic Oil makes a simple, elegant sauce for pasta and for sautéed or steamed shrimp.

> 2 small garlic cloves, peeled and minced
> 1 cup virgin olive oil

Combine the garlic and the oil in a ½-pint Mason jar, cover, and shake a few times to mix.

Chill the mixture for 1 hour in the refrigerator.

Strain the contents through a fine sieve into a 1-cup glass measuring cup.

The oil should be ready to use immediately. Rinse and dry the Mason jar and return any oil not used immediately to the jar. Store in the refrigerator for up to 1 week.

Yield = 1 cup

✧ ✧ ✧ **B**russels sprouts roasted in Garlic Oil are a favorite treat of ours. To prepare, preheat the oven to 450° F. and line a baking sheet with aluminum foil. Trim 1 pound brussels sprouts and cut an X into the bottom of each sprout. Toss with 1 cup Garlic Oil until the sprouts are thoroughly coated.

Transfer the brussels sprouts to the baking sheet and bake for 10 minutes. Flip each sprout and bake for 5 minutes more. Shake the baking sheet vigorously and bake a final 5 minutes, until the brussels sprouts have browned uniformly. The pound of brussels sprouts should serve 4 as a side dish. ✧ ✧ ✧

Basil Oil

Distinctive Basil Oil can enhance just about every course of a meal. We drizzle it on fresh tomatoes and Home Made *Smoked Mozzarella (page 112), rub it on chicken before roasting, substitute it for plain oil in preparing rice, and toss cooked pasta or noodles in it. It really perks up a pasta primavera, as well, if you sauté the vegetables first in Basil Oil.*

Try ending brunch or light summer supper with a salad dressed in a mixture of Basil Oil and Home Made *Raspberry Vinegar (page 45) or Blueberry Vinegar (page 44).*

> ½ ounce fresh basil (leaves and stems), roughly
>   chopped (about ⅓ cup)
> 1 cup extra virgin olive oil

Combine the basil and oil in the bowl of a food processor or blender and puree for 10 seconds. Transfer the mixture to a ½-pint Mason jar, cover, and set aside for about 1 hour, until the basil settles to the bottom.

Strain the contents through a fine sieve into a 1-cup glass measuring cup.

The oil should be ready to use immediately. It must be stored in the refrigerator, where it has a shelf life of up to 1 week.

Yield = 1 cup

❖ ❖ ❖ *V*ariation: For Chili Oil that makes a powerful accent to Chinese cuisine, substitute 2 fresh red finger chili peppers, chopped, for the basil. In stir-fries, mix 1 part Chili Oil with every 3 parts of the peanut oil or vegetable oil usually used. In Szechwan chicken and fish dishes that call for a sprinkle of sesame oil at the end, try 2 parts sesame oil with 1 part Chili Oil. ❖ ❖ ❖

Rosemary Oil

The woody accent of rosemary comes through clearly in this oil, which makes a great vinaigrette mixed with plain white wine vinegar or with Home Made *Peach Vinegar (page 44). Steak marinated in Rosemary Oil is robust and flavorful, while boiled new potatoes tossed in the oil give roast lamb a boost. Cooked egg noodles tossed in warm Rosemary Oil are the perfect accompaniment to goulash and other beef stews.*

2½ tablespoons dried rosemary, crumbled
1 cup canola oil

Combine the rosemary and oil in a ½-pint Mason jar, cover, and shake the jar 2 or 3 times to mix.

Let the jar sit for 2 days, until the rosemary falls to the bottom.

Strain the contents through a fine sieve into a 1-cup glass measuring cup. Rinse and dry the Mason jar and return the oil to the jar. Seal and store in a cool, dark place.

The oil should be ready to use immediately, with a shelf life of about 2 months.

Yield = 1 cup

Horseradish Oil

Horseradish Oil is a natural with seafood—mix it with white wine vinegar to top cold seafood salad, use it to sauté shellfish or any fleshy, white fish, or heat it as a seafood sauce. Spinach is tasty sautéed in the oil.

4 teaspoons finely grated fresh horseradish root
1 cup canola oil

Combine the horseradish and the oil in a ½-pint Mason jar. Cover, shake a few times to mix, and set the jar aside for about 2 hours.

Strain the contents through a fine sieve into a 1-cup glass measuring cup.

The oil should be ready to use immediately. Rinse and dry the Mason jar and return any oil not used immediately to the jar. Store in the refrigerator for up to 1 week.

Yield = 1 cup

Curry Oil

This oil is quite good in curries of all sorts and it adds an interesting accent to blander main courses—sauté pineapple rings or peach halves in Curry Oil to garnish lamb or ham steak. For a quick and easy shrimp curry, toss cooked shrimp in warm Curry Oil and serve it over rice that has been prepared with the oil.

Curry Oil makes an excellent marinade for grilled chicken or shrimp, and also pairs well with Home Made *Peach Vinegar (page 44) in vinaigrette dressing.*

> 1 tablespoon mild Indian curry powder
> 1 cup plus 1 teaspoon canola oil

Put the curry powder into a bowl and stir in 1 teaspoon of the canola oil until the oil uniformly darkens and the combination is the consistency of a crumbly paste.

Add the remaining 1 cup oil. Stir well and transfer the mixture to a ½-pint Mason jar.

Seal the jar and set it aside for about 8 hours, until the curry powder sinks to the bottom.

Taking care not to disturb the curry residue, strain the contents through a fine sieve into another ½-pint Mason jar; you'll leave a little of the oil in the first jar. Cover and store in a cool, dark place.

The oil should be ready to use immediately, with a shelf life of about 2 months.

Yield = 1 cup

Vinegars

Vinegar has been with us through much of recorded history. By the time our Victorian ancestors came on the scene, it had become an indispensable staple used in cooking, preserving, and a variety of domestic chores.

In turn-of-the-century households, vinegar was made in great quantities and with considerable labor. One set of instructions we found—for the "quick" method—calls first for constructing an apparatus that involves suspending a wooden cask within a larger cask fitted with a false bottom that is covered with flannel and a layer of sand, drilling an intricate number of holes into various of the surfaces, layering wood chips between the two casks, and affixing a spigot. Four gallons of alcohol are then recirculated through the casks every hour for 3 to 4 days.

Flavoring vinegar was no less involved an undertaking. During steeping, raspberry vinegar was strained every 24 hours for days, then decanted into a tin and boiled with sugar.

A slow version of this cask method of fermenting vinegar, which takes up to 2 years, is still used today by producers of some highly reputed vinegars, but we wouldn't recommend trying it at home.

We developed our recipes for *Home Made* vinegars to make small yields and to require only a few minutes of actual hands-on preparation. We include directions for making vinegar from scratch—without the casks, the flannel, the sand, and the wood chips—but focus on a few of the endless possibilities and combinations for flavoring plain vinegar. Let these recipes serve as guides for devising your own creations, using favorite fruits, herbs, or other flavorings.

THE BASICS

Most flavored vinegars start with white wine vinegar (for which champagne vinegar may be used interchangeably). Red wine vinegar is heavier and can turn a muddy color with some ingredients.

Wonderfully versatile fruit-flavored vinegars perk up sauces, glazes, and gravies and are excellent for deglazing sauté pans, in

Vinegar from Scratch

Contrary to both the common misconception and the literal translation of the French root *vinaigre*, vinegar is not sour wine. It is the result of a reaction that takes place when a vinegar culture or "mother" is steeped in wine.

Mothers for either red or white wine vinegar are easily obtained from commercial sources (see the Source Guide, or try a local winery). The mother, which contains the bacteria that turns the wine into vinegar, is a spongy, gelatinous white mass that comes suspended in vinegar or wine. Sealed in liquid it is inert; exposure to air is necessary to start the reaction.

To make wine vinegar, put the mother and its liquid into a large, widemouthed glass container and cover with red wine that has been uncorked and allowed to breathe for at least 2 days. We use a ½-gallon container and about 2 bottles of wine. For white wine vinegar, cover the mother and its liquid either with white wine that has been allowed to breathe full strength or with 2 parts wine to 1 part water, depending on how strong you like your vinegar.

The better the wine the better the vinegar—avoid jug wine. It is not necessary for all the wine to be of the same variety or vintage; just be sure to add only white wine to a white wine vinegar starter and red wine to a red wine vinegar starter.

Secure cheesecloth over the container, which will allow air to circulate while preventing dust from settling on the surface. Set aside for about 4 weeks, until the mixture smells and tastes like vinegar.

As you use the vinegar, replenish with wine, making sure that the mother is always covered. The remains of a bottle from a dinner party make the perfect occasional addition (remember to let it breathe for at least 2 days first). Let the mixture steep for at least 1 week after each addition, employing the "smells and tastes like vinegar" test once again for doneness. If you ever replace more than 2/3 of the vinegar with wine, steep for about 4 weeks.

Once you get your "vinegar crock" started, it just keeps on going. The mother will give off "baby" mothers, which can be preserved indefinitely covered with wine or vinegar in tight-sealing jars. (Your "babies" will probably be much in demand once word gets out!) Discard the original mother when it turns gray, but leave at least one of the babies in the vinegar crock.

To bottle some of the vinegar, strain it through a fine sieve and pasteurize by heating in a non-reactive saucepan over medium heat for about 5 minutes, just until it gives off steam (do not bring to a boil). Pour into sterilized, tight-sealing jars or bottles. Use fresh corks if putting in wine bottles.

The bottled vinegar has a shelf life of at least 1 year and can be safely shipped as a gift as long as the cork or stopper is adequately secured.

addition to their obvious merits in salad making. They provide an especially nice finish to fruit salads, either drizzled on top or incorporated into a dressing.

Fruit vinegars are made by pouring warmed vinegar over fruit, setting aside to steep, and then straining. Warming the vinegar speeds up the process, allowing the steeping to take place in 3 to 5 days instead of a matter of weeks. We like a mixture sweetened only by the fruit; if you prefer your vinegar less tart, add ½ to 1 tablespoon sugar to every pint of fruit before steeping.

To add a taste variation to fruit vinegars, combine a sprig of herb with the strained vinegar when bottling and let the mixture steep a bit longer before using.

We include recipes for several one-of-a-kind vinegars, including Ginger Vinegar, Camp Vinegar (a luscious garlic-and-anchovy-laden adaptation of a Victorian receipt), and an Oriental Vinegar that brings ginger root and lemon grass to a rice wine vinegar base. These vinegars all steep for about a week.

Our herb vinegars take a bit longer to steep, 2 to 3 weeks, but are the easiest to make. Simply mix red, white, or rice wine vinegar with the herb of your choice and steep.

Home Made vinegars should have a shelf life of at least 1 year, with no special storage requirements other than keeping them out of direct sunlight (as pretty as they might look on the windowsill). Ignore any sediment that may form over time; it's harmless. To remove sediment for cosmetic purposes, restrain through a sieve fitted with a damp coffee filter.

Peach Vinegar

Peach Vinegar remains a rare treat despite the growing popularity of more common fruit vinegars. In a light vinaigrette, it adds the perfect touch to summer fruit salads; by itself, it's a wonderful dip for steamed artichoke leaves. We also mix it with marmalade or peach jelly as a glaze for pork roast, and lightly coat peach halves with it before baking.

2 cups white wine vinegar
1 pound peaches, stoned and cut into 1-inch cubes

Put the vinegar into a medium, nonreactive saucepan and warm over low heat just until it begins to give off vapor (do not bring to a boil). Stir in the peach cubes and cook for 1 minute.

Pour the mixture into a sterilized 1-quart Mason jar and allow to cool to room temperature, 10 to 15 minutes. Place a sterilized seal on top of the jar, screw on the ring, and shake a few times to mix.

Store the jar out of direct sunlight and away from heat for 5 days, shaking it periodically, while the mixture steeps (the vinegar will absorb most of the pigment from the fruit).

Strain the contents through a fine sieve into a 4-cup glass measuring cup. Discard the fruit residue and rinse the sieve. Rinse the Mason jar and return the strained vinegar to the jar.

Dampen a flat-bottom coffee filter and fit it into the sieve. Rinse the measuring cup, place the sieve on top, and pour in the vinegar a bit at a time, allowing it to drip into the measuring cup.

Transfer the vinegar to flasks, bottles, or cruets. The vinegar should be ready to use immediately, with a shelf life of at least 1 year.

Yield = 2 cups

◇ ◇ ◇ *V*ariation: For Blueberry Vinegar, substitute 1 pint blueberries, coarsely chopped, for the peaches. ◇ ◇ ◇

◇ ◇ ◇ *T*o make Peach Mint Vinegar, place 1 sprig fresh mint in the container before pouring in the vinegar. Fill, seal, and let steep out of direct sunlight and away from heat for 1 day before using or shipping. ◇ ◇ ◇

Raspberry Vinegar

One Victorian cookbook advises, in an entry entitled "Money in Vinegar," that to build up a neighborhood trade, "it is only necessary to leave samples, with price attached, at the neighboring houses."

While we haven't yet taken to knocking on neighbors' doors, we do recommend preparing Raspberry Vinegar in quantity. It's wonderfully versatile; we use it for just about everything from deglazing to saucing (it's great in beurre blanc and a range of savory sauces).

> 6 cups white wine vinegar
> 1 pint red raspberries, plus ½ pint (optional) for decoration

In a medium, nonreactive saucepan over low heat, warm the vinegar just until it begins to give off steam (do not bring to a boil).

Put 1 pint of the raspberries into a fine sieve fitted over a sterilized ½-gallon clamp jar. Pour the warm vinegar over the berries and let it run into the jar, then add the berries to the jar. Allow the mixture to cool 20 to 30 minutes to room temperature, then seal and shake the jar gently.

Set the jar out of direct sunlight and away from heat to steep for 4 days, shaking it every so often. While steeping, the vinegar will take on a raspberry hue and the fruit will lose most of its color.

Strain the mixture through a fine sieve into a large batter bowl (with a handle) or into a large, nonreactive saucepan. Rinse the jar and return the strained vinegar to it. Rinse the bowl or saucepan.

Dump the fruit and rinse the sieve. Dampen a flat-bottom coffee filter, then line the sieve with the filter and fit it over the bowl or saucepan. Pour in the vinegar a bit at a time, allowing it to drip into the receptacle.

Transfer the vinegar to flasks or bottles. If you wish, spear 6 to 8 whole raspberries on a wooden skewer and put the skewer into the container before filling.

The vinegar should be ready to use immediately, with a shelf life of at least 1 year.

Yield = 6 cups

❖ ❖ ❖ **V**ariation: For Cranberry Vinegar, substitute 4 cups (1 pound) fresh cranberries, coarsely chopped, for the raspberries. Decorate, if you wish, with skewers of whole cranberries. ❖ ❖ ❖

❖ ❖ ❖ **R**aspberry Lemon Thyme Vinegar is a refreshing treat made by placing 1 sprig fresh lemon thyme in a flask or bottle before adding the vinegar. Fill, seal, and steep out of direct sunlight and away from heat for 1 week before using or shipping. ❖ ❖ ❖

Oriental Vinegar

We toss such steamed vegetables as string beans, asparagus, or okra in Oriental Vinegar. For Japanese-style rice, substitute about a teaspoonful of the vinegar for the butter normally used in preparing American rice. It can also be mixed to taste with soy sauce as a dipping sauce for pot stickers or Home Made *Pork Wontons (page 122).*

> 2 cups rice wine vinegar
> 6 black whole peppercorns
> 1 chunk peeled fresh ginger (about 1½ x ¾ x ⅜ inch)
> 1 thin 1-inch strip lemon zest
> 1 14- to 15-inch stalk lemon grass

Combine the vinegar, peppercorns, ginger, and lemon zest in a clean and dry 16-ounce bottle. Trim the bottom of the lemon grass, remove the outer leaf, and cut it in half crosswise. Add the lemon grass to the bottle. Seal with a cork and steep for 1 week.

The vinegar should be ready to use immediately after steeping, with a shelf life of at least 1 year.

Yield = 2 cups

Camp Vinegar

This thick, pungent vinegar is an adaptation of a recipe from the early 1900s, when a variety of "camp" goods were "put up and sold under this name for sea stores or persons going on exploring and other expeditions." We like it so much we invented Camp Mustard (page 58), the key ingredient in a Perfect Caesar Salad.

> 1 shallot, peeled and chopped
> 1 large garlic clove, peeled and mashed
> 1 tablespoon anchovy paste
> ⅛ teaspoon cayenne pepper
> ¼ cup white wine Worcestershire sauce
> 1 cup white wine vinegar

Easy Herb Vinegars

Herb vinegars are the simplest to make and among the most versatile *Home Made* flavored vinegars. Although they need to steep a bit for the flavors to meld, they require no cooking or straining. You simply stuff the bounty of your herb garden (or supermarket) into a bottle, cork, and set it aside.

These vinegars really perk up salads. Just substitute herb vinegar for the vinegar and herbs in favorite salad dressing recipes. (The herb in your vinegar doesn't have to be the same as that called for, just one with similar characteristics.) They're terrific sprinkled on steamed vegetables or used in lieu of plain vinegar whenever you feel the need for a flavor boost. Red wine–based herb vinegars flavor meat marinades nicely (but be careful not to use too much, or the acid in the vinegar will "cook" and toughen the meat.)

Combine all the ingredients in a sterilized 1-pint Mason jar. Place a sterilized seal on top, screw on the ring, and shake 2 or 3 times to mix.

Place the jar out of direct sunlight and away from heat for 1 week to steep, shaking it periodically.

Strain the contents through a fine sieve into a 2-cup glass measuring cup. Rinse the Mason jar and return the strained mixture to the jar.

Discard the solids and rinse the sieve. Rinse the measuring cup and fit the sieve on top. Lightly moisten a flat-bottom coffee filter and line the sieve with the filter. Strain the vinegar a second time, pouring the still fairly thick liquid into the sieve in batches and allowing it to drip through into the measuring cup.

Pour the vinegar into a 10-ounce bottle or cruet (which will probably be a little less than full) and seal with a cork.

The vinegar should be ready to use immediately, with a shelf life of at least 1 year.

Yield = 1¼ cups

To make an herb vinegar, put rinsed and dried herbs and any spices into a sterilized 750-ml wine bottle and add about 3 cups vinegar, filling to within ¼ inch of the top. Stop with a new cork and set aside for 2 to 3 weeks to steep. The vinegar has a shelf life of at least 1 year.

With red wine vinegar, use:
- 4 sprigs fresh curly-leaf parsley
- 2 tablespoons black peppercorns

or
- 2 sprigs fresh flat-leaf parsley
- 2 sprigs fresh basil

With white wine vinegar, use:
- 4 sprigs fresh tarragon

or
- 4 sprigs fresh rosemary

With rice wine vinegar, use:
- 4 sprigs fresh cilantro
- 2 tablespoons dried star anise

Ginger Vinegar

Dedicated with love to our many fellow ginger mavens! Sprinkle Ginger Vinegar on fruit plates—it's especially good on blood oranges—or mix with honey for a wonderful dressing for fruits and salads.

> 1 tablespoon minced fresh ginger
> 1 cup white wine vinegar

Mix the ginger and the vinegar together in a sterilized ½-pint Mason jar. Place a sterilized seal on top and screw on the ring.

Set the jar aside for 1 week to steep, out of direct sunlight and away from heat.

Strain the contents through a fine sieve into a 2-cup glass measuring cup. Clean out the sieve. Rinse the Mason jar and return the strained vinegar to the jar.

Rinse the measuring cup. Line the sieve with a moist flat-bottom coffee filter and set it over the cup. Strain the vinegar through again, a bit at a time, allowing it to drip into the measuring cup.

Pour the vinegar into an 8-ounce bottle or cruet and seal with a cork.

The vinegar should be ready to use immediately, with a shelf life of at least 1 year.

Yield = 1 cup

Condiments

"To compound catsup," one century-old set of instructions we came across begins, "select perfect fruit; always cook in porcelain, never in metal; bottle in stone and glass, and never use tin; keep in a dry, dark, cool place. If, on opening, there is mold on the catsup, remove carefully every particle of it, and the catsup will not then be injured."

While this treatise clearly reflects the period's greater concern with parsimony than with food safety, the other words of advice are well heeded—to start with the freshest ingredients, cook and bottle in nonreactive containers, and store properly.

In this section, we build not only upon such basic instructions

◇ ◇ ◇ *V*ariation: for subtly spicy Hot Pepper Vinegar, substitute 1 tablespoon crushed red pepper flakes for the ginger. ◇ ◇ ◇

Warm Vinaigrette for Spinach or Potato Salad

This simple concoction, which can be prepared in minutes, is the basis for an elegant spinach salad or a rustic, old-fashioned potato salad. For the spinach salad, it's essential that the spinach be at room temperature before starting the vinaigrette.

> 4 slices bacon
> 1 tablespoon dark brown sugar
> ½ cup red wine vinegar
> 2 tablespoons freshly squeezed lemon juice
> 2 teaspoons Dijon mustard
> 1 teaspoon Worcestershire sauce
> 10 ounces spinach, trimmed, rinsed, and drained, *or*
> 3 Yukon gold potatoes, cooked, cooled, peeled, and sliced
> 1 small red onion, peeled and thinly sliced (optional garnish for either salad)

Cook the bacon in a heavy skillet over low heat until crisp. Remove the bacon and drain on paper towels.

To the bacon fat in the skillet, stir in the brown sugar, vinegar, and lemon juice with a wooden spoon; next the mustard, then the Worcestershire sauce. Bring to a light, bubbling boil over medium heat and cook for 1 minute, stirring constantly, until the mixture thickens slightly.

Crumple the bacon over the spinach or potatoes, pour the vinaigrette over and toss well. Garnish with the onion, if desired, and serve immediately.

Yield = 4 servings

but also upon the repertoire of condiments handed down to us. We progress from the centuries-old mustards to delicate Victorian catsups, Tomato Jelly, and fresh Prepared Horseradish, and finally on to a fiery Red Pepper Jelly more in tune with modern taste buds.

THE BASICS

Trust us—turn-of-the-century catsups bear no resemblance to that watery red stuff your supermarket stocks. Each has its own unique personality, as demonstrated by the two very distinct recipes we include—for light and refreshing plum catsup and for dense, rich mushroom catsup.

Preparation, however, is similar. Boiled fruit or salted mushrooms are pureed and subsequently simmered with vinegar and flavorings. We call for hot sealing, with hot-water baths if you'll be shipping.

While the savory Tomato Jelly takes a couple of hours to cook, the Red Pepper Jelly cooks for only 11 minutes after the mixture first comes to a boil.

Home Made mustards are a combination of ground mustard seed (and sometimes mustard powder), water, vinegar, spices, and other flavorings. The consistency of the grind determines that of the mustard: coarsely ground mustard seed will yield a grainy mustard, finely ground seed a smoother variety.

The combination needs to steep a bit—anywhere from 45 minutes for the pungent Camp Mustard to overnight for the delicate Dijon-Style Mustard—to let the bitterness of the mustard seed dissipate.

Mustards are hottest when freshly made; they tend to lose some of their bite as they age. To keep the kick, refrigerate.

Plum Catsup

Subtle but intense Victorian catsups can derive their distinctive flavors from any of a variety of fruits and vegetables. Plum Catsup is sweeter than tomato catsup; although smooth in consistency, it tastes a little bit like chutney. Serve with poultry or game birds.

> 2 pounds purple plums, stoned and quartered (about 4 cups)
> 1 small yellow onion, peeled and minced (about 1/3 cup)
> 1 cup water
> 1 cup cider vinegar
> 3/4 cup granulated sugar
> 1/3 cup light brown sugar, firmly packed
> 3/4 teaspoon ground ginger
> 1/2 teaspoon salt
> 1/2 teaspoon dry mustard
> 1/2 teaspoon ground cinnamon
> 1/4 teaspoon freshly ground black pepper
> 1/4 teaspoon ground cloves
> 1/8 teaspoon ground allspice

Combine the plums, onion, and water in a medium saucepan. Bring to a boil over medium heat, reduce the heat to low, and simmer, uncovered, for 30 minutes.

Transfer the mixture to a food processor or blender and puree to a smooth consistency.

Rinse the saucepan and return the puree to the pan. Stir in the vinegar, sugars, and seasonings. Bring back to a boil over medium heat. Reduce the heat to low and cook, uncovered, for 45 minutes, or until no ring of water forms around the edge of a small amount spooned onto a saucer.

When the catsup is almost done, fill a large pot with water sufficient to cover 1/2-pint Mason jars by an inch or 2 and bring to a boil. Using tongs, submerge 3 jars into the boiling water and boil for 5 to 6 minutes, adding the seals toward the end. Keep at a boil.

Carefully remove a jar. Fit with a canning funnel and ladle the hot catsup to within 1/4 inch of the top. Clean the mouth of the jar, remove a seal and place firmly on top, and screw on the ring. Repeat the process to fill and seal the remaining jars.

Home Made Seasoning Blends

Contrary to what you may think, the folks at McCormick and Spice Islands don't possess special powers of culinary alchemy that enable them to conjure up curry powder, nor (alas) is a trip to the Côte d'Azur necessary for authentic herbes de Provence.

Creating your own mixtures—starting with basic formulas and experimenting for subtle taste variations—is a delightful way to produce fresh, aromatic seasonings.

For the best results, start with the best ingredients. If you're lucky enough to live in a city that has a spice merchant (also see Source Guide) or an old-fashioned ethnic food shop filled with vats of spices, beat a path to its door. When we lived in New York, we sometimes visited the Ninth Avenue food district just to be able to step into one of these shops and inhale, deeply and blissfully.

Seasonings are best used within 3 to 6 months; to keep them flavorful, store in tightly sealing, opaque containers. (Washed and dried prescription vials, designed to keep out light and moisture, work well. If using decorative containers for display, avoid clear glass.)

To make Poultry Seasoning (for roasting or for poultry stuffing), mix:

> 2 teaspoons dried rosemary
> 2 teaspoons dried sage

½ teaspoon ground ginger
1 teaspoon dried oregano
⅛ teaspoon ground black pepper

To make Herbes de Provence (sprinkle on chops or vegetables, or stuff under the skin of chicken before roasting), mix:

1 tablespoon dried winter savory
1 tablespoon dried thyme
2 teaspoons anise seed
1 tablespoon dried lavender (food grade)
½ teaspoon dried rosemary
¼ teaspoon ground sage

To make Curry Powder, mix:

1 teaspoon ground coriander
½ teaspoon ground turmeric
½ teaspoon ground cumin
½ teaspoon celery seed
⅛ teaspoon ground black pepper
¼ teaspoon ground ginger
¼ teaspoon ground cloves
⅛ teaspoon ground nutmeg

To make Fines Herbes, mix equal amounts of chopped fresh or dried parsley, tarragon, chives, and chervil. The classic fresh version, preferred by purists, is excellent as a garnish for salads or seafood. The modern dried rendition is used in egg dishes, poultry, or fish.

Put the jars through a 10-minute hot-water bath (see page 36) if shipping.

Turn the jars upside down on a dish towel and cool for about 2 hours. Check the seals.

The catsup should be ready to use immediately, with a shelf life of at least 1 year. Store for up to 6 months in the refrigerator after opening.

Yield = 3 cups

Mushroom Catsup

"Those who are not thoroughly conversant with the difference between the edible and poisonous varieties should buy mushrooms from a reliable dealer or buy the spawn and grow the mushrooms (themselves)," advises one early twentieth-century household encyclopedia. Although you don't really need to worry about acquiring poisonous mushrooms from the modern produce dealer, growing your own mushrooms isn't a bad idea if, like us, you use them in quantity (see page 191).

Mushroom Catsup has an assertive flavor that goes well with cold roast beef or ham; or add a little to enliven gravy. We make it in small quantities, since a little goes a long way, but the recipe can easily be doubled.

    12 ounces white button mushrooms, cleaned and
        diced
  1⅛ teaspoons pickling salt
     1 garlic clove, peeled and mashed
     1 large shallot, peeled and chopped
     6 tablespoons white wine vinegar
   ⅛ teaspoon ground white pepper
   ⅛ teaspoon ground ginger
     1 tablespoon dry sherry

Combine the mushrooms and the salt in a bowl, mixing well to coat the mushrooms. Cover loosely with a towel and set aside for about 12 hours.

Put the mushrooms in a food processor or blender. Add the garlic, shallot, and 2 tablespoons of the vinegar. Puree to a smooth consistency.

Transfer the puree to a medium saucepan. Add the pepper and ginger and bring to a boil over medium heat. Reduce the heat to low, stir in the remaining 4 tablespoons of vinegar, and simmer, uncovered, for ½ hour, or until thick enough to coat the back of a spoon. Stir in the sherry.

Meanwhile, fill a large pot with water to cover a ½-pint Mason jar by an inch or 2 and bring it to a boil. Using tongs, submerge the jar into the boiling water and boil for 5 to 6 minutes, adding the seal after 3 or 4 minutes. Leave at a boil.

Carefully remove the jar from the boiling water and fit it with a canning funnel. Ladle the hot catsup to within ¼ inch of the top of

◇ ◇ ◇ **N**ote: You can skip
the hot sealing if you store
the catsup in the refrigerator,
where it has a shelf life of up to
6 months. Let the cooked catsup
cool to room temperature and
transfer it to a tightly sealing
(preferably glass) container.

◇ ◇ ◇

the jar. Remove the seal and place firmly atop the jar, making sure
the mouth of the jar is clean, and screw the ring on.

Put the jar through a 10-minute hot-water bath (see page 36) if
shipping.

Place the jar upside down on a dish towel for about 2 hours to
cool. Check the seal.

The catsup should be ready to use immediately, with a shelf life
of at least 1 year. Refrigerate after opening.

Yield = About 1 cup

Lindsay's Tomato Jelly

*Tomato Jelly is a sweet condiment that brings out the best in smoked
sausages; warm the sausages in the jelly or serve it hot as a sauce. Cold,
it works well as a condiment for spicy meat, such as seasoned roast
beef. This version was provided by the 12-year-old daughter of our
illustrator.*

◇ ◇ ◇ **V**ariation: For Old-
Fashioned Tomato Catsup,
combine 1 medium onion,
chopped, with the tomato
chunks in the first step and
substitute 1/4 cup dark brown
sugar, firmly packed, for the
3 cups granulated sugar.

◇ ◇ ◇

3½ pounds tomatoes, cored and cut into large chunks
(about 8 chunks per tomato)
3 cups sugar
1 cup cider vinegar
3 cinnamon sticks
½ tablespoon whole cloves

Put the tomatoes into a large, nonreactive pot. Bring to a boil
over medium heat and continue to boil for about 35 minutes, stirring occasionally, until the tomatoes have fallen apart and they are
soft enough to mash. Remove the pot from the heat.

Using a slotted spoon, transfer the tomatoes in batches into a
food mill placed over a large bowl. Work the tomatoes through the
food mill until all are pureed, periodically discarding the skin and
seeds that accumulate in the mill.

Empty and rinse the pot. Return the puree to the pot and stir in
the sugar and vinegar. Wrap the cinnamon sticks and cloves in a
double thickness of cheesecloth. Tie the cheesecloth in a knot and

add the bundle to the pot. Cook, uncovered, over medium heat for 1½ hours, maintaining a gentle boil, or until thick enough to coat the back of a spoon.

After the jelly has cooked for about 1 hour, fill another large pot with enough water to cover an inch or 2 over the top of 1-pint Mason jars and bring it to a boil. Submerge 2 jars into the water, using tongs, and boil for 5 to 6 minutes, adding the seals toward the end. Keep at a boil.

Carefully remove a jar from the boiling water, fit it with a canning funnel, and ladle in hot jelly to within ¼ inch of the top. Wipe the mouth of the jar clean, remove a seal and place it on top, and screw on the ring. Repeat the process for the remaining jar.

If you are going to ship the jars, put them through a 10-minute hot-water bath (see page 36).

Flip the jars upside down onto a dish towel placed on the counter and let sit for 2 hours. Check the seals.

The jelly should be ready to use immediately, with a shelf life of at least 1 year. It will keep for up to 6 months in the refrigerator after opening.

Yield = 4 cups

❖ ❖ ❖ *F*or a great Barbecue Sauce, combine 2 cups (1 pint) Tomato Jelly, 2 tablespoons Dijon-Style Mustard, 4 teaspoons Worcestershire sauce, 2 teaspoons freshly squeezed lemon juice, ¼ teaspoon hot sauce, and ¼ teaspoon freshly ground black pepper in a small saucepan. Whisk thoroughly and cook over medium heat for 5 minutes. This will yield about 2 cups Barbecue Sauce. ❖ ❖ ❖

Prepared Horseradish

Making your own Prepared Horseradish ensures freshness, and avoids the unnecessary sugar and salt often added to commercial preparations. Whether assembling a traditional Passover seder (in which horseradish represents the bitterness of life) or just mixing up a batch of Home Made *Bloody Marias (page 76), this horseradish is so pungent, it's guaranteed to bring tears to your eyes. The recipe is easily halved or doubled, as needed.*

    3 tablespoons water
    3 tablespoons distilled white vinegar
    ½ cup finely grated fresh horseradish root

Combine the water, vinegar, and horseradish in a small bowl. Mix well, cover, and refrigerate for at least 2 hours before using. The horseradish should keep at least 3 months in the refrigerator.

Yield = ½ cup

❖ ❖ ❖ *A*dding horseradish to mashed potatoes adds such zip that it can make fans out of diners who otherwise turn up their noses at such down-home fare. We so enjoy the horseradish mashed potatoes served at Oprah Winfrey's restaurant in Chicago, where it's a house specialty, that we had to come up with our own version.

    4 large Yukon gold potatoes
    4 tablespoons butter (½ stick)
    ¾ cup half-and-half

¼ cup sour cream

2 tablespoons Prepared Horseradish

½ teaspoon ground white pepper

Cook the potatoes for 7 minutes in a microwave oven at full power. Allow to cool. Peel and rice or grate the potatoes into a bowl.

In a small saucepan, cook the butter and half-and-half over medium heat just until the butter melts and the mixture begins to give off steam (don't let it boil).

Meanwhile, add the sour cream, horseradish, and pepper to the riced potatoes. Pour in the half-and-half and beat with a fork until the potatoes are smooth and fluffy. Serve immediately.

Yield = 4–6 servings

❖ ❖ ❖

Applesauce

We think that Home Made *Applesauce is just so much . . . well, better . . . than the bland, watery commercial stuff that you'll never again buy ready-made once you try this recipe. And it's much easier than you think.*

1½ pounds McIntosh apples (or another soft variety that will fall apart in cooking), peeled, cored, and sliced

½ pound Jonathan apples (or another firm variety that will hold its shape when cooked), peeled, cored, and cut into bite-size chunks

½ cup water

Combine the apples and water in a large, nonreactive saucepan or a Dutch oven. Cover and cook for 15 minutes over medium heat.

Remove from heat and whisk the applesauce to a smooth consistency. Serve immediately, or chill before serving.

The applesauce should have a refrigerator shelf life of at least 1 week.

Yield = 3 cups

Five-Onion Relish

This relish is hearty, in both taste and texture. Its sweet and sour flavor, with a woody undertone from the balsamic vinegar, lends zest to broiled poultry or pork roast.

- ⅓ cup balsamic vinegar
- ⅓ cup light brown sugar, firmly packed
- 1 leek, well cleaned, trimmed, and very thinly sliced (about 1 cup)
- 1 small white onion, peeled and very thinly sliced (about 1 cup)
- 1 small red onion, peeled and very thinly sliced (about 1 cup)
- 5 scallions, trimmed and sliced into thin rounds (about ⅓ cup)
- 1 shallot, peeled and very thinly sliced
- ½ teaspoon dried tarragon

In a small, nonreactive saucepan, stir the vinegar and sugar and bring to a boil over medium heat. Reduce the heat to low and simmer for 3 minutes. Remove the pan from the heat and allow to cool for 10 minutes.

Combine the onions in a medium bowl and pour the cooled vinegar over. Add the tarragon and mix thoroughly. Set aside for 30 minutes, then cover and refrigerate for at least 2 hours. Before serving, drain most of the liquid from the relish.

Yield = About 1½ cups

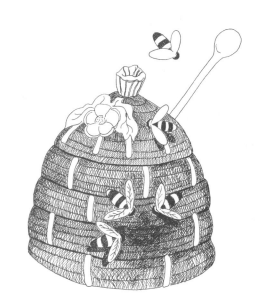

Honey Mustard

Honey Mustard sets off lighter sandwiches—ham, turkey, or vegetarian, such as avocado and sprouts—nicely. We also use it in ham glazes.

> 1 tablespoon yellow mustard seed
> ¼ tablespoon dry mustard
> 1 tablespoon water
> 2 tablespoons white wine
> ⅛ teaspoon salt
> Pinch ground turmeric
> 2 tablespoons red wine vinegar
> ½ cup honey

Grind the mustard seed to a fine consistency. Mix the ground seed with the dry mustard and water in a small bowl, cover with plastic wrap, and set aside for 2 hours.

Combine the mixture with the wine, salt, turmeric, and vinegar in a blender or mini–food processor. Puree until smooth, then return the puree to the bowl and mix in the honey.

The mustard should be ready to use immediately, with a refrigerator shelf life of 3 months.

Yield = About 1 cup

Camp Mustard

This recipe orchestrates an unusual harmony of flavors—it starts as a traditional sweet honey mustard, but the addition of Camp Vinegar introduces a hint of anchovy. It's a great base for a tangy mustard vinaigrette, and really perks up egg salad.

2 tablespoons yellow mustard seed
2½ teaspoons dry mustard
2 tablespoons water
½ teaspoon salt
1 teaspoon dried tarragon
1 garlic clove, peeled
½ teaspoon sugar
2 teaspoons honey
3 tablespoons *Home Made* Camp Vinegar (page 46)

Grind the mustard seed to a fine consistency. Transfer to a small bowl, add the mustard powder and water, and stir with a fork until blended. Set the bowl aside, uncovered, for about 45 minutes, until the mixture dries to the consistency of coarse sand.

Combine with the remaining ingredients in a blender or mini-food processor and puree until smooth.

The mustard should be ready to use immediately, with a refrigerator shelf life of 6 weeks.

Yield = ½ cup

Perfect Caesar Salad

There's nothing quite like a Caesar salad to make the meal. It's elegant, yet pungent enough to add a touch of the exotic to even the most basic steak or chop dinner.

Making Caesar salad at home, however, has always seemed a bit intimidating, especially to those whose experience was limited to watching headwaiters enact exaggerated rituals of preparation. And since traditionally the recipe calls for raw egg, a forbidden commodity since salmonella came on the scene, it began to look as though the days of preparing this cherished dish at home were limited.

This recipe makes the Perfect Caesar Salad using Home Made *components—it's simple, can be assembled in minutes, and eliminates the raw egg.*

1 tablespoon Camp Mustard
¼ cup *Home Made* Mayonnaise (page 36)
¼ cup *Home Made* Garlic Oil (page 38)
6 large leaves romaine lettuce, rinsed, dried, and ripped into bite-size pieces
1 cup seasoned croutons
2 tablespoons freshly grated Parmesan cheese

Whisk the mustard and mayonnaise in a small bowl, then whisk in the oil.

Put the lettuce into a salad bowl. Add the croutons and Parmesan cheese. Pour on the dressing and toss until the lettuce is well coated.

Yield = 4 servings

◇ ◇ ◇ *B*lack Pepper Mustard is the key ingredient in preparing a rich Mustard Chicken for 4. First, rub ¼ cup of the mustard over the skin of a quartered chicken. Put the chicken into a baking pan, cover with plastic wrap, and refrigerate for 2 hours while the flavors meld.

While bringing the chicken back to room temperature, preheat the oven to 350° F. Bake about 40 minutes, until the juices run clear when the chicken is pricked with a fork.

Meanwhile, prepare a sauce by combining another ¼ cup mustard and ½ cup heavy cream in a small saucepan over medium-low heat. Whisk and cook 3 to 4 minutes, until the sauce has thickened a bit. Spoon sauce over the chicken before serving. ◇ ◇ ◇

Black Pepper Mustard

Coarse and spicy, this is our "deli" mustard, ready to provide the perfect finishing touch to corned beef or pastrami creations, to garnish sausage and charcuterie plates, or to baste chicken.

3 tablespoons yellow mustard seed
1 tablespoon white wine vinegar
1½ tablespoons water
¼ teaspoon salt
¼ teaspoon freshly ground black pepper

Coarsely grind the mustard seed. Transfer to a small bowl, add all the remaining ingredients, and mix thoroughly with a fork. Cover with plastic wrap and set aside for 2 hours.

The mustard should be ready to use immediately, with a refrigerator shelf life of 3 months.

Yield = ½ cup

Dijon-Style Mustard

This classic, versatile mustard is almost indispensable in the modern kitchen. The recipe yields a mustard of medium consistency; if you prefer a very coarse stone-ground consistency, whisk the mustard mixture and the remaining ingredients together rather than pureeing.

2 tablespoons yellow mustard seed
½ tablespoon dry mustard
2 tablespoons water
2 tablespoons white wine
2 tablespoons white wine vinegar
¼ teaspoon salt
⅛ teaspoon ground turmeric

Grind the mustard seed to a fine consistency. Mix the ground mustard with the dry mustard powder and water in a small bowl, cover with plastic wrap, and set aside overnight.

Combine the mustards with the wine, vinegar, salt, and turmeric in a blender or mini–food processor. Puree until smooth.

The mustard should be ready to use immediately, with a refrigerator shelf life of 3 months.

Yield = ½ cup

Red Pepper Jelly

Hot and spicy, but tempered by a tinge of sweetness, Red Pepper Jelly quite literally packs a sugar-coated punch! A tasty condiment its devotees just can't seem to find enough creative uses for, it's also a highly versatile base for marinades and sauces.

For a zesty pork marinade, whisk a little oil and water into jelly that has been warmed and cool to room temperature before pouring over the meat. As a sauce for chicken or pork, combine in a 2-to-1 ratio with white wine or stock, and heat.

And if plain old hot isn't hot enough for you, substitute Home Made *Hot Pepper Vinegar (page 48) for white wine vinegar.*

> 1 pound red bell peppers, cored, seeded, deveined, and cut into chunks (about 3 cups)
> 4 large jalapeño peppers, cored, seeded, deveined, and halved lengthwise
> ¼ cup white wine vinegar
> ¼ cup water
> 2 cups sugar
> 2½ tablespoons fruit pectin

Fill a large pot with water to cover an inch or 2 over the top of ½-pint Mason jars and bring it to a boil. Using tongs, submerge

◈ ◈ ◈ **N**ote: Dispense with hot sealing for home use. Let the cooked jelly cool to room temperature and refrigerate in tightly sealing (preferably glass) containers. It should keep for up to 6 months in the refrigerator. ◈ ◈ ◈

4 jars into the water and boil for 5 to 6 minutes, adding the seals toward the end. Keep at a boil.

Meanwhile, combine the bell pepper and jalapeño pepper in a food processor and finely chop. (This can also be done in 2 batches in a blender, or by hand.)

Transfer the peppers to a medium saucepan. Add the vinegar and water, bring to a boil over medium heat and boil for 5 minutes. Stir in the sugar, bring back to a boil, and boil for another 5 minutes. Add the fruit pectin and cook 1 minute more, stirring constantly.

Carefully remove a Mason jar from the boiling water. Fit it with a canning funnel and ladle in hot jelly to within ¼ inch of the top of the jar. Wipe the mouth of the jar clean, place a seal firmly on top, and screw on the ring. Repeat the process to fill and seal all the jars.

Put the jars through a 10-minute hot-water bath (see page 36) if they will be shipped.

Set the jars upside down on a dish towel overnight. Check the seals.

Yield = 4 cups

CHAPTER 3

Beverages

O n a foggy, gaslamp-lit London street, vendors sell ginger beer and cordials from stalls. In a formal New York drawing room, a butler serves coffee and brandy after dinner. On the rambling front porch of a Midwestern farmhouse, lemonade is poured generously, while a bottle of blackberry liqueur nearby awaits uncorking after supper. And in an ornate Victorian ice cream parlor off the town square of a New England village, youngsters squeal in delightful anticipation with every ingredient added to a soda fountain creation.

Our nineteenth-century predecessors thoroughly enjoyed all sorts of beverages. A last course of fine brandy and liqueurs with the coffee was as requisite a part of civilized dining as were soup and meat. And although wines and spirits were much appreciated, a range of nonalcoholic drinks, including home-brewed sodas and fruit juice drinks that put their contemporary counterparts to shame, were also popular.

For those who indulge, proffering cordials with coffee remains very much a gracious end to a leisurely dinner. The pleasure doubles when the liqueurs presented are the hosts' own creations: What better way to celebrate the occasion and the guests than to raise a *Home Made* cordial in toast?

Home Made sodas and juices are every bit as flavorful as those enjoyed at the last turn of the century. They also enable you to eschew the artificial additives and preservatives that proliferate in commercially prepared beverages. Besides, the real thing still tastes better!

❖ ❖ ❖

INGREDIENTS

The best advice for making any beverage or liqueur at home is to start with the best ingredients—use a high-quality brandy or vodka and fresh fruit that's in season. Several recipes call for *glycerin* as a thickening agent; the drugstore variety is perfectly safe to use in the quantities specified. "Food grade" glycerin can be ordered from various sources, including beer and wine supply houses (see Source Guide).

Old-fashioned soda making requires a few special ingredients. What are commonly referred to as *extracts* are really flavor essences, and should not be confused with alcohol-based cooking extracts (including the extracts in our liqueur section). Soda extracts are available in a wide range of flavors (see Source Guide). *Champagne yeast* is available from beer and wine supply houses (see Source Guide).

EQUIPMENT

Once again in this chapter, a supply of *Ball or Kerr self-sealing Mason jars,* readily available at almost any supermarket, is indispensable. We use 1-quart jars for steeping liqueurs, ½-pint and 1-pint jars for storing syrups in the refrigerator, and ½-pint jars for steeping and storing extracts. For gifts of extracts, little apothecary bottles are perfect. The jars don't need to be sterilized for any of these recipes, just clean and dry.

Mason jars and their rings are reusable, but the flat metal seals that go atop the jar before the ring is screwed on are not. Most stores stock *replacement seals* alongside the jars.

Once they have steeped, we transfer liqueurs to *decorative decanters.* If you're using decanters fitted with *corks* rather than glass stoppers, replace the corks with each use. Look for replacements in the housewares section of larger hardware stores or see the Source Guide.

A *funnel* is needed to transfer the finished liqueur into decanters, and also for transferring soda from the large bowl or pot in which the ingredients are mixed to the bottles.

Several recipes call for straining ingredients through *fine-mesh sieves,* unlined or fitted with *flat-bottom coffee filters,* into *glass mea-*

Decorative Decanter Labels

What better way to finish your gift of *Home Made* liqueur than to hang a hand-painted label on the decanter? Decanters festooned with decorative labels also make a handsome addition to your own home bar.

The oven-bake clay from which the labels are made is available in a range of colors from crafts shops, as are acrylic paints. For the ceramic lettering brushes and silk cord try your crafts shop or see the Source Guide.

For each label, you will need:
· A strip of oven-bake clay about 2 x 5 x ⅝ inches (about 2 ounces)
· 2 sheets wax paper
· Rolling pin
· 2½- to 3-inch oval cookie cutter
· Toothpicks
· Ceramic lettering brush
· Acrylic paint
· 10 inches of brightly colored silk cord

Preheat the oven to about 250 to 265° F., according to the clay manufacturer's directions.

suring cups. Use a medium-size sieve with a 2- or 4-cup measuring cup, as specified in individual directions.

Save *soda bottles* in various sizes to bottle your *Home Made* soda; they are designed to withstand the pressure of fermentation. If your bottles don't have screw-on caps, substitute *crown caps* (see Source Guide).

Our old-fashioned soda recipes call for lukewarm water that is between 95 and 100° F., which is easily determined with an *instant-read thermometer.*

One of the juice recipes, as well as one for a syrup, call for extracting the juice of fresh fruit that has been wrapped in a double layer of *cheesecloth.*

We sometimes specify *nonreactive containers or pots.* Glass, enamel, stainless steel, or anodized aluminum (such as Calphalon or Magnalite) will do fine, but copper, plain aluminum, and cast iron can combine with some ingredients to cause an unwanted chemical reaction. Enameled cast iron is nonreactive, but we hesitate to use it lest the enamel coating become stained.

Knead each strip of clay with clean hands for about 2 minutes, until malleable. Roll it out between the sheets of wax paper to a thickness of about 3/16 inch. (This can also be done by flattening the clay a bit by hand and then putting it through the thickest setting on a pasta machine. If using this method, dispense with the wax paper.)

Cut the clay into an oval with the cookie cutter. Make a hole at each end of the oval with a toothpick. Place the clay on a baking sheet and bake for about 20 minutes, until hard and shiny.

Remove the baked clay from the oven and set it aside for about 10 hours to cool thoroughly.

Using a ceramic lettering brush, write the name of the decanter's contents onto the label with acrylic paint. Allow the paint to dry for about 2 hours.

Knot an end of the silk cord and thread the cord back-to-front through one of the holes in the label (so that the knot catches on the back of the label). Pass the cord front-to-back through the hole on the other end of the label, knot it in the back, and suspend the label from the neck of the decanter.

Liqueurs

"The temperance movement has made great advance[s]," notes the author of a 1901 book on entertaining, "since the days when it was not considered etiquette for a man to leave the table sober, and also from recent times when men lingered at the table after the ladies had withdrawn, to partake of strong liquors with their cigars." However, nipping a bit after dinner was down but apparently not out, as the same treatise goes on to advise that "a superior quality of brandy and various liqueurs are usually served with coffee. In buying [wines and spirits] it is always best to go directly to a reliable merchant and take his advice...A man's wine merchant should stand in as close relation to him as his lawyer or his physician."

Despite the seemingly mixed—and arguably chauvinistic—attitude toward spirits that characterized the late 1800s, wines and liqueurs were much in evidence on menus of the day. The cocktails that came into vogue a few decades later had not yet been perfected; we found a recipe for one that actually combined rum and gin, sweetened with maple syrup.

In these recipes, we show how to make a variety of liqueurs, including an updated version of the very Victorian blackberry cordial as well as renditions of such popular contemporary cordials as Frangelico (Hazelnut Liqueur), Grand Marnier (Orange Brandy Cordial), Amaretto (Almond Liqueur), and Kahlúa (Coffee Liqueur).

We've found the art of making liqueurs particularly entertaining (to say nothing of economical, if you've purchased any of late). Bringing out decanters of your own *Home Made* cordials for taste testing is a sure way to end a leisurely dinner party on a memorable note.

THE BASICS

Creating *Home Made* liqueurs begins with infusing alcohol with fruit, nuts, and other flavorings. You don't need a distillery in your basement, just a supply of vodka and brandy. Select a fairly good grade, just as you would if you were going to drink the liquor straight up, rather than use them in mixed drinks.

Fruits are crushed and nuts chopped to release their flavor before they are added to the alcohol. (Be sure to rinse, dry, and pick over the fruit first.) In most recipes, the flavored vodka or brandy is set aside to steep in a cool, dark place for 10 days to 6 weeks. Don't steep in the refrigerator. If you don't have a pantry, choose a cabinet away from the stove, a countertop out of sunlight, or any other nook removed from direct heat and strong light.

Straining is usually done twice, through a plain sieve and then again through the sieve lined with a damp coffee filter. The second straining will catch residual bits of fruit or nuts, leaving a clarified liquor.

Add sugar syrup to sweeten, and in some recipes glycerin to thicken, and you have a liqueur. Set it aside a few days for the flavors to meld, and enjoy! *Home Made* liqueurs continue to mellow with age for 2 to 3 months, after which time the flavors begin to dissipate.

ᗛ ᗛ ᗛ

Liqueur-Flavored Desserts

You may not be able to have your cake and eat it too, but you *can* have your liqueur and eat it too! *Home Made* liqueurs add a grand finishing touch to a host of desserts.

Cakes: Add Orange Brandy Cordial, Sour Cherry Vodka, or any of the raspberry cordials to flavor chocolate cake; Hazelnut Liqueur, Almond Liqueur, or Coffee Liqueur to flavor sponge cakes; and, of course, Orange Brandy Cordial to flavor orange cake. Almond Liqueur is a nice touch in flourless chocolate cake recipes that call for almonds. After a cake has baked—and is still warm and still in the pan—poke holes across the top with a tester or toothpick. Pour about 2 ounces of liqueur over and allow it to drip down into the cake.

And don't forget the possibilities of flavoring frostings with liqueurs; adding a little Coffee Liqueur to chocolate, for example, makes a mocha frosting.

Brownies: Infuse a batch of fudge brownies with Almond Liqueur following the directions above for cakes.

Pies: Apple pie is better than Mom's when you first toss the apples in ½ cup Orange Brandy Cordial, and berry pies of all persuasions benefit from tossing the berries in ½ cup Raspberry Vodka Cordial, Raspberry Brandy Cordial, or a blend of the two.

Fresh Fruit: Everybody's favorite, strawberries, takes on a new dimension when macerated for 2 hours in Orange Brandy Cordial. For fruit compote, add a jigger of Blackberry or Raspberry (Vodka or Brandy) Cordial for every 6 cups of fruit and top with a generous dollop of *Home Made* Crème Fraîche (page 88).

Blackberry Cordial

We've updated the traditional after-dinner glass of blackberry brandy or wine that your grandmother took "for digestive purposes." Vodka lends a bit of a punch and the orange peel a pleasing accent. We think your grandmother will probably approve of the changes, but her grandmother might have found this a somewhat bitter concoction—a nineteenth-century recipe we unearthed called for adding a pound of white sugar to a similar yield of blackberry cordial.

1 pint blackberries
2 1 x 4-inch strips of orange peel, pith removed
1/4 teaspoon ground cloves
1 1/2 cups vodka
1 1/2 cups brandy
2/3 cup sugar
1/3 cup water
1/2 teaspoon glycerin

Put the blackberries into a shallow dish and lightly crush them with a fork. Transfer the berries and their juice to a 1-quart Mason jar. Add the orange peel, cloves, vodka, and brandy. Seal the jar and shake it to mix. Set the jar aside in a cool, dark place for 4 weeks.

Strain the mixture through a fine sieve into a 4-cup glass measuring cup, pressing down on the fruit with a wooden spoon to extract as much fluid as possible. Discard the solids, and rinse the sieve and the Mason jar thoroughly. Fit the sieve with a damp coffee filter and strain the liquid back into the jar.

Combine the sugar and water in a small saucepan. Heat for 5 minutes over medium-low heat, stirring constantly, until the sugar dissolves, leaving a clear syrup. Remove the pan from the heat and cool to room temperature.

Add the syrup and the glycerin to the jar. Reseal the Mason jar and shake gently to blend. If you wish, transfer the liqueur to decanters.

The Blackberry Cordial should be ready to drink in 2 or 3 days and has a shelf life of 2 to 3 months.

Yield = 3 cups

Orange Brandy Cordial

This hearty liqueur, with its pronounced orange flavor, is highly versatile. It's great by itself and it holds up well in sauces and desserts.

> 2 large navel oranges
> 1 whole clove
> 2 cups brandy
> 1 cup sugar
> ¼ cup water
> 1 teaspoon glycerin

Thinly peel the oranges in long strips with a vegetable peeler, taking care not to include any pith. Cut the strips into ¼-inch segments.

Put the orange peels and the clove into a 1-quart Mason jar, top with the brandy, and seal. Shake the jar to mix and set it aside in a cool, dark place for 10 days.

Strain the liquid through a fine sieve into a 4-cup glass measuring cup and discard the solids. Rinse the sieve and the Mason jar thoroughly. Fit the sieve with a damp coffee filter and strain the flavored brandy back into the jar.

Combine the sugar and water in a small saucepan. Heat for about 5 minutes over low heat, stirring constantly, just to the boiling point. Remove the pan from the heat and let the sugar syrup cool for 5 minutes.

Add the sugar syrup and glycerin to the flavored brandy. Reseal the Mason jar and shake it gently to blend. If you wish, transfer the liqueur to a decanter.

The Orange Brandy Cordial should be ready to drink in 2 or 3 days and has a shelf life of 2 to 3 months.

Yield = 2 cups

Spiked Coffee, Tea, and Cocoa

Perking up hot beverages with a shot of liqueur is a phenomenon of relatively recent origins. Our turn-of-the-century predecessors most likely would have considered the idea curious. Indeed, they seemed to be perplexed about the nature of the common cup of coffee or tea. "Coffee and tea have power to sustain under fatigue and privation," counsels one source. "Hunger is better borne by their aid. Tea disposes to mental cheerfulness and activity, and clears the brain . . . They are both to be recommended. Cocoa possesses in a milder degree the properties of tea or coffee, but it differs from them in possessing much higher nutritive powers."

"Tea should not be used early in the morning," cautions a critic, "as the body needs immediate nourishment in a larger quantity; and it should at all times be taken moderately, both in quantity and strength."

"With regard to the quality of coffee, the best is the cheapest," advises one cookbook. "Don't buy poor, cheap tea and coffee," counters another, "it is simply impossible to make them fit to drink." Yet another sagely observes, "The making of coffee is a very simple operation, but the nicety and care with which it is prepared mark the difference between the good and bad decoction. The best quality of coffee carelessly made is not as acceptable as that well made from an inferior bean."

Brew your coffee as you will and stand forewarned about the evils of tea drinking in the morning, but by all means take time out from these controversies to enjoy an occasional mug of coffee, tea, or cocoa flavored with a warming liqueur and all the trimmings.

Hazelnut Cocoa: Mix a cup of cocoa with a jigger of Hazelnut Liqueur. Add a cinnamon stick.

Orange Coffee: Add a jigger of Orange Brandy Cordial to a cup of Viennese roast coffee. Top with a twist of orange peel.

Creamy Almond Coffee: In a large mug, combine 3 parts coffee to 1 part scalded heavy cream, and add a jigger of Almond Liqueur.

Chilled Mexican Coffee: Put a scoop of Vanilla Ice Cream (page 98) into a mug. Pour a jigger of Coffee Liqueur over. Fill with chilled strong coffee.

Berry Tea: To a cup of freshly brewed tea, add a jigger of Raspberry Vodka Cordial, Raspberry Brandy Cordial, or Blackberry Cordial. Add a lemon slice and honey to taste.

Grown-up Cocoa: Add 2 tablespoons Sour Cherry Vodka to a cup of hot cocoa. Top with whipped cream and a little shaved chocolate or cocoa powder.

Sour Cherry Vodka

This Scandinavian delight is crisp and refreshing, fruity but just tart and pungent enough to set it apart from most other cordials. It also makes a superb sauce for duck or goose: Mix ½ cup Sour Cherry Vodka with 1 cup of pitted cherries and thicken with arrowroot.

> 1¼ pounds sour cherries, pitted (about 2¾ cups)
> 1 cup sugar
> 2 cups vodka

Put the cherries into a 1-quart Mason jar, and cover with the sugar. Seal the jar and shake it several times, until the cherries are well coated with sugar.

Add the vodka, reseal, and shake the jar a few more times to mix. Set aside in a cool, dark place for 4 weeks.

Strain the mixture through a fine sieve into a 4-cup glass measuring cup. If desired, transfer the liqueur to a decanter.

The Sour Cherry Vodka should be ready to drink immediately and has a shelf life of 2 to 3 months.

Yield = 2 cups

Almond Liqueur

Home Made *Almond Liqueur is lighter than the traditional version; you get a strong almond flavor, with none of the heavy, syrupy taste.*

    1 pound almonds, shelled
    2 cups vodka
    ½ vanilla bean
    ½ cup sugar
    ¼ cup water
    1 teaspoon vanilla extract
    ½ teaspoon glycerin

Coarsely chop the almonds by hand or in a food processor (a blender will produce too fine a chop). This should yield 1⅓ to 1½ cups chopped nuts.

Combine the nuts, vodka, and vanilla bean in a 1-quart Mason jar. Seal the jar, shake to mix, and set it aside in a cool, dark place for at least 10 days.

Strain the liquor through a fine sieve into a 4-cup glass measuring cup and discard the residue in the sieve. Rinse the sieve and the Mason jar thoroughly. Fit the sieve with a damp coffee filter and strain the flavored vodka back into the jar.

Combine the sugar and water in a small saucepan. Bring to a boil over low heat, stirring until the sugar dissolves. Continue to boil for 2 minutes, until a clear syrup forms. Remove the pan from the heat and cool to room temperature.

When the syrup is cool, add it to the Mason jar. Add the vanilla and glycerin. Seal the jar and shake it gently to blend. The liqueur can be transferred to a decanter.

The Almond Liqueur should be ready to drink in 2 or 3 days and has a shelf life of 2 to 3 months.

Yield = 2 cups

✧ ✧ ✧ **V**ariation: For a rich, nutty Hazelnut Liqueur, substitute 1 pound hazelnuts, shelled, for the almonds and omit 2 tablespoons of the sugar, 1 tablespoon of the water, and the vanilla extract and glycerin. ✧ ✧ ✧

Home Made *Extracts*

It's quite easy to make extracts at home, and it's practical, too. Vanilla and Lemon Extracts, especially, are frequently called for in recipes. We also include a recipe for Orange Extract, which is used in custards, ice creams, sponge and angel food cakes, or as a substitute for Lemon Extract. Any would be a lovely addition to a gift basket.

To make an extract, simply combine ingredients in a ½-pint Mason jar and set aside to steep for at least 3 days. Each recipe yields ¾ cup extract, which can be stored anywhere and should keep for up to a year.

If you want to give a gift of an extract, strain a portion (for aesthetics), transfer it to a little apothecary bottle, and add a piece of vanilla bean, or a spiral of lemon or orange peel.

For Vanilla Extract, combine 2 vanilla beans, cut in half lengthwise and then chopped (about 1 tablespoon), ½ cup brandy, and ¼ cup water.

For Lemon Extract, thinly peel 1 lemon with a vegetable

peeler, taking care not to include any pith. Dice the peel (about 2 tablespoons) and combine it with ½ cup vodka and ¼ cup water.

For Orange Extract, thinly peel ½ navel orange (as above), and cut the peel into chunks (about 1½ tablespoons). Combine with ¼ cup vodka and ½ cup water.

❖ ❖ ❖ *Variation*: **For velvety Vanilla Liqueur, omit the first step. Combine 1 cup boiling water with the sugars and proceed as with Coffee Liqueur, increasing the amount of vanilla to 3 tablespoons.**
❖ ❖ ❖

❖ ❖ ❖ *Home Made* **liqueurs can easily be made into cream liqueurs for a luscious treat. We especially like Coffee Cream Liqueur, but you can make a cream version of any *Home Made* cordial that strikes your fancy.**

To 1½ cups (12 ounces) liqueur, add 7 ounces sweetened condensed milk and 5 ounces evaporated milk. Chill thoroughly before serving.

Yield = **3 cups**
❖ ❖ ❖

Coffee Liqueur

Our Coffee Liqueur is considerably smoother and more delicate than commercial varieties. It's best sipped as a cordial or poured over ice cream, rather than mixed in drinks.

> 2 cups ground coffee beans (select a strong, full-bodied blend, such as French Roast)
> 3 cups boiling water
> 1½ cups granulated sugar
> ½ cup light brown sugar, firmly packed
> 1 teaspoon glycerin
> 1 teaspoon *Home Made* Vanilla Extract
> 3 cups vodka

Put the ground coffee and boiling water into a bowl and mix thoroughly. Line a fine-mesh sieve with a coffee filter and strain immediately into a 4-cup glass measuring cup.

Combine the coffee and the sugars in a medium saucepan. Heat for 5 minutes over low heat, stirring constantly, just until the mixture begins to steam (do not bring to a boil). Remove the pan from the heat and let cool.

Stir in the glycerin, vanilla, and vodka. Using a funnel, divide the liqueur between two 20-ounce decanters.

The Coffee Liqueur should be ready to drink in 3 or 4 days and has a shelf life of 2 to 3 months.

Yield = 5 cups

Raspberry Vodka Cordial

We love raspberries in almost any way, shape, or form, and enjoy raspberry liqueur in several varieties, each subtly different. Raspberry Vodka Cordial should appeal to those who find traditional liqueurs too sweet or too heavy for their taste; here, the vodka provides a neutral background for the intense flavor of the berries.

1½ pints red raspberries
2½ cups vodka
1 cup sugar
½ cup water
½ teaspoon glycerin

Put the raspberries into a large, shallow dish and mash with a fork or potato masher. Transfer the fruit and its juice to a 1-quart Mason jar and cover with the vodka. Seal the jar, shake to mix, and set it aside in a cool, dark place for 6 weeks.

Strain the contents of the jar through a fine sieve into a 4-cup glass measuring cup. Discard the fruit; rinse the sieve and the Mason jar thoroughly. Fit the sieve with a damp coffee filter and strain the flavored vodka back into the jar.

Combine the sugar and water in a small saucepan. Bring to a boil over medium heat, stirring until the sugar dissolves. Reduce the heat to low and simmer for 5 minutes, or until a clear syrup forms. Remove the pan from the heat and cool to room temperature.

Add the cooled syrup and the glycerin to the liqueur. Reseal the jar and shake gently to blend. Using a funnel, divide the liqueur between two 10-ounce decanters.

The Raspberry Vodka Cordial should be ready to drink in 2 or 3 days and has a shelf life of 2 to 3 months.

Yield = 20 ounces (2½ cups)

◇ ◇ ◇ **Variation: For Raspberry Brandy Cordial, substitute 2¾ cups brandy for the vodka and use only 1 pint red raspberries. Or try our favorite raspberry liqueur, derived by mixing 2 parts Raspberry Vodka Cordial with 1 part Raspberry Brandy Cordial.** ◇ ◇ ◇

Making Beer and Wine

"Everything old is new again," the saying goes. The long-abandoned Victorian penchant for making beer and wine at home has resurfaced as a hobby in the 1990s. Luckily, we can dispense with the sometimes cumbersome apparatuses used in the 1800s, and use instead any number of kits available from beer and wine supply houses (see Source Guide).

Essentially, beer-making kits come in two varieties. The simpler version, which is ideal for novices or for a party novelty, is virtually idiot-proof. These provide a disposable fermenting sack that already contains pre-measured amounts of malt, sugar, and hop extract, along with the needed supply of brewer's yeast. They make 30 to 40 servings of beer, served from a built-in spigot. With the kit we tried, we simply added hot water to the sack, mixed, added cold water and the yeast, and set aside for the ale to ferment. A thicker, stoutlike beer could be made by adding less cold water. Fermentation took 21 days, and the quality of the beer improved during its subsequent 3-month shelf life.

For more diehard aficionados, basic kits can be had that include reusable fermenting tanks (some divide the process into stages and also include a settling tank) and a bottler. You can then buy ingredient kits with premeasured supplies for making everything from pilsners to bitters.

Wine-making starter kits contain a reusable fermenting vessel. For the equivalent of jug wine, some fermenters come equipped with a spigot attachment. For a more sophisticated approach, corkers are available.

If the first image that comes to mind when you think of making wine is that of Lucy and Ethel stomping grapes in the infamous old *I Love Lucy* episode, perish the thought. Although you *can* purchase a press if there just happens to be a vineyard in your backyard, you can also readily obtain concentrated grape juices for producing a wide range of varietals, as well as concentrated fruit juices for making fruit wines.

Sodas, Juices, and Syrups

You are what you eat, so the saying goes. By extension, you also are what you drink, and you need not be captive to those bland, fizzy, mass-produced soft drinks that tickle the nose rather than the taste buds, that quench the thirst but leave the soul dry.

Better, we think, to have a drink worth savoring. Our versions of classic beverages are timeless, evoking recollections of the past.

A frosty lemonade or ginger beer inspires thoughts of a Victorian gazebo, town green, or sprawling lawn where it might have been sipped so many summers ago. A mug of hot mulled apple juice on Halloween brings to mind "The Legend of Sleepy Hollow" and scents of burning leaves. And a rich, silky ice-cream soda can still soothe the hurt of a bruised knee, or a bruised ego, as readily as it did when you were a child—or when your grandfather was a child, for that matter.

THE BASICS

The key ingredient to making old-fashioned sodas at home is a type of extract available in dozens of flavors (see Source Guide), including ginger beer and root beer.

The initial step, combining sugar, water, extract, and a yeast mixture, takes but a matter of minutes. You then set the stuff aside for a few days to do its thing (technically known as fermentation). For those who can't wait, we offer Quick Root Beer that can be drunk immediately, made from a concentrate stocked in many grocery stores.

Sodas can also be made from *Home Made* syrups (Vanilla Syrup for cream soda, Lemon Syrup for lemon soda), but syrups have life beyond soda making. Chocolate Syrup, for example, serves as a base for cocoa and egg creams; all can be used to flavor milk or milk shakes. Most *Home Made* syrups are made by adding flavoring to a simple sugar-and-water syrup and chilling to thicken.

Home Made juices are as versatile as they are easy. Apple Juice can be made without a juice extractor and transformed quickly into a warming mulled beverage. Front Porch Lemonade takes on new life as Pink Lemonade with a little help from Grenadine. Classic Tomato Vegetable Juice serves as the base for our spicy Bloody Maria mix—either can be hot sealed for savoring long after the last tomato has been harvested.

Old-Fashioned Ginger Beer

Use empty soda bottles for this recipe, as they are designed to withstand the pressure of the yeast reaction. Rinse them out thoroughly with very hot tap water first; glass bottles can also be put through a dishwasher. If the bottles do not have screw-on resealable caps, substitute "crown" caps (see Source Guide). Reduce the amount of sugar if you wish, but don't increase it, as this could alter the nature of the reaction and cause the bottles to explode.

For a refreshing picnic beverage, derived from an old English formula, mix ginger beer and light ale in equal proportions.

⅛ teaspoon champagne yeast
¾ cup lukewarm water (95–100° F.)
2¼ cups sugar
12 cups hot water (120–125° F.)
4 teaspoons ginger beer extract

Add the yeast to the lukewarm water, and stir just enough to moisten the yeast. Set aside for 10 minutes, uncovered.

Combine the sugar and hot water in a large (at least 3-quart) nonreactive bowl or pot. Stir until the sugar is totally dissolved, then stir in the extract. Add the yeast mixture and combine thoroughly. Using a funnel, transfer to the soda bottles, leaving at least 1 inch at the top of each bottle. Cap the bottles.

Stand the bottles upright in a warm place (70–80° F.) for 5 to 6 days, until the soda is effervescent. Refrigerate before serving.

The ginger beer should be ready to drink as soon as it has chilled.

Yield = About 13 cups

❖ ❖ ❖ *T*o make Old-Fashioned Root Beer, substitute an equal amount of root beer extract for the ginger beer extract. For a classic Root Beer Float, add 2 scoops *Home Made* Vanilla Ice Cream (page 98); for a truly decadent rendition, use *Home Made* Ann's White Chocolate Ice Cream (page 100). ❖❖❖

Quick Root Beer

This recipe is for those who want their soda when they want it, and don't have the patience to wait for it to ferment. It produces a drink that is somewhat less effervescent than the old-fashioned variety. The recipe is for a single glass, but can easily be converted to increase the yield. Look for the root beer concentrate in the spice section of the supermarket.

3 tablespoons sugar
1 cup water
1 teaspoon root beer concentrate
½ teaspoon baking soda
½ teaspoon cream of tartar

In a tall glass, dissolve the sugar in the water. Stir in the root beer concentrate, baking soda, and cream of tartar.

Add ice and serve.

Yield = One 8-ounce glass

Tomato Vegetable Juice

Fresh tomato juice is always a nice change from the commercial variety. In this version, onion, carrot, celery, and celery seed add flavor.

>   7 pounds very ripe Italian plum tomatoes, cored and
>   cubed
>   1 medium onion, peeled and minced
>   2 large carrots, peeled and minced
>   2 celery stalks, trimmed and minced
>   ½ teaspoon celery seed

Combine all the ingredients in an 8-quart pot. Cook for about 30 minutes over medium-low heat, stirring occasionally, until the tomatoes are very soft.

Transfer the mixture (including liquid) in batches into a food mill placed over a large bowl. Work it through the food mill until all ingredients are pureed, periodically discarding the tomato skin and seeds that accumulate. Stir and transfer the juice to a large pitcher. Chill before serving.

The Tomato Vegetable Juice will keep in the refrigerator for 1 week.

Yield = 6 cups

❖ ❖ ❖ *I*f you want to extend the shelf life of the Tomato Vegetable Juice, hot seal it in three 1-pint Mason jars and put it through a 15-minute hot water bath. Allow to cool, check the seals, and store for up to 1 year. (See the directions for hot sealing, hot-water baths, and checking seals on page 6.) ❖ ❖ ❖

Bloody Marias

The Bloody Mary has become an American institution. Everyone has a favorite version; ours has a slightly south-of-the-border accent.

To make "Bloody Maria" mix, follow the directions for Tomato Vegetable Juice, adding 2 tablespoons seeded and minced jalapeño pepper, ½ cup chopped fresh basil, and ¼ cup chopped fresh dill to the pot.

After the mixture has been put through a food mill, stir in 4 teaspoons *Home Made* Prepared Horseradish (page 54), 4 teaspoons freshly squeezed lemon juice, ½ teaspoon freshly ground black pepper, ¼ teaspoon salt, and an additional ¾ teaspoon celery seed.

Chill the Bloody Maria mix before serving and store it in the refrigerator for up to 1 week. (It can also be hot sealed and put through a hot-water bath to store for up to one year.)

If you're really into hot and spicy, mix Bloody Marias with pepper vodka.

Yield = About 6 cups

◈ ◈ ◈ *H*ot mulled Apple Juice is a thoroughly warming drink for chilly autumn nights, and it's lighter and easier to make from scratch than with cider.

In a medium saucepan, combine 4 cups Apple Juice, 1 cinnamon stick, and 4 whole allspice berries. Stick 4 whole cloves into ½ navel orange and add it to the pan. Heat for 5 minutes over low heat. Ladle the juice into 4 mugs and garnish each with a cinnamon stick. If desired, stir 1 ounce brandy into each mug. ◈ ◈ ◈

Apple Juice

Fine apple juice varies greatly according to the type of apple used, just as fine wine varies according to the grape. We prefer the crisp, slightly tart taste produced by McIntosh apples; for variety, try tarter pippins or sweeter Jonathans.

This recipe employs a quick, simple manual method of juicing. You can, of course, use a juice extractor. Surprisingly, there is a noticeable difference: The manual method yields a thicker, sweeter juice.

For a single glass of juice, use 1 ¼ pounds (about 4) apples.

5 pounds apples, cored and quartered

Finely chop the apple segments in a food processor and transfer them to a large double layer of cheesecloth. Wrap the cheesecloth tightly into a ball and squeeze the juice out into a large bowl. Chill the juice before serving.

The Apple Juice will keep in the refrigerator about 1 week.

Yield = 4 cups

Front Porch Lemonade

What could possibly conjure up images of summertimes past faster than an ice-cold pitcher of freshly squeezed lemonade? Even if your "front porch" is a balcony on the thirty-third floor and there is no rocking chair in sight, close your eyes, take a sip, and listen to the wind rustling through the elms on the lawn out by the gazebo.

◈ ◈ ◈ *K*ids of all ages appreciate how Pink Lemonade adds a festive touch to parties. Mixed with vodka, it makes a cool and refreshing warm-weather drink for grown-up kids. To make Pink Lemonade, use ½ cup lemon juice and substitute ¾ cup plus 2 tablespoons Grenadine for the sugar. ◈ ◈ ◈

⅔ cup sugar
1 cup freshly squeezed lemon juice, strained (juice of 4 large lemons)
4 cups cold water

Combine the sugar and lemon juice in a large pitcher. Stir in the water.

Chill well and serve over ice.

Yield = About 5 cups

Grenadine

Used in Pink Lemonade and a variety of mixed drinks, grenadine is derived from glossy red pomegranate seeds. Be sure to discard all the white membrane around the seeds.

    1½ cups pomegranate seeds (about a 1-pound
          pomegranate)
    2 cups sugar
    ½ cup water

Combine all the ingredients in the bowl of a food processor and process briefly to break up the seeds. (The mixture need not be a smooth consistency.) Transfer to a 1-quart Mason jar and set the jar aside for 3 days in a cool, dark place, but don't refrigerate.

Strain the contents through a fine sieve into a 4-cup glass measuring cup. Allow the liquid to drip through; this could take up to 30 minutes.

Transfer the strained liquid to a medium nonreactive saucepan. Bring just to a boil over low heat, about 10 minutes. Remove from the heat and cool to room temperature before using.

Store the Grenadine in the refrigerator, where it should keep for up to 6 months.

Yield = 2 cups

✧ ✧ ✧ *F*or a "blast from the past," albeit the recent past rather than the 1800s, stir a tablespoon of Grenadine in 6 ounces of ginger ale over ice and garnish with a maraschino cherry... remember the Roy Rogers and Shirley Temple "kiddy cocktails" your parents would order for you before dinner? ✧ ✧ ✧

Lemon Syrup

Use Lemon Syrup to make lemon soda, without all the additives and preservatives that come with store-bought drinks. Just add 4 tablespoons to 8 ounces club soda or seltzer.

    ½ cup sugar
    ¼ cup water
    ⅓ cup freshly squeezed lemon juice

Combine the sugar and water in a small nonreactive saucepan and stir. Bring to a boil over medium heat and boil for 5 minutes.

Remove the pan from the heat, stir in the lemon juice, and cool to room temperature. Chill the syrup for at least 2 hours before using. The Lemon Syrup has a refrigerator shelf life of 3 to 4 weeks.

Yield = ⅔ cup

✧ ✧ ✧ *A* popular drink during the Victorian era, Raspberry Shrub was made by diluting raspberry vinegar with sugar and water. A tart but surprisingly thirst-quenching version can be made by mixing 3 tablespoons Lemon Syrup, 1 tablespoon *Home Made* Raspberry Vinegar (page 45), and 8 ounces club soda or seltzer. Serve chilled over ice. ✧ ✧ ✧

◈ ◈ ◈ **L**egions of ex–New Yorkers around the country— including us—grow misty-eyed at the very thought of a native soda creation known as an "Egg Cream" (which, incidentally, contains no egg). A classic egg cream, made with a brand of chocolate syrup available only in the New York City area, just can't be had anywhere else.

For a close approximation that's a lot cheaper to come by than an airplane ticket, mix 1 tablespoon Chocolate Syrup and 2 ounces light cream in a 10- to 12-ounce glass. Slowly fill the glass with about 6 ounces of seltzer. The mixture will bubble up fiercely, producing a frothy layer of foam on top. ◈ ◈ ◈

◈ ◈ ◈ **F**or Cream Soda, the quintessential old-fashioned soft drink, combine 6 tablespoons Vanilla Syrup, 2 tablespoons corn syrup, and 6 ounces seltzer or club soda in a 12-ounce glass. Add ice and serve. ◈ ◈ ◈

Chocolate Syrup

The pure, rich taste of cocoa permeates this syrup, which is considerably less sweet than most commercial syrups. And speaking of cocoa . . . for the perfect hot chocolate, stir 2 tablespoons syrup into ¾ cup scalded milk; for chocolate milk, add 2 tablespoons to 1 cup cold milk.

> ⅔ cup cocoa powder
> 6 tablespoons corn syrup
> ½ cup boiling water
> ½ cup sugar

Mix the cocoa powder and corn syrup in a small nonreactive saucepan. Slowly whisk in the boiling water. Heat over low heat for 3 minutes. Add the sugar, whisking until it has completely dissolved.

Let the syrup cool to room temperature and chill for 2 hours before using. Store in a tightly sealing container. The Chocolate Syrup has a refrigerator shelf life of 3 to 4 weeks.

Yield = 1¼ cups

Vanilla Syrup

We think vanilla has been a "sleeper" flavor for far too long, and it just might rise again in this back-to-basics era. It was popular with our ancestors, who appreciated its subtlety and richness long before chocolate pushed it aside. Chocolate makes a great soda and is indispensable to an egg cream, but there's nothing like a vanilla milk shake.

> 2 vanilla beans
> 1 cup sugar
> ½ cup water

Cut the vanilla beans in half crosswise and then again lengthwise.

Combine all the ingredients in a small nonreactive saucepan and stir to mix. Bring to a boil over medium heat; boil for 5 minutes. Strain the syrup through a fine sieve into a 1-cup glass measuring cup.

Allow the syrup to cool to room temperature and chill it for at least 2 hours before using. Vanilla Syrup has a refrigerator shelf life of 3 to 4 weeks.

Yield = 1 cup

Strawberry Syrup

The all-time favorite of kids of all ages, Strawberry Syrup turns a glass of milk into a treat! It's also good in milk shakes and spooned over ice cream.

> 1 pint strawberries, hulled
>
> 1 cup sugar

Put the strawberries into a medium nonreactive saucepan and smash them with a potato masher. Cook over low heat for about 5 minutes, until the berries are soft and fork-tender.

Line a fine sieve with a 2-foot square of cheesecloth folded in half, and position it over a 2-cup glass measuring cup. Scrape the berries and juice into the sieve, gather the cheesecloth into a ball, and allow the mixture to drip through. This should yield about ¾ cup strawberry juice. Discard the cheesecloth.

Rinse the saucepan and return the strawberry juice to the pan. Stir in the sugar. Bring to a boil over medium heat and boil for about 1 minute, until a clear syrup forms. Remove the pan from the heat.

Rinse the sieve, and strain the syrup through again. Skim any foam off the top. Cool to room temperature and chill the syrup for at least 2 hours before using. The Strawberry Syrup has a refrigerator shelf life of 1 week to 10 days.

Yield = 1 cup

Quick Coffee Syrup

Quick Coffee Syrup can be made in minutes using instant coffee. Stir it into chilled milk, use it to flavor milk shakes, or spoon over ice cream.

> 1 tablespoon instant coffee granules
>
> 1 tablespoon boiling water
>
> ½ cup water
>
> 1 cup sugar

Combine the coffee granules and the boiling water in a small bowl and mix until the coffee is thoroughly dissolved.

Put the water into a small nonreactive saucepan. Stir in the sugar. Bring to a boil over medium heat and boil for 5 minutes.

The Home Soda Fountain

It wasn't all that long ago when every urban neighborhood and small town had its own soda fountain. Each one had a distinctive feel, reflecting the personality of the community; America lost an important resource with the closing of so many in recent years.

The long, cool marble counters, the ornate soda dispensers, and the ice-cream tables are only a memory in all too many communities today—but one that can still be conjured up by making your own fountain creations at home.

Although the possible flavors for *Home Made* ice-cream sodas are exhaustive, they all follow a simple formula: In a 10- to 12-ounce glass, stir together 2 tablespoons syrup and 4 ounces milk. Add 4 ounces soda or seltzer and a generous scoop of ice cream. Here are a few combinations that we think go together especially well.

With Chocolate Syrup, try: seltzer and Coffee Ice Cream (page 100)
or
Old-Fashioned Root Beer and Vanilla Ice Cream (page 98)

With Strawberry Syrup, try: seltzer and Ann's White Chocolate Ice Cream (page 100)
or
seltzer and Strawberry Ice Cream (page 98)

With Coffee Syrup, try: seltzer and Chocolate Ice Cream (page 97)

With Vanilla Syrup, try: cola and Vanilla Ice Cream (page 98)
or
seltzer and your favorite flavor of *Home Made* ice cream.

Remove the pan from the heat and stir in the coffee. Let the syrup cool to room temperature and chill for at least 2 hours before using. The coffee syrup has a refrigerator shelf life of 3 to 4 weeks.

Yield = 1 cup

Eggnog

4 cups light cream
3 large eggs, separated
½ cup granulated sugar
1 teaspoon vanilla extract
2 cups brandy
3 tablespoons confectioners' sugar
Ground nutmeg to garnish

Combine 3 cups of the cream and the egg yolks in a medium saucepan. Stirring constantly, cook over very low heat for 4 to 5 minutes, just until the mixture is thick enough to coat the back of the spoon. Remove the pan from the heat.

In a large bowl, combine the granulated sugar, vanilla, and brandy, stirring with a wooden spoon until the sugar is dissolved. Whisk in the cream and egg yolk mixture thoroughly.

Put the egg whites into the top of a double boiler over boiling water and beat them to soft peaks, using an electric mixer at medium speed. Gradually beat in the confectioners' sugar. Continue to beat until stiff peaks form.

Gently fold the beaten egg whites into the large bowl; stir in the remaining cup of cream. Cover and refrigerate for at least 1 hour. To serve, ladle into small cups and dust each with a little nutmeg.

Dairy Products

ew foods evoke pastoral images as readily as dairy products. Even in today's world of factory farms and mass production, we retain mental snapshots of cows grazing in bucolic pastures, and somewhere in the back of our taste buds lingers the flavor of real, farm-fresh products sampled years ago.

It's really but a small step back in time to a nineteenth-century farmhouse, where out behind the kitchen, cream rises to the top of pails of fresh milk, and sweet butter hardens in the churn. In a trough nearby, whey drains from the milk curds that will be used in making cheese. And on the front porch, children crank an ice-cream freezer in anticipation of the delights to follow.

Although these scenes are but a memory, the pleasures of freshly made, ever so rich and creamy butter, cheese, ice cream, and other dairy products can still be a part of our daily lives.

Thanks to modern ingenuity, butter can be churned in a food processor or electric mixer, curds and whey can be separated in a small cheesecloth sack suspended over a bowl rather than a trough, and the cumbersome ice-cream freezer of yore is supplanted by compact ice-cream makers that produce pints or quarts in a matter of minutes.

THE BASICS

"Procure a calf's rennet," begins one turn-of-the-century instruction for cheesemaking—surely words to strike terror—or at the very least, confusion—into the heart of the modern cook. But rest assured that we include only updated recipes that require a minimum of special equipment and that render small quantities in keeping with smaller households.

And although two recipes do use rennet as a thickening agent, we spare the calf and call instead for handier, if less picturesque, rennet tablets.

We provide directions for preparing a variety of delectable soft cheeses, from Herbed Chèvre and Cream Cheese to Raspberry Dessert Cheese and Mascarpone, that can be made with little fuss and few esoteric ingredients—and recommend that you continue to rely on the neighborhood cheese monger for hard cheeses, which require molds, presses, special starters, and more time than you likely have to spend.

Most *Home Made* cheeses are produced, essentially, by introducing an acidic substance (such as vinegar, buttermilk, or citrus juice) into heated milk or cream to induce coagulation, and then allowing the liquid whey to drip from the curds for 2 to 24 hours.

For Cream Cheese, the acid is added to room-temperature milk and set aside for 20 hours to coagulate before heating. The time it takes for curds to form may vary, depending on the temperature of the kitchen; the ideal temperature is 70 to 72° F. If the temperature of your kitchen is in the high seventies or above, subtract about 2 hours from the time allowed; if below 70° F., add 1 to 2 hours.

Yogurt Cheese is made by simply draining yogurt, with no additional ingredient or cooking required. Mozzarella is the most complicated recipe, with cutting the curds and immersing them in boiling and then iced water—but one you'll find well worth the extra effort.

Crème Fraîche and Nonfat Yogurt are made by mixing ingredients and setting them aside at room temperature. Crème Fraîche ages best at 70 to 72° F., with some allowance for variation in temperature. Yogurt needs a "hot spot," such as atop a radiator or a warming oven.

Making plain and flavored butter is a simple two-step process—put the bowl and mixing apparatus of a food processor or stationary mixer into the freezer to chill for a few hours, then "churn" the cream in it for 10 minutes.

Home Made ice creams fall into 2 categories. The extra-rich versions (Ann's White Chocolate and Chocolate Ice Cream) start with a cooked custard base, while the almost as good, but quicker, mix-and-freeze varieties (Strawberry, Vanilla, and Coffee Ice Cream) go directly into the ice-cream maker with no cooking.

INGREDIENTS

In preparing *Home Made* dairy products, the fresher the milk or cream you start with, the better the end result will be. If you have access to milk and cream from a dairy, by all means use them.

Our recipes that require *whole milk* or *skim milk* are written to accommodate the common homogenized variety. When we call for *buttermilk, goat's milk,* or *cream,* use nonhomogenized products. For *buttermilk* and *heavy cream,* this is not really a concern, as most brands on the market are nonhomogenized. *Goat's milk* comes in both varieties; check labels. The *light cream* used to make Mascarpone must be nonhomogenized; most sold in supermarkets is homogenized, but nonhomogenized is available from dairies and will be special ordered by many grocers.

The *rennet tablets* called for in the Mozzarella and Cream Cheese recipes can be found in many natural and health food stores, or may be ordered from cheese supply houses (see Source Guide). Don't use the "junket" rennet sold in supermarkets; it's a different strength and contains several unwanted additives.

Look for the *citric acid* used for Mozzarella in supermarket spice sections or order it from cheese supply houses. *Tartaric acid,* used in making Mascarpone, is available from many pharmacies, as well as from cheese supply houses.

For Tiramisu, Jill's Cheesecake, and the ice creams, we prefer to use *Nest Eggs*® brand eggs (see Source Guide) or another brand of eggs from "uncaged" hens fed a drug-free diet.

EQUIPMENT

In many recipes, we specify the use of *nonreactive bowls or cookware.* Glass, enamel, stainless steel, or anodized aluminum (such as Calphalon or Magnalite) will do fine, but copper, plain aluminum,

Yogurt and Cheese Kits

We developed the recipes for *Home Made* dairy products to make dabbling in the art as easy as possible. They are formulated to take advantage of the natural bacteria in milk, cream, or yogurt, with no special "starters," or bacterial cultures, needed.

For those who wish to progress to a more advanced level, starter cultures are available that enable a greater degree of control over subtle variations in the taste of yogurt or soft cheeses. In addition, cultures are essential for making sour cream and hard cheeses.

Basic kits for making soft cheeses, hard cheeses, and yogurt come with a variety of starter cultures (the yogurt kits usually include cultures for sour cream as well). The kits, which can be ordered from cheese supply houses (see Source Guide), include just about everything you'll need—including a dairy thermometer, molds, recipes, rennet and acid, and cheesecloth, in addition to the starter cultures.

or cast iron (enameled or plain) can affect the flavor of the dairy product.

We often call for *stainless steel spoons,* which are nonreactive and much easier to keep clean and free of bacteria that could ruin the recipe than wooden spoons. *Slotted stainless steel spoons* are specified for heating ingredients because they facilitate even distribution of heat and incorporating additional ingredients.

A glass *dairy thermometer* is necessary to monitor the temperatures to which various ingredients must be heated. (A glass candy thermometer can be used as long as it is impeccably clean and free of sugar residue.) Dairy thermometers are stocked by many kitchenware stores and by cheese supply houses (see Source Guide).

Cheesecloth is used in many recipes. Fine-grade cheesecloth can be ordered from cheese supply houses (see Source Guide) and does not need to folded to a double thickness. The more readily available commercial grade will suffice as long as it is used in double thickness or greater for dripping curds.

Long-handled wooden spoons or other utensils are used to suspend cheesecloth-encased curds allowing the whey to drip into a receptacle. For smaller-yield recipes (8 ounces or less), a *sturdy wooden chopstick* will also work.

Use either an *ice-and-salt-chilled ice-cream maker or a compact freezer* to make *Home Made* ice-cream recipes.

TECHNIQUES

Before making Crème Fraîche, Nonfat Yogurt, or any *Home Made* cheese, carefully *wash the work surface and all utensils* with soap and hot water. This will prevent introducing bacteria that could hinder the desired reaction and keep the ingredients from coagulating or alter the taste.

When *monitoring temperatures with a dairy thermometer,* make sure that the thermometer isn't touching the bottom of the pan; many thermometers have clips that will hold them in place on the side of the pan. Read the temperature with the thermometer suspended in the contents, rather than removing it first.

To *drain liquid whey from solid curds* for cheese, suspend the curds in a cheesecloth bag from the handle of a wooden spoon over a receptacle. (The setup resembles an old hobo's sack on a stick.) Unless otherwise directed, allow the whey to drip naturally; squeezing the whey from the curds will produce a drier cheese than is normally desired.

Herbed Chèvre

This zesty fresh goat cheese makes a superb first course or a sophisticated snack. For fancier presentation, mix 2 tablespoons cracked black pepper, chopped fresh basil or chives, or pignoli into the cheese before forming into a log, or roll the log in 1 tablespoon pepper, basil, or chives, or 2 tablespoons pignoli before chilling.

   It's also tasty tossed in pasta with cream sauce.

> 4 cups (1 quart) nonhomogenized goat's milk
> 1 tablespoon *Home Made* Parsley Basil Herb Vinegar (page 47)
> 2 teaspoons *Home Made* Parsley Peppercorn Herb Vinegar (page 47)

Heat the milk in a medium, nonreactive saucepan over medium heat until it reaches 180° F. on a dairy thermometer. Reduce the heat as low as possible and cook for another 10 minutes, maintaining the heat at 180 degrees as closely as possible. (Check every 3 minutes, adjusting the heat or removing the pan from the heat temporarily.)

After 10 minutes, remove the pan from the heat. Add the vinegars, stirring with a slotted stainless steel spoon just to incorporate, and set the pan aside for 15 minutes while the milk curdles.

Line a colander with a moist double thickness of cheesecloth. Place the colander in the sink and pour in the curdled milk, allowing the excess liquid to drain through. Gather the 4 corners of the cloth to form a bag and secure in a knot; slip a wooden spoon under the knot.

Suspend the bag over a deep, nonreactive bowl or clean pot so that the bag falls clear of the sides and has at least a 1-inch clearance from the bottom of the receptacle. Let the mixture drip at room temperature for 2 hours. Discard the liquid.

Remove the cheese from the cheesecloth, form into 1 long log or 2 short logs about 1½ to 2 inches thick, cover, and chill for 2 hours before serving. Store it in the refrigerator, where it should keep for up to 1 week.

Yield = About 11 ounces

✧ ✧ ✧ *A*dd flavor and shelf life to the chèvre by marinating it in herbed oil. Instead of forming the cheese into a log, roll it into 1-inch balls, using about 2 tablespoons for each ball. Place in a tightly sealing jar, cover with extra-virgin olive oil, and add a sprig or 2 of fresh rosemary or thyme. Marinate in the refrigerator for at least 2 days before using. The Marinated Goat Cheese has a refrigerator shelf life of about 1 month. ✧ ✧ ✧

Crème Fraîche

In France, the thickness and subtle tang of crème fraîche is obtained by letting unpasteurized cream sit; we replicate the classic by adding buttermilk to pasteurized cream. Think of Crème Fraîche as something of a cross between whipped cream and sour cream—heavenly spooned on naturally sweet fresh fruit, yet versatile enough to flavor and thicken savory soups and sauces.

> 1 cup (½ pint) heavy cream, at room temperature
> 2 tablespoons buttermilk, at room temperature

Pour the heavy cream into a nonreactive bowl. Add the buttermilk and stir. (Do not whisk—you don't want to add air to the mixture.)

Cover the bowl with cheesecloth to keep dust out but let air circulate, and set it aside at room temperature for 20 hours. Chill for 4 hours more before serving.

The Crème Fraîche must be kept in the refrigerator, where it has a shelf life of about 1 week.

Yield = ½ pound

Mozzarella

Although this recipe entails a bit more hands-on preparation than most Home Made *cheeses, anyone who has tasted fresh Mozzarella will vow that it is time well invested. Try it with tomato slices topped with a drizzle of* Home Made *Garlic Oil (page 38). For a summertime treat, we are especially fond of Smoked Mozzarella (see page 112).*

> 1½ teaspoons citric acid
> 6 tablespoons lukewarm water
> 5 quarts skim milk
> ¼ rennet tablet
> 6 tablespoons coarse kosher salt
> 16 cups (4 quarts) water
> 8 cups (2 quarts) cold water
> 4 ice cubes

In a small, nonreactive bowl, dissolve the citric acid in 4 tablespoons of the lukewarm water, stirring with a slotted stainless steel spoon.

Pour the milk into a large, nonreactive stockpot. Add the dissolved citric acid, stirring for 1 minute with the stainless steel spoon to distribute well. Heat to 88° F. on a dairy thermometer over medium heat, which will take 3 to 5 minutes.

Meanwhile, dissolve the rennet in the remaining 2 tablespoons lukewarm water, crushing the tablet and stirring with the steel spoon. When the milk mixture reaches 88° F., remove from the heat and stir in the dissolved rennet. Cover the pot and set it aside for 20 to 25 minutes, until the milk has coagulated into a thick, custardlike mixture.

Using a long knife, cut the milk into approximately ½-inch curds (cut through, but do not break up). Recover the pot and set it aside for 5 minutes more.

Uncover and return the pot to a very low heat for about 15 minutes, stirring constantly with the steel spoon, until the mixture reaches a temperature of 106° F. Remove from the heat and continue to stir for 20 minutes. By now, the curds will have hardened into pellets surrounded by the liquid they have given off.

Line a colander with a moist double thickness of cheesecloth and place it in the sink. Pour the mixture into the cheesecloth and let the liquid drain for 15 minutes.

Meanwhile, bring the 4 quarts of water to a boil.

The curds will have solidified while draining; remove the mass from the colander. Cut into long strips about 1 inch by 1 inch and place them into a large bowl.

Add the salt to the boiling water and stir with a wooden spoon until the salt dissolves. Pour the salt water over the strips. With the wooden spoon, stir the strips for 7 to 10 minutes, pushing down and then pulling up so as to stretch them, until a glossy, stringy mass is formed.

Transfer the mass to a cutting board and knead for about 2 minutes to form a ball.

Place the ball in a medium bowl with the cold water and ice cubes for 5 minutes. Remove the cheese and dry it with paper towels.

The Mozzarella should be ready immediately. To store, wrap it in plastic wrap and refrigerate for up to 2 weeks.

Yield = ¾ pound

Chocolate Tiramisu

The classic Mascarpone-based Italian dessert is currently enjoying almost cult popularity in locations as far-flung as the United States and Japan. Tiramisu literally translates to "pick me up," which we've always found to be exactly the effect. Our version adds bittersweet chocolate for a twist on the old-time favorite.

3 large egg yolks

⅓ cup granulated sugar

¼ cup *Home Made* Coffee Liqueur (page 71)

1 ounce bittersweet chocolate, chopped

½ pound Mascarpone, at room temperature

2 cups heavy cream

1 12-ounce sponge cake loaf, cut into ¼-inch slices (27 slices)

½ cup *Home Made* Quick Coffee Syrup (page 80)

2 tablespoons confectioners' sugar

1 tablespoon unsweetened cocoa powder (preferably Dutch process)

Bring water to a boil in the bottom of a double boiler.

Meanwhile, put the egg yolks in the top of the double boiler (off the heat) and whisk until pale yellow. Whisk in the granulated sugar and Coffee Liqueur. Place the top of the double boiler over the boiling water. Reduce the heat to medium-low and cook for about 10 minutes, whisking constantly, until the mixture thickens and reaches 140° F. on a dairy thermometer.

Remove the double boiler from the heat and whisk in the chocolate. With an electric mixer set at medium speed, beat the mixture for about 1 minute while it cools.

Put the Mascarpone in a large bowl and mash it a bit with a rubber spatula until smooth. Fold in the cooled chocolate mixture.

Whip 1 cup of the cream until soft peaks form and fold into the Mascarpone-chocolate mixture.

Place 9 slices of the sponge cake in a single layer on the bottom of an 11 x 7 x 2 ½-inch baking dish. Brush ⅓ of the coffee syrup over the cake. Spread ½ of the chocolate mixture evenly on top. Repeat with another layer of cake, syrup, and the remaining chocolate. Top with the remaining cake and syrup.

Combine the remaining cup of cream and the confectioners' sugar in a bowl and whip until soft peaks form. Spread the whipped cream evenly over the top layer in the baking dish. Dust with the cocoa powder.

Refrigerate the Tiramisu for 3 to 4 hours before serving.

Yield = 10–12 servings

Mascarpone

Perhaps best known as the key ingredient in Tiramisu, the classic Italian cheese Mascarpone is tangier and somewhat less dense than cream cheese. We serve it with olives and crackers as an appetizer; for dessert, spoon it over fresh fruit or whip candied fruit into the cheese.

Look for nonhomogenized light cream at a local dairy or health food store.

> 1 quart light cream (nonhomogenized)
> ¼ teaspoon tartaric acid

In the top of a nonreactive double boiler over boiling water (or in a medium nonreactive saucepan placed in a large pot of boiling water), heat the cream over medium heat until it reaches 180° F. on a dairy thermometer. Remove the double boiler from the heat.

Stir in the tartaric acid with a slotted stainless steel spoon and continue to stir for 1 to 2 minutes, just until curds begin to form. Remove the top half of the double boiler (or the pan from the stockpot). Continue to stir for about 2 minutes more, until coagulated.

Line a colander with a moist double thickness of cheesecloth and place it in the sink. Pour in the mixture and allow it to drain for 1 hour. Gather the 4 corners of the cheesecloth to form a bag and secure in a knot; slip a wooden spoon under the knot.

Suspend the bag over a deep, nonreactive bowl so that it falls clear of the sides and has at least a 1-inch clearance from the bottom of the bowl. Refrigerate and allow the cheese to drip for 8 hours.

The Mascarpone should be ready to use immediately, with a refrigerator shelf life of about 1 week. Store in an airtight plastic container.

Yield = ½ pound

Raspberry Dessert Cheese

We call this a dessert cheese because its fruity undertone makes it such a natural for a refreshing last course, but it can also be served as an appetizer.

> 1 quart whole milk
> 1 tablespoon *Home Made* Raspberry Vinegar
> (page 45)

Heat the milk in a medium, nonreactive saucepan over medium heat until it reaches 180° F. on a dairy thermometer. Reduce the heat as low as possible and continue to cook for 10 minutes, maintaining the temperature as close as possible to 180° F. (Check every 3 minutes, adjusting heat or removing the pan from the heat temporarily as needed.)

After 10 minutes, remove the pan from the heat. Add the vinegar, stirring with a slotted stainless steel spoon just to incorporate. The milk will begin to curdle almost immediately; set it aside for 15 minutes.

Line a colander with a moist double thickness of cheesecloth and place it in the sink. Pour in the curdled milk and allow the excess liquid to drain through.

Gather the 4 corners of the cloth to form a bag and secure in a knot; slip a wooden spoon under the knot.

Suspend the bag over a deep, nonreactive bowl or clean pot so that it falls clear of the sides and has at least a 1-inch clearance from the bottom of the receptacle. Let the mixture drip at room temperature for 2 hours.

Remove the cheese from the cheesecloth, form into a wheel or a log, cover, and chill for 2 hours before serving.

Store the Raspberry Dessert Cheese in the refrigerator, where it has a shelf life of about 1 week.

Yield = About 10 ounces

❖ ❖ ❖ *F*or variety, mix in ¼ cup dried currants, dried raspberries, pignoli, or *Home Made* preserves (pages 20–23) after the cheese has drained and before chilling, or roll the cheese in 2 tablespoons chopped pistachios or hazelnuts to coat. ❖ ❖ ❖

Jill's Cheesecake

We asked our friend Jill Van Cleave to create a simple, rich Victorian cheesecake using Home Made *ingredients. As the proprietress of the popular JR's Bakery in Chicago, Jill has a job many consider the adult equivalent of being a kid in a candy store.*

> 10 ounces refrigerator sugar cookie dough
> 1¼ pounds Cream Cheese, at room temperature
> ¾ pound Baker's Cheese, at room temperature
> 1½ cups sugar
> 5 large eggs
> 2 tablespoons all-purpose flour
> 1 teaspoon grated orange zest
> 2 teaspoons *Home Made* Vanilla Extract
> ⅓ cup heavy cream

Preheat the oven to 350° F. Roll out the cookie dough between 2 sheets of wax paper. Remove the top sheet. Place the bottom of a 9-inch springform pan upside down on top of the dough. Flip the bottom and dough right side up. Remove the remaining sheet of wax paper and trim the excess dough overlapping the outer edge of the circle. Place the pan bottom and dough into the springform and lock it closed.

Put the pan in the center of the oven and bake until golden brown, 10 to 12 minutes. Remove to a wire rack to cool.

Lower the oven temperature to 325° F. Place a baking pan ¾-filled with water on the bottom rack of the oven.

Meanwhile, combine the Cream Cheese and Baker's Cheese in a bowl. Beat with an electric mixer at medium speed until smooth. Add the sugar and continue to beat until well blended. Add the eggs, one at a time, and beat until each is well incorporated. Reduce the mixer speed to low and beat in the remaining ingredients.

Pour the batter into the springform pan over the crust.

Set the pan on top of a cookie sheet and place on the rack in the center of the oven, over the pan of water. Bake for 60 to 70 minutes, just until the center is set and the top is light golden.

Remove the springform pan from the cookie sheet to a wire rack and allow the cake to cool for at least 2 hours. Cover with plastic wrap and refrigerate for 4 hours before serving.

Yield = 8–10 servings

Baker's Cheese

In this recipe, you literally squeeze as much liquid as possible out of the curdled milk mixture, leaving a dry, crumbly cheese that is ideal for baking. This is the cheese that's used in firm, cakelike cheesecake and for stuffing cheese blintzes. Try it as well in place of ricotta cheese in lasagna.

> 6 cups whole milk
> 6 tablespoons freshly squeezed lemon juice
> 6 tablespoons freshly squeezed lime juice

Pour the milk into the top of a nonreactive double boiler over boiling water (or into a medium, nonreactive saucepan placed in a large pot of boiling water). Heat over low heat until the milk reaches 100° F. on a dairy thermometer.

Remove from the heat and stir in the lemon juice and lime juice with a slotted stainless steel spoon. Let the mixture sit undisturbed for 15 minutes.

Line a colander with a moist double thickness of cheesecloth and place it in the sink. Transfer the mixture into the cheesecloth, allowing the excess liquid to drain through.

Gather the 4 corners of the cloth to form a bag and secure in a knot; slip a wooden spoon under the knot.

Suspend the bag over a deep, nonreactive bowl or clean pot so that it falls clear of the sides and has at least a 1-inch clearance from the bottom of the receptacle. Let the mixture drip at room temperature. After it has dripped for 1 hour, lift the bag by the stick and twist the cheesecloth from the knot downward to squeeze out

as much liquid as possible. Let it drip for another hour.

The Baker's Cheese should be ready to use immediately and has a refrigerator shelf life of about 1 week.

Yield = ¾ pound

Cream Cheese

Silky smooth, extraordinarily rich, and with a hint of sweetness, this Cream Cheese is the perfect accompaniment to Home Made *Egg Bagels (page 158) and smoked fish (see Chapter 5) for a brunch to remember.*

> 6 cups heavy cream, at room temperature
>
> 2 cups (1 pint) whole milk, at room temperature
>
> ¼ cup buttermilk, at room temperature
>
> ¼ rennet tablet
>
> ¼ cup water

Mix the cream, milk, and buttermilk together in a large, nonreactive bowl.

Dissolve the rennet in the water, crushing the tablet and stirring with a stainless steel spoon. Stir the dissolved rennet into the milk mixture, and continue to mix for 8 minutes. Cover with cheesecloth to prevent dust from settling on the surface. Set aside at room temperature for about 20 hours, until a thick, custardy mixture has formed beneath the liquid on the top of the bowl.

Cut the mixture into approximately 1-inch curds (cut through, but do not dislodge).

Rinse and squeeze dry a 3-foot square of cheesecloth. Fold the cheesecloth in half and then half again, producing a 4-thickness piece of cheesecloth. Center it over a colander placed in the sink. Pour in the contents of the bowl, allowing the excess liquid to drain through. Rinse and dry the bowl.

Gather the 4 corners of the cheesecloth to form a bag and secure in a knot; slip a wooden spoon under the knot.

Suspend the bag over the bowl so that it falls clear of the sides and has at least a 1-inch clearance from the bottom. Let the mixture drip at room temperature for 5 hours.

Lift the bag by the stick and twist the cheesecloth from the knot downward to squeeze out any excess liquid. If the cheese is not yet as thick as desired, allow to drip for 1 hour longer.

Chill the Cream Cheese for 1 hour before using. Store it in the refrigerator, where it will keep for 4 to 5 days.

Note: Adding ⅛ teaspoon salt to the Cream Cheese before chilling will extend the refrigerator shelf life to 1 week. (This is not recommended if you are going to use the cheese for baking.)

Yield = 12 ounces

Boursin

This wonderfully smooth and spicy spreadable cheese is great light party fare. It's easy to make using Home Made *Cream Cheese, Yogurt Cheese, or Herbed Chèvre. Each lends slightly different character to the Boursin—the distinctive flavor of Herbed Chèvre, the tang of Yogurt Cheese, or the silkiness of Cream Cheese.*

> 4 tablespoons (½ cup) butter, at room temperature
>
> 1 cup Cream Cheese, Yogurt Cheese, or Herbed Chèvre, at room temperature
>
> 1 garlic clove, peeled
>
> 2 teaspoons peeled and very finely minced white onion
>
> 1 teaspoon *Home Made* Herbes de Provence (page 51)

Combine the butter and cheese in a bowl and mash until smooth with a sturdy spoon. Press the garlic into the mixture. Add the onion and Herbes de Provence. Mix well. Serve at room temperature with cocktail rye, apple slices, or dried fruit.

Yield = About ¾ pound

Nonfat Yogurt

This yogurt is creamy, custardy—and nonfat. To flavor before serving, stir in crushed fresh fruit, Home Made *Cooked Berry Preserves (page 20) or Freezer Fruit Preserves (page 21),* Home Made *Lemon Syrup (page 78) or Strawberry Syrup (page 80), or a few drops vanilla extract.*

Be sure to save 2 tablespoons as the starter for your next batch.

> 1¼ cups nonfat dry milk
> 2 cups water
> 2 tablespoons plain nonfat yogurt

Fill the sink with the hottest possible tap water and place a 1-quart glass casserole and its cover into it.

Combine the dry milk and water in a medium nonreactive bowl and mix until the powder has dissolved. Add the yogurt and stir thoroughly.

Remove the casserole and cover from the hot water and dry them. Pour the milk into the casserole, cover, and wrap with a large towel to contain the heat. Set the casserole aside in a warm place. You want to try to find a spot that is at least 80° F., such as on a

❖ ❖ ❖ **To make Yogurt Cheese, line a fine-mesh sieve with a coffee filter and suspend it over a large, nonreactive bowl. Put 1 cup Nonfat Yogurt into the sieve and refrigerate for at least 12 hours. The solid curd remaining in the sieve is pure Yogurt Cheese, which will keep for about 1 week in the refrigerator. It can be substituted for cream cheese in most baking recipes, producing a lighter dessert with a somewhat zestier flavor.**
❖ ❖ ❖

radiator, on top of an oven turned on to the warming setting (140° F.), or atop a refrigerator.

Leave the casserole for 16 to 24 hours until the Nonfat Yogurt is thick and as tangy as desired. The time needed to thicken varies upon the temperature of the spot in which the Nonfat Yogurt sits; the longer it sits, the tangier it gets.

Refrigerate for at least 2 hours before serving. When chilled, it should have a custardy consistency. Store the Nonfat Yogurt in the refrigerator, where it should keep for about 1 week.

Yield = 2 cups

Butter

Rich and creamy, this Home Made *version makes butter worth the calories!*

To make an attractive Butter Log, transfer the Butter, before chilling, onto a sheet of wax paper and fold the paper over the Butter until the ends meet. Place a hard-edged ruler on top, and hold it firmly against the Butter. While holding the ruler, grab the end of the top layer of wax paper and slowly pull it toward you; this will form the Butter into the shape of a log. Roll the paper around the log and chill. Serve whole or cut off medallions as needed.

> 1 cup (½ pint) heavy cream

Place the bowl and blade of a food processor into the freezer to chill for 4 to 5 hours.

Refit the bowl and blade, turn on the food processor, and pour the cream through the feed tube. Continue to process for about 10 minutes, until the Butter has hardened around the blade, leaving the liquid that has separated from the cream in the bottom of the bowl.

Transfer the Butter to a fine sieve and shake 2 or 3 times over the sink to allow any excess liquid to drain. Put the Butter in a bowl, cover, and chill for at least 1 hour before using. Store it in the refrigerator, where it has a shelf life of about 1 week.

Yield = 10–12 tablespoons (²⁄₃–¾ cup)

◇ ◇ ◇ **B**utter can also be made using a heavy, stationary electric mixer.

Place the metal bowl and metal paddle attachment in the freezer for 4 to 5 hours. Refit the bowl and paddle, pour in the cream, and drape a clean towel over the bowl to catch the liquid that will spatter. Mix at high speed for 10 minutes, drain the Butter as above, and chill for at least 1 hour before using.
◇ ◇ ◇

Flavored Butter

To flavor, prepare *Home Made* Butter to the draining stage. (You can also use a good grade of commercial butter, softened to room temperature.)

FOR WHIPPED FRUIT BUTTER:

Return the butter to the food processor bowl and add ½ cup fresh raspberries, strawberries, blueberries, or blackberries (or an equal amount of thawed and well-drained frozen berries). Process for 3 to 4 minutes, until well blended. Serve on hot muffins, waffles, or pancakes.

FOR GARLIC CHIVE BUTTER:

Put the butter in a small bowl. Press in 3 peeled garlic cloves, add 1½ tablespoons chopped fresh chives, and mix with a wooden spoon. Serve on steamed vegetables, grilled fish, or, for a distinctive garlic bread, on a baguette of *Home Made* Classic French Bread (page 156).

FOR BASIL PIGNOLI BUTTER:

Put 1 cup fresh basil leaves, 1 tablespoon pignoli, and 1 teaspoon freshly squeezed lemon juice into a food processor. Pulse to chop. Add the butter and process about 1 minute, until well blended. Serve on pasta, baked potatoes, or grilled chicken.

FOR WASABI BUTTER:

Combine the butter, 2 teaspoons wasabi powder, 1 teaspoon soy sauce, 1 finely diced trimmed scallion, 1 peeled and finely minced garlic clove, 1 teaspoon sesame seeds, and 1 teaspoon sesame oil in a small bowl. Mix thoroughly with a wooden spoon. Serve on broiled or grilled fish, baked potatoes, or steamed white rice.

Chocolate Ice Cream

Thick and creamy, our Chocolate Ice Cream will remind you of a rich Italian gelato—with a dark hue and a dense taste. Combined with milk and Home Made *Chocolate Syrup (page 79), it makes a truly decadent chocolate milk shake.*

> 1 cup (½ pint) heavy cream
> 3 large egg yolks
> ½ cup sugar
> 4 ounces bittersweet chocolate, roughly chopped (about ¾ cup)
> 1 cup (½ pint) light cream
> 1 teaspoon vanilla extract

In a medium saucepan, scald the heavy cream over medium heat, just until the milk gives off steam and bubbles begin to form around the edge. Remove the pan from the heat.

In a medium bowl, whisk the egg yolks until they turn a pale lemon color. Add the sugar and whisk to dissolve. Slowly whisk in ¼ cup of the scalded cream until completely incorporated. Pour this mixture into the saucepan and whisk to blend with the scalded cream.

Over low heat, whisk the cream mixture constantly for about 5 minutes, until it has thickened and reached a temperature of 178 to 180° F., registered on an instant-read or a dairy thermometer. Remove the pan from the heat.

Add the chocolate, whisking until it is thoroughly melted and incorporated. Whisk in the light cream and vanilla.

Transfer the mixture to a *medium* bowl, cover, and refrigerate for at least 8 hours. Prepare the ice cream in an ice-cream maker according to manufacturer's directions.

Store the ice cream in the freezer, where it has a shelf life of about 1 week.

Yield = 1 pint

Vanilla Ice Cream

Ice cream eaten too rapidly, cautions one newspaper columnist of the late 1800s, "cools the stomach, prevents digestion, and causes . . . unseemly belchings, if not actual chill, which in feeble persons endangers life."

> 1 cup (½ pint) heavy cream
> 1 cup (½ pint) light cream
> ⅓ cup sugar
> ½ vanilla bean, slit open lengthwise
> ¼ teaspoon vanilla extract

Whisk the creams together in a bowl, then whisk in the sugar until dissolved. Add the vanilla bean and extract, whisking to blend.

Cover the bowl with plastic wrap and refrigerate for 2 hours.

Remove the vanilla bean and scrape out the inside of the bean with the back of a knife. Return these flecks of vanilla to the cream and whisk to blend; discard the bean.

Prepare the ice cream in an ice-cream maker according to manufacturer's directions.

Store the ice cream in the freezer, where it has a shelf life of about 1 week.

Yield = 1 pint

Strawberry Ice Cream

This easy treat is made without cooking. It has a simple, satisfying strawberries-and-cream flavor. Although you want some bits of berry in the strawberry-sugar puree, process until the chunks are very small. Larger pieces of strawberry will allow air pockets to form and the fruit can become icy when frozen.

> 1 pint strawberries, hulled and rinsed
> ⅓ cup sugar
> 1 cup heavy cream
> 1 teaspoon vanilla extract

Combine the strawberries and sugar in the bowl of a food processor and pulse to a coarse puree.

In a medium bowl, whisk the cream until frothy, about 30 seconds. Whisk in the vanilla, then the strawberry puree.

Prepare the ice cream in an ice-cream maker according to manufacturer's directions.

Store the ice cream in the freezer, where it has a shelf life of about 1 week.

Yield = 1 pint

Coffee Ice Cream

Good, old-fashioned Coffee Ice Cream, our favorite, is all too scarce in many parts of the country—you may want to double the ingredients to yield a quart if you have an ice-cream maker with sufficient capacity.

> 1 cup (½ pint) heavy cream
> ⅓ cup sugar
> ½ cup milk
> 1 teaspoon vanilla extract
> ½ cup extra-strong brewed coffee

In a medium bowl, whisk the cream and sugar until the sugar has dissolved completely and the mixture is frothy. Add the milk, vanilla, and coffee. Whisk until well blended.

Cover the bowl with plastic wrap and chill in the refrigerator for 1 hour.

Prepare the ice cream in an ice-cream maker according to manufacturer's directions.

Store the ice cream in the freezer, where it has a shelf life of about 1 week.

Yield = 1 pint

Ann's White Chocolate Ice Cream

Sinful is the word that first comes to mind when describing this exceptionally rich ice cream, which tastes a bit like liquid white chocolate. It's the brainchild of our food-lover friend Ann Bloomstrand. We like it so much we make a quart at a time, but the recipe is easily cut in half to yield a pint.

> 1 quart heavy cream
> 8 large egg yolks
> 1 cup sugar
> ½ large vanilla bean, slit open lengthwise
> ½ pound white chocolate, chopped (about 1½ cups)

Scald 2 cups of the cream in a medium saucepan over medium heat, just until the milk gives off steam and bubbles begin to form around the edge. Remove the pan from the heat.

In a medium bowl, whisk the egg yolks until they have a pale lemon hue. Add the sugar and continue to whisk until dissolved. Slowly whisk in ½ cup of the scalded cream. When the mixture is thoroughly blended, whisk it into the scalded cream in the saucepan. Add the vanilla bean.

Return the saucepan to low heat and whisk the cream constantly for about 5 minutes, until it has thickened and reached a temperature of 178 to 180° F., as registered on an instant-read or a dairy thermometer. Remove the pan from the heat.

Remove the vanilla bean from the pan, then whisk in the white chocolate, until it is melted and thoroughly incorporated. Scrape out the inside of the vanilla bean with the back of a knife and add these flecks to the pan. Whisk in the remaining cream.

Transfer the mixture to a bowl, cover, and refrigerate for at least 8 hours. Prepare the ice cream in an ice-cream maker according to manufacturer's directions.

Store the ice cream in the freezer, where it has a shelf life of about 1 week.

Yield = 1 quart

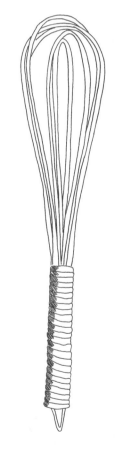

Smoked Foods & Sausages

Just as they needed to pickle and preserve the bounty of the harvest to keep through the coming months, our nineteenth-century forebears found it necessary to preserve meat and fish for the future as well; smoking and sausage making were two of the most common methods.

Smoking was often done by suspending foods in a barrel over a smoldering fire of wood chips or corncobs. A more elaborate household may have been equipped with a freestanding smokehouse; bacon or kippers might simply have been hung from the chimney over the hearth.

Sausages were made by first curing the meat in a mixture of salt, sugar, and saltpeter, then either stuffing the meat into casings and smoking, or stuffing it into muslin sacks, coating with lard, and hanging up to dry.

While commercial preservatives, refrigerator-freezers, and the omnipresent corner deli may have eliminated the imperative to preserve foods in the old ways, smoked meats, smoked fish, and sausages of all sorts remain ever popular.

Perhaps the lasting appeal of smoking and sausage making lies in their link to our culinary roots. Sausage making is a universal phenomenon, all the more interesting in its ethnic and regional variations. Smoking is timeless—the taste of smoked foods being our most tangible reminder of a heritage of cooking over the open fire that dates from prehistoric days.

❖ ❖ ❖

EQUIPMENT

The majority of our smoking recipes are executed in the popular *kettle grill,* which has a deep firepan and comes with a cover. This grill's design allows you to build an "indirect" charcoal fire that smokes foods while they cook. *Charcoal briquets,* the most convenient of which are instant-lighting, are burned to produce the fire. Adding *applewood, mesquite,* or *hickory wood chips* or *larger chunks* produces an aromatic smoke that flavors the food.

Our Hickory-Smoked Brisket is cooked in a *water smoker,* a portable, cylindrical contraption that resembles R2D2 of *Star Wars* fame. This is a slower method of smoke cooking that keeps food moist by constantly emanating steam from a water pan positioned above the fire.

Foods can smoke on the stovetop in a *covered wok*—or *straight-sided fry pan* or *stockpot,* depending upon the size needed. Use a *small wire rack* to raise the food above the sugar and seasonings placed in the bottom of the utensil.

The Minted Smoked Salmon and the Basil-Smoked Shrimp and Scallop Kebabs can also be prepared in a *portable indoor hot smoker,* a device designed specifically for stovetop smoking (see Source Guide).

The primary requirement for making sausage is a *meat grinder.* An electric grinder or a grinder attachment to a multipurpose stationary electric mixer is easiest to use, but a manual grinder will also get the job done. Meat grinders come with discs featuring holes of different sizes which regulate the coarseness of the grind.

Meat can also be ground in some heavy-duty *food processors;* ingredients for seafood sausages can be pureed in any model.

Our recipes require only *cheesecloth* or *plastic wrap* to encase sausages so that they hold their shape until cooked. Ingredients may also be stuffed into *sausage casings,* which are available in many supermarkets and meat markets; this will require a *sausage stuffer.* You can use either a manual sausage stuffer or a stuffer attachment to a multipurpose stationary electric mixer.

A few recipes call for an *instant-read thermometer* to test doneness.

TECHNIQUES

To *smoke in a kettle grill,* first put the wood chips or chunks to be used in a bowl, cover with water, and set them aside to soak for 1 hour.

Place a rectangular metal pan (such as a shallow baking pan or the bottom of a broiler pan) in the center of the bottom rack. Mound half of the charcoal briquets on each side of the pan. Open the bottom vents on the grill. Light the charcoal and allow the fire to burn until the briquets are ashen and glowing, about 25 minutes.

Drain the wood chips or chunks and distribute them over the hot charcoal. Position the food on the grilling rack directly over the metal pan, not the briquets. Cover the grill, open the cover vents, and cook the food for the length of time indicated in the individual recipe. Check periodically to see if more charcoal briquets need to be added to keep the fire hot. Once you remove the cooked food from the grill, close all vents to extinguish the fire.

To *smoke in a water smoker,* see the directions for preparing Hickory-Smoked Brisket (page 111).

To *smoke indoors on the stovetop,* line a wok, straight-sided fry pan, or stockpot with a double thickness of aluminum foil. Put the sugar and other smoking ingredients in the bottom. Insert a low rack— one that will clear the sugar mixture but still allow the pot to be covered tightly. Place the food on the rack and cover.

If using a wok, ring the cover with 2 wet towels, along the exposed inner surface of the wok, to keep the smoke from escaping. If using a stockpot or fry pan, drape a wet towel over the cover and secure it tightly with string or a rubber band. Smoke the food according to individual recipe directions.

Remove the pot from the heat (leaving the towels intact) and set it aside for 5 minutes before uncovering, to allow the smoke to dissipate.

For a portable indoor hot smoker, assemble the ingredients and components of the smoker according to manufacturer's directions.

Smoked Foods

Until electric freezers came on the scene a few decades ago, meat and fish were commonly preserved by curing and then smoking. The process, which could take weeks, was laborious and cumbersome. After curing in a salt mixture or brine, the foods were either cold smoked, or hot smoked over a fire that gave off sufficient heat to cook them as they smoked.

While we no longer need to wrestle whole carcasses from the salting trough to the smokehouse, or hang hams in the chimney, we nonetheless retain an appreciation for the distinctive smoky taste these classic methods of preservation impart to foods.

THE BASICS

Most home smoking today is a variation of the old hot-smoking method. We aren't really preserving foods, but rather using smoke to flavor them as they cook. The curing step is often skipped, and cold smoking is limited largely to commercially prepared fish, cheese, and some meats.

In a few recipes, our abbreviated version of curing extracts excess fat and adds flavor. Chinese Tea-Smoked Duck is first salted, and Smoked Salmon and Minted Smoked Salmon sit for 24 hours in a salt-and-sugar mixture before being smoked.

The fastest and easiest way of smoke cooking, which we use in many *Home Made* recipes, is in a kettle grill. Once the charcoal briquets become white and ashen, wood chips or chunks that have been soaked in water are added to the fire, producing dense smoke that is trapped when the grill is covered. Hickory-Smoked Brisket, which would cook too fast and dry out in a kettle grill, requires a water smoker, which steams the meat while it smokes. In this recipe, we dispense with charcoal and burn dry wood chunks, adding a couple of damp chunks when the fire is hot.

City dwellers who lack even the few square feet of outdoor access necessary for grilling need not be deprived of home-smoked foods, since we offer recipes for smoking chicken, duck, salmon, and shrimp and scallop kebabs on the stovetop. While portable indoor hot smokers specifically designed for this purpose are available, we've written these recipes to allow you to use a wok (which is ideal), a stockpot, or fry pan. The duck and the chicken, which require longer cooking than the seafood, are steamed prior to smoking.

The key to smoking on the stovetop without setting off all the smoke alarms on your floor is to seal the covered pot with damp towels, trapping the smoke inside. Remove the pot from the heat and let it sit for 5 minutes before removing the toweling, during which time the smoke will have dissipated.

Leftover portions of most *Home Made* smoked foods can be stored in the refrigerator for up to a week. For the few dishes that really are best eaten immediately, we dispense with notes on shelf life.

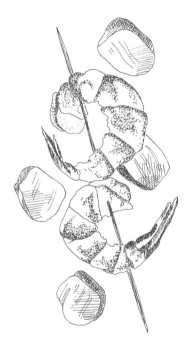

Honey-Basted, Hickory-Smoked Ham

"Hang [the hams] up in the smoke house under a barrel or any suitable receptacle and smoke," advises a 100-year-old reference. "Chips or saw-dust from hickory or beech wood or corncobs are the most suitable fuel with which to smoke hams . . . The process may be continued for 8 or 10 hours or for several weeks . . . Some persons who burn wood exclusively as fuel smoke hams by sewing them up in a coarse cloth and hanging them up in the chimney, but this method is not suitable if coal is used."

While preparing this recipe in a kettle grill may lack some of the ro-mance of smoking the ham for weeks in a barrel, it's a lot easier!

> 1 8- to 9-pound sugar-cured ham (uncooked)
> ¼ cup honey
> 2 cups small hickory chunks

Coat the ham thoroughly with the honey. Cover with plastic wrap and refrigerate for 12 hours.

Soak the hickory chunks in water for 2 hours.

Put a large rectangular metal pan in the center of the bottom rack of a kettle grill and mound about 30 charcoal briquets on each side of the pan. Open the bottom vents on the grill. Light the char-coal and allow the fire to burn until the briquets are ashen and glowing, about 25 minutes.

Drain the hickory chunks and distribute them over the charcoal. Place the ham on the grilling rack so that it is directly over the pan. Cover the grill, open the cover vents, and smoke the ham for 2 hours, until blackened and crusty on the outside.

Store the ham in the refrigerator, where it has a shelf life of 5 to 7 days.

Yield = 8–10 servings

Black Bean Chowder

This is just one of the countless uses we've found for *Home Made* Honey-Basted, Hickory-Smoked Ham. (We recently smoked one on a weekday evening for the following weekend, only to find a nearly bare bone in the refrigerator come Saturday morning.)

> 1 cup dried black beans, rinsed, drained, and picked over
> 2 cups water
> ¼ cup finely diced ham fat
> 1 small yellow onion, peeled and chopped (about 1 cup)
> 3 garlic cloves, peeled and minced
> 1 stalk celery, chopped
> 1 small carrot, peeled and chopped
> ½ tablespoon ground cumin
> ½ teaspoon dried thyme
> ½ cup chopped fresh cilantro
> 4 cups chicken stock
> ½ cup cubed Honey-Basted, Hickory-Smoked Ham
> 2 tablespoons freshly squeezed lime juice

Combine the beans and water in a medium saucepan and bring to a boil over high heat. Continue to boil for 5 minutes, then cover the pan and remove it from the heat; let the beans sit for about 45 minutes.

Sauté the fat in a large, heavy-bottomed saucepan over medium heat until melted; discard the crispy brown pieces that remain. Add the onion, garlic, celery, and carrot and cook for 3 minutes, stirring occasionally. Cover, reduce the heat to low, and cook for about 10 minutes more, until the vegetables are limp but not browned.

Stir in the cumin, thyme, cilantro, and chicken stock. Stir in the beans and bring back to a boil over medium heat. Reduce the heat to low and simmer, partially covered, for about 1 ½ hours, until the beans are tender enough to mash easily with the back of a spoon. Every so often, skim any foam that forms on the top.

Transfer about half of the solid ingredients from the saucepan to the bowl of a food processor or blender and puree. Return the puree to the pan. Add the ham and lime juice, and cook for an additional 10 minutes, until the ham is heated through. Garnish with finely chopped jalapeño pepper and serve immediately with Harry's Long-Awaited Corn Rye (page 154).

Yield = 6 servings

❖ ❖ ❖ *W*hat better Sunday brunch fare than Smoked Salmon served on *Home Made* Egg Bagels (page 158) topped with *Home Made* Cream Cheese (page 94) or, for an intriguing twist, with *Home Made* Crème Fraîche (page 88)? ❖ ❖ ❖

Smoked Salmon

This delicacy is reminiscent of the classic Scandinavian gravad lax, which is also salt cured. However, our version is then hot smoked, which cooks the fish, so you needn't worry about bacteria. Smoked Salmon makes a simple, elegant appetizer or snack by itself, but adding a little to a variety of dishes, from scrambled eggs to pasta in cream sauce, enlivens them considerably.

- ½ pound fresh salmon fillet
- 1 tablespoon sugar
- 1 tablespoon coarse kosher salt
- ¼ teaspoon coarsely ground black pepper
- 1 cup hickory chips

Rinse the salmon and pat it dry. Fold a 30-inch-long sheet of aluminum foil in half. Lay the salmon skin side down on the foil.

Combine the sugar, salt, and pepper in a small bowl. Spread the mixture over the fish and rub it in.

Close the foil around the salmon securely and transfer it to a medium baking dish. Place a second, smaller dish on top of the fish and weigh it down with a bag of rice or sugar, or with a large, heavy can. Place the baking dish in the refrigerator for 24 hours.

Soak the hickory chips in water for 1 hour.

Put a small, rectangular metal pan in the center of the bottom rack of a kettle grill and mound 15 charcoal briquets on each side of the pan. Open the bottom vents on the grill. Light the charcoal and allow the fire to burn until the briquets are ashen and glowing, about 25 minutes.

Drain the hickory chips and distribute them over the charcoal. Unwrap the salmon and set it lengthwise on the grilling rack directly over the metal pan. Cover the grill, open the cover vents, and smoke the salmon for 15 minutes.

Serve room temperature or chilled.

The Smoked Salmon will keep in the refrigerator for up to 5 days.

Yield = About ½ pound

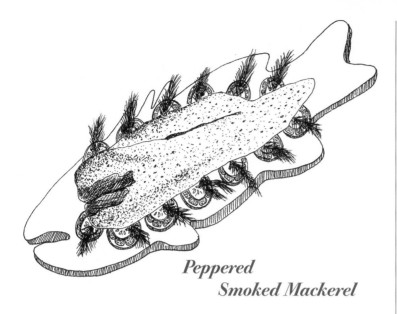

Peppered Smoked Mackerel

Instead of preparing the mackerel in a barrel in the smokehouse out back as in prior centuries, use a kettle grill on the terrace or patio. We add a healthy dose of pepper for accent, but this delicate appetizer derives its character principally from the mesquite.

> ½ cup mesquite chips
> 2 4-ounce mackerel fillets
> 1 teaspoon coarsely ground black pepper
> 1 medium lemon, peeled and cut into 8 wedges

Soak the mesquite chips in water for 1 hour.

Put a small, rectangular metal pan in the center of the bottom rack of a kettle grill and mound 15 charcoal briquets on each side. Open the bottom vents on the grill. Light the charcoal and allow the fire to burn until the briquets are ashen and glowing, about 25 minutes.

Meanwhile, rinse the mackerel fillets and pat them dry. Remove any small bones, if necessary, with tweezers. Put the fish on a plate, skin side down, and sprinkle the pepper evenly over both fillets.

When the fire is ready, drain the mesquite chips and add them to the charcoal, along with the lemon wedges. Place the mackerel on the grilling rack so that it sits over the pan. Cover the grill, open the cover vents halfway, and smoke the fish for 15 minutes. Serve immediately.

Yield = 4 appetizer servings

❖ ❖ ❖ **O**ur favorite way to serve Peppered Smoked Mackerel is to top with horse-radish sauce and a sprinkle of capers. To make about ¾ cup horseradish sauce, mix 1 table-spoon freshly grated horseradish root or *Home Made* Prepared Horseradish (see page 54), 1 peeled and minced shallot, ½ cup sour cream, and ¼ tea-spoon ground white pepper. Cover and chill for about 30 minutes. ❖ ❖ ❖

Down-home Texas barbecue is as
legendary as it is succulent.
Everyone has a favorite source,
and in tracking a few of ours,
we've visited some real hole-in-
the-wall back road smokehouses—
usually to find the more dilapi-
dated the surroundings, the better
the barbecue!

    This recipe departs a bit
from the purist school of Texas
barbecue—the Home Made
Hickory-Smoked Brisket is not
marinated, and is smoked over
hickory rather than mesquite.

16–20 thin slices Hickory-
        Smoked Brisket
  1 cup *Home Made*
      Barbecue Sauce
      (page 54)
  4 hamburger buns or
      kaiser rolls

Preheat the oven to 275° F.
Enclose the brisket slices
securely in aluminum foil, place
in a baking dish, and bake for 1
hour. Remove the baking dish
from the oven, unwrap the meat,
and set it aside.

    Bring the barbecue sauce to a
simmer over low heat in a large
saucepan. Add the meat and
cook for 5 minutes more. Serve
on hamburger buns or kaiser
rolls.

    Yield = 4 servings ❖ ❖ ❖

Hickory-Smoked Brisket

*This is the only smoking recipe in which we call for specialized equip-
ment, a water smoker (see page 104), since the meat dries out too much
in a kettle grill. Those who have access to a water smoker will appreciate
the result—tender beef that's great plain and also the essential ingredient
for Texas-style Barbecue Sandwiches.*

  18 medium to large hickory chunks
    1 large garlic clove, peeled and finely minced
  3-pound whole boneless beef brisket
  ¼ teaspoon coarsely ground black pepper
    2 cups beer
    4 cups water
    4 bay leaves

Soak 2 of the smaller hickory chunks in a bowl of water for
1 hour.

Rub the garlic into the fatty side of the brisket and sprinkle with
pepper.

Make a pyramid of the remaining hickory chunks on the coal
rack of a hot smoker. Light the wood chunks and allow the fire to
burn until they become ashen, about 25 minutes, then carefully
spread them into a single layer. Drain and add the 2 hickory
chunks that have been soaked.

Combine the beer, water, and bay leaves in the water container
and fit it into the smoker.

Position the grill rack on the smoker and put the brisket onto the
grill. Cover and smoke the brisket for 5 to 6 hours, until the meat
reaches an internal temperature of 170° F. on an instant-read thermometer. Check periodically, and add charcoal briquets if needed
to keep the fire glowing.

Remove the brisket to a cutting board and allow it to sit for
10 minutes. Slice the meat across the grain and serve warm.

The brisket can be stored in the refrigerator for 4 to 6 days.

Yield = 6–8 servings

Smokehouse Hickory Spare Ribs

These are old-fashioned smokehouse ribs—flavorful and a bit chewy—not the bland, parboiled variety. We call for grilling, but they can also be prepared indoors: Cover the ribs with aluminum foil and bake for 1 hour in a 350° F. oven. Remove the foil and broil them for 2 to 3 minutes per side, until crusty.

> 3½ pounds baby back ribs
> 2 cups *Home Made* Barbecue Sauce (page 54)
> 1 cup hickory chips

Score both sides of the ribs with a sharp knife, cutting to the bone on a 45-degree angle every 2 inches. Place the ribs in a single layer in a large baking dish (cut the slab if necessary to fit the ribs in a single layer).

Coat the ribs on both sides, using 1 cup of the Barbecue Sauce. Cover with plastic wrap and refrigerate for at least 2 hours.

Soak the hickory chips in water for 1 hour.

Put a large rectangular metal pan in the center of the bottom rack of a kettle grill and mound 15 charcoal briquets on each side. Open the bottom vents on the grill. Light the charcoal and allow the fire to burn until the briquets are ashen and glowing, about 25 minutes.

Drain the hickory chips and distribute them over the charcoal. Place the ribs on the grilling rack so that they are directly over the pan. Cover the grill, open the cover vents, and smoke the ribs for 1 hour and 15 minutes.

Warm the remaining cup of Barbecue Sauce. Cut the ribs and serve them immediately with the Barbecue Sauce on the side.

Yield = 4 servings

❖ ❖ ❖ *We* smoke cheese as an appetizer to serve while the ribs cook. Prepare the grill as directed and smoke the cheese before the ribs. Place 1-pound blocks of *Home Made* Mozzarella (page 89), Swiss, or Gouda on squares of foil. Place the foil in the center of the grilling rack. Cover the grill, open the vents, and smoke the cheese for 10 minutes. Allow it to cool to room temperature, cover with plastic wrap, and refrigerate for at least 30 minutes before serving. ❖ ❖ ❖

A Dickens Christmas, Updated

What would any proper Victorian hostess have brought to the table for the Christmas feast? Why, a goose, of course—even Mrs. Cratchit, in her humble circumstances due to the stinginess of Scrooge and Marley, served her family a Christmas goose.

We've evolved an admittedly offbeat ritual of serving Apple-Smoked Goose at holiday dinners, and we've found that family and friends love both the goose and the novelty of its having been prepared outdoors at Christmastime.

This menu is an updated Dickens feast for 6, featuring our Apple-Smoked Goose as the centerpiece.

GIBLET GRAVY (OR TRY
Home Made APRICOT
ORANGE SAUCE, PAGE 23)

Giblets and neck from
the goose
2 cups chicken stock
1 cup dry white wine
1 teaspoon salt
1 bay leaf

Trim excess fat from the giblets and neck.

Combine all the ingredients in a small saucepan and bring to a boil over medium heat. Reduce the heat to low and simmer, uncovered, for 1½ hours. Cover and continue to cook over low heat for 30 minutes more.

Remove the pan from the heat. Discard the bay leaf and transfer the giblets and neck to a cutting board; remove the neck meat from the bone. Coarsely chop the giblets and neck meat and transfer them to the bowl of a food processor or blender. Pour in the chicken stock and process until the mixture is thick and smooth.

Return the gravy to the saucepan and heat for 5 minutes over medium heat. Transfer to a gravy boat and serve at once.

Apple-Smoked Goose

Goose figured prominently on the Victorian table, and it's also a favorite dish of ours for special occasions. Smoking goose in a kettle grill is one of the easiest ways to prepare it and lets you add applewood chips, which lend a subtle, fruity accent.

We've found that making slits along the bottom of the breast allows a substantial amount of fat to drain from the goose as it cooks, producing a much leaner bird than usual.

1 cup applewood chips
9-pound goose
¼ teaspoon freshly ground black pepper

Soak the applewood in water for 1 hour.

Put a large rectangular metal pan in the center of the bottom rack of a kettle grill and mound 15 charcoal briquets on each side. Open the bottom vents on the grill. Light the charcoal and allow the fire to burn until the briquets are ashen and glowing, about 25 minutes.

Meanwhile, rinse the goose and pat it dry. Using a sharp knife, make a 3-inch-long slit, just deep enough to break the skin, under each wing along the bottom of the breast. Turn the wings under. Remove the excess fat from the cavity of the goose, then sprinkle the pepper into the cavity.

When the fire is ready, drain the applewood chips and distribute them on the coals. Place the goose on the grilling rack, slit side down, so that it is directly over the pan. Cover the grill, open the cover vents, and smoke the goose for about 3 hours, until it reaches an internal temperature of 170° F. on an instant-read thermometer and the thigh juices run clear.

Remove the bird from the grill and set it aside for at least 20 minutes before carving. Store any leftover goose in the refrigerator, where it will keep for 5 to 7 days.

Yield = 6 servings

CHESTNUT STUFFING

- 3 cups canned chestnut meat, rinsed and drained
- ½ cup light cream
- ½ cup (1 stick) unsalted butter, melted
- ½ cup chopped white onion
- 1 cup bread crumbs
- 1 teaspoon salt
- ¼ teaspoon ground white pepper
- ¼ teaspoon ground sage

Preheat the oven to 350° F. Coarsely mash the chestnuts in a large bowl. Add the remaining ingredients and mix well. Transfer the mixture to a lightly buttered 1-quart baking dish and bake for 30 to 40 minutes, until the top of the stuffing has browned.

Home Made Meatless Mincemeat (page 28), served as a relish

PLUM PUDDING WITH HARD SAUCE

Pudding:

- 1 ½ cups golden raisins
- 1 cup dried currants
- ¼ cup chopped candied citron
- ½ cup finely chopped suet
- 3 cups pumpernickel bread crumbs
- 2 teaspoons ground cinnamon
- 1 teaspoon ground nutmeg
- ¼ teaspoon ground cloves
- ¼ teaspoon ground mace
- ½ teaspoon salt
- 1 cup granulated sugar
- 4 large eggs
- ½ cup milk
- 6 tablespoons brandy

1/3 cup unsalted butter, at room temperature

1 teaspoon brandy

1 cup confectioners' sugar

In a large bowl, combine the raisins, currants, candied citron, suet, bread crumbs, spices, salt, and granulated sugar. Mix well and set aside.

In a medium bowl, beat the eggs until frothy using an electric mixer at low speed. Beat in the milk and brandy. Fold the mixture into the large bowl and combine thoroughly.

Set a rack into the bottom of a large stockpot. Fill the pot with enough water to come halfway up the sides of a round 2-quart baking dish when set on the rack. Bring to a boil over medium heat.

Meanwhile, lightly butter the baking dish. Pour the batter into the baking dish, cover with a double thickness of aluminum foil, and secure the foil with string.

When the water in the pot has come to a boil, carefully place the baking dish onto the rack. Reduce the heat to low, cover the pot, and gently boil for 5 hours. Add more water as needed to maintain a water level about halfway up the sides of the baking dish. Remove the baking dish from the pot and set the pudding aside to cool for a few minutes.

To make the Hard Sauce, cream the butter until pale and fluffy with an electric mixer at medium speed. Gradually beat in the brandy and confectioners'

Minted Smoked Salmon

Along with pork, fish was one of the foods often preserved by smoking in olden days. While our ancestors would have smoked salmon in the chimney or in a smoker fashioned from a wooden barrel, we've adapted the technique to the stovetop and use nothing more exotic than a wok or a fry pan.

Mint adds a unique flavor to salmon, which is more typically paired with dill. Serve the salmon warm as an appetizer, along with a little Home Made Prepared Horseradish (page 54).

1/2 pound fresh salmon fillet

1 teaspoon dried mint

1/2 tablespoon coarse kosher salt

1/8 teaspoon coarsely ground black pepper

1/2 tablespoon granulated sugar

1/2 cup light brown sugar, firmly packed

1/2 cup dark brown sugar, firmly packed

Rinse the salmon and pat it dry. Fold a 30-inch-long sheet of aluminum foil in half and lay the salmon, skin side down, on the foil. Sprinkle the mint onto the salmon.

Combine the salt, pepper, and granulated sugar in a small bowl. Spread the mixture evenly over the fish, pressing it into the flesh.

Close the foil around the salmon securely and transfer it to a baking dish. Place a second, smaller dish on top of the fish and weigh it down with a bag of rice or sugar, or with a large, heavy can. Place the baking dish in the refrigerator for 24 hours.

Unwrap the salmon and rinse off the sugar, salt, and any loose mint (some mint will adhere to the surface of the fish).

Line a wok or a straight-sided fry pan with a double thickness of aluminum foil and dump in the brown sugars. Insert a low rack that clears the sugar but still allows a cover to fit.

Place the salmon on the rack and cover the pan. If using a wok, ring 2 wet towels around the cover to keep the smoke from escaping; for a fry pan, drape a wet towel over the cover and fasten it tightly with string or a rubber band.

Smoke the salmon for 15 minutes over medium heat. Remove the pan from the heat (leaving the toweling intact) and set it aside for 5 minutes before uncovering.

The Minted Smoked Salmon has a refrigerator shelf life of 5 days.

Yield = 4 appetizer servings

Basil-Smoked Shrimp & Scallop Kebabs

In this recipe, we actually wood smoke indoors! Using wet towels to insulate the wok or fry pan contains the pervasive woody aroma and keeps the smoke from spreading through the house.

- ½ cup applewood chips
- ½ pound large shrimp (about 12 shrimp), peeled and deveined
- ½ pound sea scallops (about 12 scallops)
- 1 cup chopped fresh basil (leaves and stems)

Soak the applewood chips in water for 1 hour.

Soak four 6-inch bamboo skewers in water for 15 minutes.

Thread the shrimp and scallops alternately onto each skewer.

Line a wok or a straight-sided fry pan with a double thickness of aluminum foil. Drain the applewood chips and combine them with the basil in the bottom. Insert a low rack that will keep the skewers raised but still allow a cover to fit.

Place the skewers across the rack and cover the pan. If using a wok, ring 2 wet towels around the cover; for a fry pan, drape a wet towel over the cover and secure it tightly.

Smoke the kebabs for 15 minutes over medium-high heat. Remove the pan from the heat and set it aside for 5 minutes before uncovering. Serve immediately.

Yield = 2 main course servings, or 4 servings as an appetizer

Chinese Tea-Smoked Duck

Tea smoking lends this dish a truly one-of-a-kind taste. It makes a wonderful buffet dish, since the duck is equally good warm or room temperature.

- 1 5- to 6-pound duck
- 3 tablespoons coarse kosher salt
- ½ teaspoon coarsely ground black pepper
- 1 tablespoon dry sherry
- 2 pieces peeled fresh ginger, each about 2 x 1 x ½ inch thick
- 4 cups water, approximately
- ¾ cup dark brown sugar, firmly packed

sugar. Continue to beat until the mixture is creamy.

Invert the Plum Pudding onto a serving plate and slice it; top each portion with a dollop Hard Sauce.

Yield = 4 servings

❖ ❖ ❖ *W*e serve the smoked shrimp and scallops on a bed of mixed greens with Cranberry Mustard Vinaigrette: Whisk 1 tablespoon *Home Made* Dijon-Style Mustard (page 59) with 1 ½ tablespoons *Home Made* Cranberry Vinegar (page 45). Drizzle in ¼ cup olive oil, whisking until the oil is absorbed and the dressing is thickened. ❖ ❖ ❖

❖ ❖ ❖ *V*ariation: For Lemon Tea-Smoked Chicken, substitute a 4- to 5-pound broiler for the duck. Instead of coating the bird with the salt and pepper paste and refrigerating it for 5 hours, just rub the skin with the juice of 1 lemon before steaming; add the pulp of the lemon and ¼ cup dry sherry to the boiling water in the bottom of the pot. Steam the chicken for 45 minutes and proceed with the recipe directions for the duck. ❖ ❖ ❖

Tea-Smoked Duck Salad

Chinese Tea-Smoked Duck makes a distinctive salad; serve this on a bed of mixed greens for a light and elegant meal. For variety, substitute Lemon Tea-Smoked Chicken for the duck.

- ½ Chinese Tea-Smoked Duck, skinned, deboned, and cubed (about 2 cups)
- ¼ cup sliced water chestnuts
- ¼ cup cubed green bell pepper
- ½ cup whole cashews
- 1 tablespoon minced fresh cilantro
- 2 tablespoons soy sauce
- 1 tablespoon sesame oil
- 1 tablespoon canola oil
- 2 tablespoons mayonnaise
- 1 tablespoon dry sherry
- ½ tablespoon dark brown sugar, packed
- 2 garlic cloves, peeled and minced

Combine the duck, water chestnuts, green pepper, cashews, and cilantro in a large bowl. Mix well.

In a small bowl, whisk the soy sauce, oils, mayonnaise, sherry, brown sugar, and garlic thoroughly. Pour over the poultry and toss.

Cover and chill for at least 1 hour before serving.

Yield = 2–3 servings

¾ cup black Chinese tea leaves

1 tablespoon sesame oil

Rinse and pat the duck dry, and set it aside.

In a small, heavy fry pan over medium heat, toast the salt and pepper for about 5 minutes, stirring constantly, until the salt is a light tan hue. Transfer to a bowl, and stir in the sherry to make a coarse paste.

Rub half of the paste evenly around the cavity of the duck and the remaining half over the skin. Cut 1 piece of ginger into 4 matchstick slices and place them into the cavity. Cover the duck with plastic wrap and refrigerate it for at least 5 hours.

Unwrap the duck and rinse the paste thoroughly from the cavity and the skin. Discard the ginger slices. Pat the duck dry.

In a wok or stockpot, place a low rack that keeps the duck raised but allows a cover to fit. Add 4 cups water and bring to a boil over medium heat. Pour off a bit of water if it boils over the rack.

Place the duck onto the rack, cover, and steam over medium heat for 1½ hours.

Remove the pot from the heat, transfer the duck to a plate, and set the rack aside. Dump the water. After the pot has cooled enough to handle, line it with a triple thickness of aluminum foil. Put the brown sugar and tea in the bottom, mixing to break up the sugar. Refit the rack.

Place the duck on the rack and cover the pot. If using a wok, ring 2 wet towels around the cover to keep the smoke from escaping; for a stockpot, secure a wet towel tightly over the cover.

Smoke the duck for 3 minutes over medium-high heat, then reduce the heat to medium and smoke it for 12 minutes longer. Remove the pot from the heat and set it aside for 5 minutes before uncovering.

Transfer the duck to a cutting board and brush the entire surface of the bird with the sesame oil. Cut the duck in half lengthwise, then cut off the wings. Separate the legs from the breasts, then cut each quarter into 4 long pieces (cutting through the bones with a cleaver).

Store any leftover duck in the refrigerator, where it has a shelf life of 5 to 7 days.

Yield = 4–6 main-course servings, or 5–7 servings as an appetizer

Sausages

One nineteenth-century home economist advised that the meat for sausage "can be chopped in a wooden tray by means of a cleaver."

For the casing, "remove from the pig's intestines the loose fat and outer membranes. Turn them inside out and cleanse them thoroughly in borax water. Bleach by letting them soak for 24 hours or more in water containing 1 ounce of chloride of lime to the gallon . . . Finally, wash them thoroughly several times in warm water.

"Or sausages may be packed," she continues, "in cases of muslin or other clean white goods . . . [then] dipped in melted lard and hung up to dry."

Contrary to one's first impression upon reading these instructions, the art of seasoning finely chopped meat and stuffing it into some form of casing has changed little since the days when cookbook authors advised their readers to undertake sausage making wielding a cleaver—it's much the same as the sausage-making practices of several preceding centuries, for that matter. What has changed dramatically is the relative ease with which it can now be accomplished.

THE BASICS

Today, we are most likely to prepare sausage meat with a grinder, fill ready-made casings with a sausage stuffer (or to dispense with the traditional casings altogether), and throw any sausages that won't be cooked right away into the freezer.

Whereas our ancestors made sausages mostly from pork, *Home Made* sausages are made of chicken, turkey, veal, and seafood as well.

Although we provide instructions for stuffing sausage meat into traditional casings, most *Home Made* recipes utilize alternative methods that are easier and quicker, and don't require a sausage-stuffing apparatus.

The sausage meat for *Home Made* Hickory-Smoked Andouille is rolled in cheesecloth so that it will hold its shape while smoking in a kettle grill; our Cajun Boudin Blanc is steamed in cheesecloth. Salmon Sausage and Veal Bratwurst are encased in long sheets of plastic wrap and twisted into links that can be separated easily and unwrapped once the sausages have simmered.

We form Chicken Sausage and Turkey Breakfast Sausage into patties for easy frying, but leave the Chorizo and Italian Sausage in bulk so they can be cooked in a variety of dishes.

Sausage making is multicultural, which we've tried to reflect in our selections. Hickory-Smoked Andouille and Boudin Blanc hail from Cajun Louisiana and reflect the region's French influence. Our Veal Bratwurst is a lighter, updated rendition of the old German specialty prized in Wisconsin.

Other ethnic recipes include the aforementioned ever-popular Italian Sausage and spicy Chorizo, which has traveled in recent years from Mexico to Latin communities across the country; another specialty from afar is featured here—Chinese Pork Wontons, a departure from the mainstream in that the sausage meat is wrapped in pastry dough.

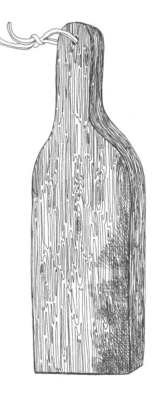

Turkey Breakfast Sausage

"If you like to know what you are eating, have your sausage meat pre-pared at home or by some one you can trust," advises one cookbook au-thor of the 1880s. "Season highly with salt, pepper, and sage . . . and cook in a frying-pan until brown." Wise words still, though we've added a few spices for zip.

3¼ pounds turkey legs, deboned (do not skin or trim fat)

½ tablespoon coarse kosher salt

1 tablespoon ground sage

½ teaspoon freshly ground black pepper

1 teaspoon dried rosemary

¼ teaspoon ground ginger

½ teaspoon dried oregano

⅛ teaspoon cayenne pepper

2 tablespoons water

Work the turkey through a meat grinder, using the disc with the largest holes. Add the remaining ingredients to the ground turkey and mix thoroughly by hand. Form the mixture into patties, using about ¼ cup for each.

Preheat a medium nonstick fry pan over medium-low heat. Transfer the patties to the pan in batches. Cover and cook for about 10 minutes over medium-low heat, flipping the patties after 5 minutes, until they are brown and crusty on both sides.

The turkey sausage will keep for up to 5 days in the refrigerator or for 6 months, uncooked, in the freezer.

Yield = 12–14 sausage patties

Hickory-Smoked Andouille

Andouille, a spicy Louisiana staple, is often cold smoked, and then cooked in dishes like gumbo and jambalaya. Since we hot smoke the sausage, it cooks while smoking and can be served right off the grill as an hors d'oeuvre. Just slice it and garnish with Home Made *Black Pep-per Mustard (page 59). We also add chunked Andouille to pastas and casseroles.*

Sausage Stuffing

Most *Home Made* sausage recipes use easy "stuffing" methods that utilize readily available materials, such as plastic wrap or cheesecloth, to hold the ingredients together. In others, we simply form the ingredients by hand into patties or leave the sausage meat in bulk form.

However, you may want to experiment with traditional sausage casings, which are available from many supermarkets and meat markets. (If you don't see them in the meat case, ask the butcher.) Casings require a manual sausage stuffer, a stuffer attachment to a meat grinder, or a stuffer attachment to a multipurpose stationary electric mixer (the last being the easiest to use).

Casings come packed in salt and have a long refrigerator shelf life. Each casing resembles a very long, thin deflated balloon, open at both ends. They may be cut to any length desired (if, for example, you estimate that you have enough sausage to stuff 1½ casings).

Separate the casings you will be using and soak them in hot water for 2 hours.

Open one end of the first casing and affix it to the faucet of the kitchen sink. Run cold water through briefly, inflating the casing. Then attach an end to the cylindrical spout on the stuffer. Knot the other end of the casing about 2 inches in and bunch the casing onto the spout up to the knot.

Work the ingredients through the stuffer; they will come out the spout, inflating and filling the casing. Release the bunched casing from the spout a little at a time as the casing fills. Twist the stuffed casing 2 or 3 times every 6 or 7 inches, to form individual links. Leave about 2 inches of casing unfilled at the end, remove it from the spout, and tie a knot to seal the sausage.

Repeat the process to stuff any additional casings.

Follow recipe directions for cooking.

2¾ pounds pork shoulder, butt portion (do not trim fat), cut into large chunks
4 teaspoons sugar
1 tablespoon coarse kosher salt
2 teaspoons coarsely ground black pepper
¾ teaspoon cayenne pepper
¾ teaspoon crushed red pepper flakes
¾ teaspoon dried thyme
1 tablespoon hot paprika
¾ cup hickory chips

Work the pork through a meat grinder, using the disc with the largest holes. Add the sugar, salt, peppers, thyme, and paprika. Mix thoroughly. Cover and refrigerate for at least 1 hour.

Lay a 20 x 10-inch single thickness of cheesecloth on a countertop. Liberally paint a 4-inch-wide strip along the long side of the cheesecloth with vegetable oil. Arrange 1 cup of the pork into a long thin strip along the inner border of the oil. Fold the oiled cheesecloth over the pork and roll the strip back and forth to form an even sausage about 12 inches long. Roll the sausage up in the cheesecloth and tie each end in a knot or secure with string. Repeat with five more pieces of cheesecloth and the remaining meat until you have 5 sausages.

Soak the hickory chips in water for a half hour.

Put a rectangular metal pan in the center of the bottom rack of a kettle grill and mound 15 charcoal briquets on each side. Open the bottom vents on the grill. Light the charcoal and allow the fire to burn until the briquets are ashen and glowing, about 25 minutes.

Drain the hickory chips and distribute them over the charcoal. Place the sausages on the grilling rack so that they are over the pan. Cover the grill, open the cover vents, and smoke the sausages for about 1 hour and 10 minutes, until they reach an internal temperature of 160° F. on an instant-read thermometer.

Move the sausages to the edges of the grill, directly over the charcoal. Cook for 3 minutes, flip the sausages over, and cook for 3 minutes more on the other side.

Remove the sausages from the grill. When they have cooled enough to handle, peel off the cheesecloth.

When cooked, the Andouille has a refrigerator shelf life of 5 days and may be frozen for up to 6 months.

Yield = Five 12-inch sausages

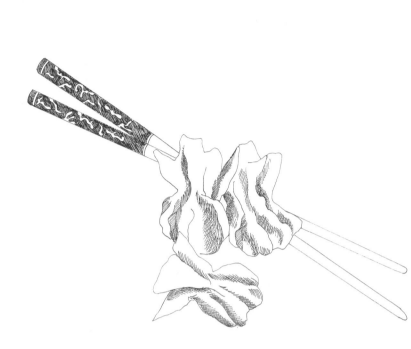

Pork Wontons

These little treats, consisting of sausage meat encased in dumplings, are incredibly easy to make. Since they're almost everyone's favorite hors d'oeuvre, we suggest making them on a rainy weekend—resisting the temptation to cook and eat them immediately—and freezing to have on hand for last-minute get-togethers.

In addition to their merits as finger food, Wontons also make a tasty addition to bowls of hot chicken soup.

½ pound pork shoulder, butt portion (with a little fat left on)
1 tablespoon soy sauce
1 tablespoon dry sherry
2 scallions, trimmed and finely chopped
¼ cup chopped fresh spinach
1 large egg yolk
48 wonton wrappers (available from Oriental markets)
2 cups vegetable or canola oil (if frying)

Work the pork through a meat grinder, using a small-holed disc. Thoroughly mix in the soy sauce, sherry, scallion, spinach, and egg yolk.

For each wonton, spoon 1 teaspoon of the pork onto the center of the wrapper. Moisten a finger in a bowl of water and dab water along all 4 borders of the wrapper. Fold the wonton in half to form a triangle. Crimp the edges together and curl the

Cajun Boudin Blanc

Unlike the French version, Cajun Boudin Blanc includes rice, and is much spicier. Traditionally, the casings are slit open and the meat scooped out. We dispense with casings, using cheesecloth instead, and then cut the cooked sausages into chunks as an appetizer or slice each into 2 or 3 main course portions.

2 pounds pork shoulder, butt portion (do not trim fat), cut into large chunks
4 cups water
1 small dried hot chili
12 whole black peppercorns
3 bay leaves
2½ teaspoons coarse kosher salt
5 garlic cloves, peeled

2 points of the triangle together until they meet.

To fry the Wontons, heat the oil to smoking in a wok or medium fry pan. Add the Wontons in batches and cook for about 2 minutes over medium heat, until browned all over, and drain on paper toweling. To boil, bring a large pot of water to a boil, add the Wontons, and cook over medium heat for 5 to 7 minutes, until they rise to the top of the pot.

Uncooked Wontons have a refrigerator shelf life of 5 days and may be frozen for up to 6 months; thaw in the refrigerator before cooking.

Yield = 48 wontons

❖ ❖ ❖ *W*e use leftover **Boudin Blanc to make a spicy breakfast hash. Break up the sausage into a nonstick fry pan and warm for about 10 minutes over medium heat, until it begins to form a light crust. Transfer to a plate and top with poached eggs.** ❖ ❖ ❖

1 medium white onion, peeled and cut into 8 long wedges

1 small green pepper, seeded, cored, deveined, and cut into 8 long strips

1 tablespoon dried sage leaf, broken up (not ground sage)

1¾ cups cooked white rice

1 teaspoon dried marjoram

1 teaspoon cayenne pepper

1 teaspoon crushed red pepper flakes

3 scallions, trimmed and chopped

⅛ cup chopped fresh cilantro

¼ teaspoon freshly ground black pepper

Combine the pork and water in a large saucepan. Bring to a boil over high heat, then reduce the heat to low. Skim off any foam that accumulates on top. Add the dried chili, peppercorns, bay leaves, and ½ teaspoon of the salt. Cut one garlic clove in half and add it. Cover and cook for about 1 hour, until the pork is fork-tender. Remove the pork with a slotted spoon.

Work the pork, onion, green pepper, and remaining 4 garlic cloves through a meat grinder, using a small-holed disc and alternating ingredients as you grind.

Add the remaining ingredients and mix thoroughly by hand, making sure that the spices are well distributed.

Lay a 20-inch-square single thickness of cheesecloth on a countertop. Paint a 4-inch-wide strip along a side of the cheesecloth liberally with vegetable oil. Arrange half of the pork mixture into a long thin strip along the inner border of the oil. Roll the mixture up in the cheesecloth, creating a solid sausage and leaving 2 to 3 inches of cheesecloth on each end. Form the sausage into a coil and tie each end in a knot, or with string. Repeat with a second piece of cheesecloth to form a second sausage from the remaining pork.

Steam the coiled sausages over about 1 inch of water for 15 minutes over medium heat. Remove the sausages from the steamer, and set them aside to cool for 5 minutes before cutting away the cheesecloth. Serve hot.

The Boudin Blanc may be stored in the refrigerator for 5 days or frozen, uncooked, for up to 6 months.

Yield = Two 15-inch sausages

Chicken Sausage

Chicken, used in lieu of pork, is a contemporary twist on the age-old art of sausage making. This sausage is one of our favorites—light, subtly spiced, flavorful, and versatile. We fry it in patties and serve it hot with a salad as a main course, or in sandwiches. The Chicken Sausage can also be stuffed into sausage casings (see page 120) and broiled or grilled with equally good results.

2½ pounds chicken legs and thighs, deboned (do not skin or trim fat)

½ pound pork fat, cut into large chunks

3 garlic cloves, peeled and minced

1½ teaspoons coarse kosher salt

¼ teaspoon ground white pepper

½ teaspoon ground cinnamon

⅛ teaspoon ground allspice

¼ teaspoon dry mustard

1 teaspoon dried basil

1 teaspoon dried tarragon

1 teaspoon dried parsley or 1 tablespoon minced fresh parsley

¼ cup white wine

1 teaspoon balsamic vinegar

Work the chicken and pork fat through a meat grinder, using a small-holed disc and alternating ingredients.

Add all the remaining ingredients and combine thoroughly. Form the mixture into patties, using about ½ cup for each.

Preheat a medium nonstick fry pan over medium-low heat. Add the patties, cover, and cook for 5 to 7 minutes or until lightly browned. Flip the patties and cook for another 5 to 7 minutes.

The Chicken Sausage has a refrigerator shelf life of 5 days and may be frozen, uncooked, for up to 6 months.

Yield = About 8 sausage patties

Home Made *Pâtés*

COUNTRY CHICKEN PÂTÉ

4 cups Chicken Sausage

¾ cup French bread crumbs

1 large egg

¼ cup *Home Made* Herbed Chèvre (page 87) or Cream Cheese (page 94)

2 tablespoons brandy

Preheat the oven to 350° F. and butter a 9 ¼-inch loaf pan liberally.

Mix all the ingredients together well and transfer the mixture to the loaf pan. Put the pan into a baking dish filled with 2 inches of boiling water. Bake for about 1 ½ hours, until the inside of the loaf reaches 170° F. on an instant-read thermometer.

Remove the baking dish from the oven. Take the loaf pan out of the baking dish and set it on a rack for 1 hour to cool.

Cut a piece of wax paper to fit on top of the loaf. Lightly butter one side and press onto the loaf, buttered side down. Cover loosely with aluminum foil. Place another 9¼-inch loaf pan on top, and weigh it down with a 5-pound bag of sugar or comparable weight. Refrigerate for at least 24 hours.

PÂTÉ EN CROÛTE

1¼ cups Italian Sausage

2 teaspoons dried thyme Dough for 1 *Home Made* Classic French Bread Baguette (page 156)

2 tablespoons *Home Made* Dijon-Style Mustard (page 59)

1 cup shredded *Home Made* Mozzarella (page 89)

1 egg, beaten

Preheat the oven to 350° F.; lightly butter a baking sheet and dust it with flour.

Cook the sausage and thyme in a heavy skillet over medium heat until the meat is crumbly but not browned, breaking it up while it cooks. Drain the sausage on paper towels.

Turn the dough out onto a 2-foot sheet of wax paper and cover with a second sheet of wax paper. Roll the dough into a rectangle about ½ inch thick. Remove the top sheet of wax paper.

Coat the dough with the mustard. Layer the sausage onto the dough, leaving a thin border around the edge, and top with the cheese. Raise a short side of the wax paper and roll the dough up about ⅔ of the way lengthwise. Fold the other side over, then crimp the edges.

Place the filled dough onto the prepared sheet, seam side down, tucking the ends under. Brush with the beaten egg. Make 2 shallow incisions diagonally on the top of the dough, using a sharp knife.

Bake about 30 minutes, until a tester comes out clean. Transfer to a platter and serve immediately, sliced on the diagonal.

Bulk Italian Sausage

This sausage lends itself to advance preparation. We freeze it in 2-cup measures for future use in spaghetti or lasagna, and by the cup for Home Made Pizza (page 168).

2 ½ pounds pork shoulder, butt portion, trimmed and cut into large chunks

½ tablespoon coarse kosher salt

1 tablespoon dried anise

½ teaspoon freshly ground black pepper

⅛ teaspoon cayenne pepper

½ teaspoon dried oregano

½ teaspoon dried thyme

2 tablespoons water

½ pound pork fat, cut into large chunks

4 garlic cloves, peeled

Put the pork into a large bowl. Add the salt, anise, peppers, oregano, thyme, and the water. Mix well to coat the meat.

Work the seasoned pork, pork fat, and garlic through a meat grinder, using the disc with the largest holes and alternating ingredients as you grind.

The Italian Sausage may be stored for up to 5 days in the refrigerator or 6 months in the freezer.

Yield = 3 pounds bulk sausage meat (6 cups)

Veal Bratwurst

This version is lighter than the Old World German specialty, and employs the quick plastic-wrap method of forming the links; use sausage casings if you wish (see page 120). We like to serve veal brats with a sampling of Home Made *Mustards (pages 57–59),* Home Made *Warm Vinaigrette Potato Salad (page 48), and plenty of beer.*

    2 pounds veal shoulder (do not trim fat), cut into
      large chunks
    ¾ pound pork shoulder, butt portion (do not trim
      fat), cut into large chunks
    ½ pound pork fat, cut into large chunks
    1 medium yellow onion, peeled and halved
    2 garlic cloves, peeled
    ⅛ teaspoon ground ginger
    1 teaspoon ground allspice
    ½ teaspoon ground white pepper
    2½ teaspoons coarse kosher salt
    1 large egg
    ¾ cup milk
    4 cups water

Work the veal, pork, pork fat, onion, and garlic through a meat grinder, using a small-holed disc and alternating ingredients as you grind.

In a small bowl, combine the ginger, allspice, pepper, and 2 teaspoons of the salt. Whisk in the egg and milk. Add the mixture to the ground meat and combine thoroughly. Cover and refrigerate for 1 hour.

Lay 5 pieces of 18 x 12-inch plastic wrap on a countertop. Put 1½ cups of the meat on each, roll it up lengthwise, and form into 12-inch logs about 1 inch in diameter. Crimp each log in the middle and tie with string to form 2 links. Tie the ends with string. Prick 4 holes in each link with a pin or the tip of a knife.

Combine the water and the remaining salt in a medium saucepan and bring to a boil over high heat. Place the sausage into the boiling water, reduce the heat to low, cover, and simmer for about 20 minutes, until the links are firm. Carefully remove the sausage from the water, cut the links apart, and remove the plastic wrap. Serve hot.

Fruit-Flavored Sausages

Adding a little fruit can lend a light and refreshing twist to several *Home Made* sausages. Make the addition to the Veal Bratwurst before refrigerating.

The Chicken Sausage and Turkey Breakfast Sausage will need to be stuffed in casings to hold together with the additional moisture given off by the fruit. Add the fruit with the other ingredients after grinding the meat, and stuff according to the directions on page 120.

To flavor Veal Bratwurst, add ⅓ cup *Home Made* Dried Raspberries (page 194) that have been soaked in 3 tablespoons dry white wine for 15 minutes.

To flavor Chicken Sausage, add ⅓ cup peeled and chopped apple.

To flavor Turkey Breakfast Sausage, add ½ cup peeled and finely chopped peach.

The Veal Bratwurst have a refrigerator shelf life of 5 days and may be frozen, uncooked, for up to 6 months.

Yield = Ten 6-inch sausage links

Chorizo

We make this spicy Mexican sausage in bulk and freeze it to have on hand for a number of dishes. Add sautéed Chorizo to tomato sauce for pasta or combine it with diced bell pepper and onion in scrambled eggs. Fire-eaters may want to increase the cayenne pepper to up to ½ teaspoon.

1½ pounds pork shoulder, butt portion, trimmed and cut into large chunks
½ pound pork fat, cut into large chunks
1½ teaspoons coarse kosher salt
⅛ teaspoon ground white pepper
⅛ teaspoon cayenne pepper
½ teaspoon crushed red pepper flakes
½ teaspoon ground coriander
¾ teaspoon ground cumin
3 tablespoons hot paprika
½ teaspoon sugar
3 tablespoons red wine vinegar
2 garlic cloves, peeled and minced
1 teaspoon chili powder
⅛ teaspoon ground cloves

Fit a meat grinder with the large-holed disc and work half of the pork chunks through it. Change to a small-holed disc and work the remaining pork and the pork fat through the grinder.

Add all the remaining ingredients to the ground pork and mix thoroughly by hand.

The Chorizo may be stored for up to 5 days in the refrigerator or 6 months in the freezer.

Yield = 2½ pounds bulk sausage meat (5 cups)

❖ ❖ ❖ **S**tuffed vegetables take on new life when Chorizo is substituted for ground beef. Just mix it with an equal amount of cooked rice, spoon into seeded green bell peppers or acorn squash, cover, and bake in a shallow baking dish in a 350° F. oven for 45 minutes. ❖ ❖ ❖

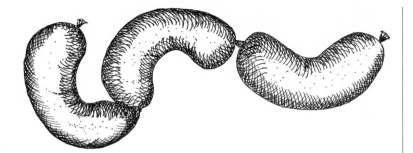

Salmon Sausage

The Victorian obsession with oysters may have been why they were used in sausage of the day, but we much prefer salmon. The resulting sausage has an elegant and light texture, but a distinct and robust flavor. For perfect luncheon or warm-weather fare, slice each link into rounds and serve on a bed of mixed greens, or fan them around a plate of Home Made *Perfect Caesar Salad (page 58).*

 1 10-ounce salmon fillet, skinned
 6 tablespoons heavy cream
 1 large egg white
 ⅛ teaspoon ground white pepper
 ¼ teaspoon hot paprika
 1½ teaspoons coarse kosher salt
 ¼ cup minced mushroom
 1 tablespoon finely chopped fresh cilantro
 ¼ teaspoon dried anise
 1 scallion, trimmed and minced
 ½ teaspoon dried tarragon
 ½ teaspoon canola oil

Cut 2 ounces of the salmon into small pieces and set it aside. Cut the remaining 8 ounces into large chunks and place them in the bowl of a food processor. Puree until smooth, about 15 seconds. Add the cream, egg white, pepper, paprika, and ½ teaspoon of the salt, and process until everything is well blended, about 5 seconds.

Transfer the puree to a medium bowl and fold in the reserved salmon, mushroom, cilantro, anise, scallion, and tarragon. Cover and refrigerate the mixture for 1 hour.

Bring a large pot of water and the remaining teaspoon salt to a boil over high heat.

Meanwhile, lay an 18 x 12-inch piece of plastic wrap on a countertop and lightly coat it with canola oil. Place the salmon puree onto the plastic wrap, roll the puree up lengthwise to form a 12-inch log about 1 inch in diameter. Crimp the log at 3-inch intervals and tie with string to form 4 links. Tie the ends with string.

Place the sausage in the boiling water. Reduce the heat to low, cover, and simmer for 10 minutes. Carefully remove the sausage from the water, cut the links apart, and remove the plastic wrap. Serve warm or at room temperature.

The Salmon Sausage will keep for 3 to 5 days in the refrigerator.

Yield = Four 3-inch sausage links

Candy

Savoring delicate little morsels fashioned from chocolate, nuts, sugar, and other goodies is an age-old pleasure—one that should be cherished all the more and indulged with heightened discrimination in this age of health consciousness.

Making candy is an ancient art, and to those of us whose families long ago forsook the chocolate pot for the nearest Godiva outlet, it's one shrouded in mystery. But with all due respect to the world's great candy makers, the simple truth is that half the fun is really in the making.

From dipping elegant little chocolates to making toffee and brittle, to tossing glazed nuts in caramel syrup, the pleasure doubles when you get to lick the bounty fresh off your fingers.

Candy making not only provides enjoyment, but also carries a certain degree of social clout, as evidenced by the hovering masses at the kitchen door ("Is it candy yet?") and by the following words of wisdom from an early 1890s treatise on entertaining:

"Candy making should be taught and acquired as one of the most useful of accomplishments. Like every other art that calls for skill and intelligence, it has an educational value. And the universal fondness for sweets renders the candy maker a popular favorite. Thus the mother who can make good candy and is fond of practicing her skill, or teaches and encourages [her children] to do so, will not only make her home attractive to her own family, but will also acquire an enviable reputation as an entertainer."

❖ ❖ ❖

THE BASICS

We've tried to simplify candy making for the enjoyment of the entire family (it's one that fathers, as well, can pass on to their progeny). While all children should be kept away from pans of boiling sugar syrup that's the first step in many recipes, older kids can help dip ingredients into chocolate and even the youngest can inscribe a heartfelt, if somewhat rudimentary, message onto a chocolate greeting card with cake decorating gel.

In *Home Made* candy recipes that start with a simple sugar syrup, the degree of readiness of the sugar mixture can be measured with a candy thermometer, but perhaps a little theory is in order.

In lieu of a thermometer, stages of boiled sugar syrup can also be discerned by gauging the reaction when a little syrup is dropped into a glass of cold water:

Temperature/Recipe	Stage	Reaction
234–240° F. (Cashew Butter Fudge)	Soft-Ball	The syrup forms a ball that flattens when removed from the water.
250–268° F. (Greg's Creamy Caramels)	Hard-Ball	The syrup forms a firm ball in the water.
270–290° F. (English Walnut Toffee, Sally Cohen's Macadamia Brittle)	Soft-Crack	The syrup forms long, firm threads in the water.
300–310° F. (Root Beer Lollipops)	Hard-Crack	The syrup forms long, brittle threads in the water.

Our fudge requires heating a sugar, cream, and milk mixture just to a soft-ball stage and stirring for a few minutes off the heat. While only a little more patience and elbow grease for stirring produce the hard-ball stage needed for old-fashioned creamy sucking caramels, we heat ingredients to the soft-crack stage for our brittle and toffee. Beyond the hard-crack stage, the syrup begins to brown and caramelize, a stage we reach only for the caramel corn.

INGREDIENTS

Chocolate contains both cocoa butter and cocoa powder. Choose high-quality chocolate with a high (60 percent or greater) cocoa butter content for its natural sweetness. This means you add less sugar, so your candy is smoother and less grainy.

For Cashew Butter Fudge and its variations, and for the Chocolate-Covered Almond Butter Balls, we use fresh *nut butters* readily available from health food stores and natural foods supermarkets.

Have a little extra butter or oil on hand, in addition to amounts specified in ingredient listings, as many recipes require greasing pans or cutting boards.

EQUIPMENT

The primary requirement for successful candy making made easy is a glass *candy thermometer*, available from some kitchenware stores or from candy supply houses (see Source Guide). Calibrated to register higher temperatures than a glass dairy thermometer, these clip onto the side of a pan, keeping the mercury away from the hot pan so you can accurately monitor the candy's temperature, and have a free hand to stir.

The second requirement is a *candy dipping set,* also available from some kitchenware stores or from candy supply houses. The set includes a long, thin-tined fork for dipping and skimming candy along the surface of melted chocolate and a thin wire dipping "spoon" for submerging round candy in the chocolate.

We use a *double boiler* to melt chocolate. If you don't already have one, double boiler inserts that can fit into a 2- or 3-quart saucepan are available as open stock selections in many lines of cookware. In recipes where the mixture is so thick that a wooden spoon might snap, we call for stirring ingredients with a *metal spoon.*

As a *flat surface* for cooling candies, we use cutting boards and cookie or baking sheets. Some recipes specifically call for a baking dish or cake pan, in which the rims or sides are needed to contain the candy as it cools; for those that don't, a marble slab may also be used.

Paper or foil *candy cups* are available from some kitchenware stores or from candy supply houses. Mini–muffin cups may also be used for candy; they can be obtained at most supermarkets.

Also available from some kitchenware stores or from candy supply houses are *lollipop sticks* and *wrapper bags.* Look for the *root beer concentrate* in the spice section of many supermarkets. Order the oil-based *candy flavorings* used in fruit-flavored lollipops from a candy supply house; they may also be stocked by a few kitchenware stores.

TECHNIQUES

Before *melting chocolate,* break it into pieces to prevent the cocoa butter from burning, and to facilitate melting by exposing more of the surface to heat. Bulk chocolate is often scored so that it can easily be separated into 1-ounce squares.

Melt the chocolate in the top of a double boiler over boiling water. This exposes the chocolate to a gentle and indirect heat that prevents it from "blooming"–developing an undesirable film caused by overheating–and for melting half of the chocolate over the heat and stirring in the remainder off the heat, which will approximate the glossiness also achieved by tempering.

For *chocolate dipping,* dip the candy into the melted chocolate and turn it over with the dipping fork or rotate it with the dipping spoon to coat, then drag it across the surface of the chocolate with the fork to skim off the excess. With the fork, transfer gently to a sheet of wax paper (in many recipes, coated lightly with vegetable oil to prevent sticking) and slide the fork out.

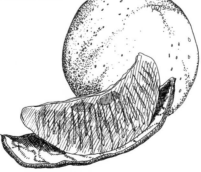

Sally Cohen's Macadamia Brittle

Macadamia nuts are pretty special and pretty indulgent—just what we figured our friend Sally needed a few days before she was to defend her doctoral dissertation. Let this sophisticated adult brittle work its restorative powers on a friend of yours in need. (In Sally's case, it proved to be just what "the doctor" ordered!)

> 1½ cups sugar
> ½ cup light corn syrup
> ¼ cup water
> 1¼ cups roughly chopped macadamia nuts
> 1 teaspoon baking soda

Butter a cookie sheet and set it aside.

Combine the sugar, corn syrup, and water in a large, heavy-bottomed saucepan. Cook over medium-low heat for about 35 minutes, stirring constantly with a metal spoon, until the mixture reaches 280° F. on a candy thermometer.

While stirring, slowly add the nuts, taking care not to let the temperature drop. Quickly add the baking soda, stir twice more, and pour the mixture onto the prepared cookie sheet. Spread it into an even thin layer with a rubber spatula.

Let the brittle cool and harden for 20 minutes, then break it up into chunks.

The Macadamia Brittle will keep for 2 to 3 months in an airtight container.

Yield = 1¼ pounds

Spicy Glazed Pecans

Traditional sugared pecans make a tasty snack, but we think these Spicy Glazed Pecans are better—they're simultaneously sweet, salty, and spicy. They're perfect with an aperitif.

> ½ cup sugar
> ¼ cup (½ stick) unsalted butter
> ⅛ teaspoon cayenne pepper
> 1 tablespoon water
> 1½ cups pecan halves
> 1½ teaspoons salt

Spread a 24 x 12-inch sheet of aluminum foil on a countertop and coat it lightly with vegetable oil.

Combine the sugar, butter, cayenne pepper, and water in a medium saucepan over medium-low heat. When the butter has melted, add the pecans. Continue to cook for about 10 minutes, stirring constantly.

Pour the pecans onto the prepared foil. Quickly spread out and separate the pecans. Sprinkle the salt over and let the pecans cool for 30 minutes.

The Glazed Pecans can be stored in an airtight container for up to 2 weeks.

Yield = 1½ cups

English Walnut Toffee

"To boil sugar is one of the niceties of cooking . . . it requires much experience to tell the exact point at which to arrest the cooking, and on this the success depends," one well-known cook told her readers in 1901. "The professional cook's method of testing it by dipping in the fingers is not practicable for ordinary use . . . but with a thermometer it can easily be determined with perfect exactness and much less trouble."

To serve or package this old-fashioned treat as a gift, break it up into irregular pieces—don't try to cut it into neat little squares. The consistency of toffee is such that it will snap easily, but prove near impossible to cut.

1 cup (2 sticks) unsalted butter
1 cup sugar
2 tablespoons water
1 teaspoon light rum
1 cup walnut pieces
½ cup semisweet chocolate chips
⅓ cup chopped walnuts

Lightly butter a baking sheet and set it aside.

Melt the butter in a medium saucepan over low heat. Stir in the sugar, water, and rum. Once the sugar has dissolved, add the walnut pieces and bring to a boil over medium heat. Continue to boil until the syrup registers 285° F. on a candy thermometer, about 9 minutes.

Pour the toffee onto the prepared baking sheet. With a flat spatula,

✧ ✧ ✧ *For a slight variation on the classic, substitute an equal amount of hazelnut pieces for the walnut pieces in the toffee mixture and of finely chopped hazelnuts for the chopped walnuts scattered on top.* ✧ ✧ ✧

work it into a narrow end of the sheet, squaring off the outer border, until it fills about ⅔ of the sheet. Let the toffee cool for 10 minutes.

Meanwhile, put the chocolate chips into a glass bowl and microwave them for 2 minutes at 50 percent power, then stir until smooth. (If unmelted bits of chocolate remain after a few seconds of stirring, microwave for an additional 30 seconds.)

Spread the melted chocolate evenly over the toffee. Scatter the chopped walnuts on top and put the baking sheet into the refrigerator for 30 minutes.

Lift the toffee off of the sheet with a spatula and break it into pieces.

The toffee will keep for up to 2 weeks in an airtight container.

Yield = About 2 pounds

Greg's Creamy Caramels

This recipe is an adaptation of an old family formula provided by our friend Greg Snider, a mild-mannered bookkeeper who turns into a zealot when he dons his candy-making apron. These old-fashioned sucking caramels provide endless pleasure as long as you don't try to chew them, a sure exercise in futility.

> 1 tablespoon unsalted butter, plus extra for greasing
> 2 cups heavy cream
> 1 cup sugar
> ½ cup light corn syrup
> 2 teaspoons vanilla extract

Thoroughly butter the bottom and sides of an 8 x 8 x 2-inch cake pan, working it carefully into the crevices, and set the pan aside.

Combine the butter with the cream, sugar, and corn syrup in a medium saucepan. Cook over low heat, stirring constantly, until the mixture reaches 250° F. on a candy thermometer; this could take 30 minutes or more.

Remove the pan from the heat and stir in the vanilla. Pour the mixture into the prepared cake pan and let it sit for about 20 minutes, until the caramel is cool enough to handle but still pliable (it will shift when the pan is rocked).

Slide the caramel out onto a cutting board, shaking the pan if needed to dislodge. Push in the sides until you have a block of caramel about 6 inches square. Cut the caramel into 1-inch squares with a sharp knife. Wrap each in a 6-inch square of wax paper and twist up the ends.

The caramels will keep up to 3 months in an airtight container.

Yield = 36 pieces

Caramel Corn with Nuts

One cookbook author, circa 1908, advises us to "choose for this purpose a quality of popcorn which pops light and tender, and select only kernels that are fully open, discarding burned or partially opened kernels. Shake the corn in a coarse sieve to free it from dust and chaff."

While one can generally dispense with the last step these days, her other words of wisdom remain useful—the better the popcorn you start with, the better the caramel corn you end up with. The perfect weekend movie nosh, Caramel Corn with Nuts is also a great last-minute hostess gift.

> 8 cups freshly popped popcorn
> ¾ cup whole almonds
> ¾ cup (1½ sticks) unsalted butter, plus extra for greasing
> ¾ cup dark brown sugar, firmly packed
> ¼ cup light corn syrup

Preheat the oven to 200° F.

Line a large baking sheet with aluminum foil and lightly butter it. Spread the popcorn onto the sheet in a single layer and scatter the almonds on top. Put the pan into the oven to keep warm.

Melt the butter over low heat in a small saucepan, then stir in the sugar and corn syrup. Raise the heat to medium-low and bring to a boil. Continue to boil until the mixture reaches 335° F. on a candy thermometer, about 5 minutes.

Remove the baking sheet from the oven and raise the oven temperature to 275° F.

Drizzle the hot caramel over the popcorn and almonds, tossing to coat. Return the caramel corn to the oven and bake for 15 minutes, tossing every 5 minutes. Remove the baking sheet from the oven and let the caramel corn cool for 10 minutes before breaking it up.

The caramel corn can be stored for about 1 week in an airtight container.

Yield = About 9 cups

Edible Chocolate Greeting Cards

A luscious backdrop for all sorts of messages that linger in memory long after receipt—edible chocolate greeting cards rekindle your sentiment with each scrumptious nibble. While Valentine's Day and birthdays are obvious occasions for this special treatment, don't limit your imagination. A promotion earned or a deadline met, a game won, or a conflict resolved are all deserving events; sometimes a simple, unexpected "thinking of you" can prove to be the sweetest message of all.

> 4 ounces bittersweet or white chocolate, broken up
> 1 small tube white or brown cake decorating gel

Lightly coat the bottom of an 11 x 7-inch baking dish with vegetable oil and set it aside.

Melt half of the chocolate in the top of a double boiler over boiling water. Remove the pan from the heat, add the remaining chocolate, and stir until melted. Remove the top of the double boiler from the bottom and continue to stir for at least 10 minutes more, until the chocolate thickens and cools to room temperature.

Pour the chocolate into the prepared baking dish and spread it evenly with a rubber spatula. Let sit for 10 minutes. Cut the chocolate in half crosswise with a sharp knife. For fluted borders, first run a pizza cutting wheel around the entire outer border of the chocolate, then cut in half. Transfer the dish to the refrigerator and chill for about 30 minutes, until the chocolate has hardened.

Remove the baking dish from the refrigerator. Holding both Chocolate Cards intact, turn the dish upside down and gently dislodge onto a counter.

Decorate and inscribe your message on each card with the cake decorating gel (use white gel on a bittersweet Chocolate Card, and brown gel on a white Chocolate Card). Refrigerate the cards for an additional 10 minutes after decorating.

Yield = Two 5½ x 7-inch Chocolate Greeting Cards

◇ ◇ ◇ **For variety, substitute almond butter or peanut butter (the fresh variety found in a health food store, not the supermarket stuff) for cashew butter. Stir in ⅓ cup chopped cashews, almonds, or peanuts with the vanilla and nut butter for a little crunch.** ◇ ◇ ◇

Cashew Butter Fudge

Cashew butter, available at most health food stores, lends this fudge a rich, nutty flavor that we find a refreshing alternative to maple or vanilla. For a smooth, creamy texture, free of the graininess that can mar an otherwise great fudge, don't skimp on the final stirring.

> 2 cups sugar
> ⅓ cup heavy cream
> ½ cup milk
> ⅛ teaspoon coarse kosher salt
> 1 teaspoon vanilla extract
> 1 cup cashew butter, at room temperature

Butter an 8 x 8 x 2-inch baking dish or cake pan, working it into all the crevices.

Combine the sugar, cream, milk, and salt in a medium saucepan. Cook over medium heat, stirring constantly until the sugar dissolves. Once the mixture begins to bubble, stir frequently until it reaches 235° F. on a candy thermometer, about 15 minutes.

Remove the pan from the heat. Stir in the vanilla and cashew butter; continue stirring for about 5 minutes, until the cashew butter has been completely absorbed, and the fudge is smooth, free of lumps, and very thick.

Transfer the candy into the prepared pan, spreading it evenly with a rubber spatula. Set the dish aside for about 1 hour for the fudge to cool and harden. Cut it into 1-inch squares.

Store the fudge in an airtight container that has been lined with wax paper. It has a shelf life of 1 month, or can be stored for up to 2 months in the refrigerator.

Yield = 64 pieces

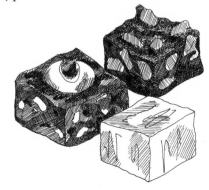

Root Beer Lollipops

These are traditional hard "suckers." In this recipe, the sugar mixture is heated too high to go into plastic molds; use metal molds (see Source Guide) or shape with cookie cutters or into free-form circles on an acrylic cutting board.

> 2 tablespoons plus 2 teaspoons light corn syrup
> ⅓ cup water
> ½ cup sugar
> 1 teaspoon root beer concentrate

Grease 8 metal lollipop molds or an acrylic cutting board well with vegetable oil and set aside.

Combine the corn syrup, water, and sugar in a small saucepan over medium-low heat, stirring just until the sugar dissolves. Once the mixture comes to a boil, reduce the heat to low and continue to cook until it reaches 300° F. on a candy thermometer. (It will take about 15 minutes total.) If crystals begin to form around the edge of the pan, carefully brush them back with a moistened pastry brush. Remove the pan from the heat and quickly stir in the root beer concentrate.

Fill each prepared lollipop mold with about 1 tablespoonful of the mixture, according to the size of the molds, or set cookie cutters onto the prepared cutting board and spoon about 1 tablespoonful into each. For each 3-inch free-form circular lollipop, spoon 2 tablespoonfuls directly onto the prepared cutting board.

Insert a stick into each lollipop, pushing it about ¼ inch into the syrup and smoothing over the stick so that it will be secure when hardened.

Set the lollipops aside for 20 to 25 minutes, until hardened. Remove from the molds or cookie cutters. Wrap each in a lollipop bag and store them in an airtight container, where they should keep for up to 6 months.

Yield = 4–8 lollipops

◇ ◇ ◇ **B**esides root beer, you can make lollipops in a variety of fruit flavors using oil-based candy flavorings (see Source Guide). Substitute ½ teaspoon of candy flavoring for the teaspoon of root beer concentrate. To color, add 2 drops of food coloring with the candy flavoring (red coloring for cherry lollipops, green for peppermint lollipops, etc.). ◇ ◇ ◇

Edible Chocolate Gift Box

Presenting Home Made *candy in a Chocolate Gift Box will fulfill any chocoholic's wildest fantasy. This labor of love takes a little patience, but produces an offering that is truly good to the last bite!*

Although we call for the standard square gift box you probably have around the house, plastic box molds in a variety of shapes are available as well from candy supply houses and some kitchenware stores (see Source Guide); if using molds, dispense with the aluminum foil lining.

- 8 ounces bittersweet, semisweet, milk, or white chocolate, broken up
- A cardboard box, approximately 6 inches square and 2 inches deep, with shallow cover

Line the inside of the box and the cover with sheets of aluminum foil, smoothing out any wrinkles in the foil, and set them near the stove.

In the top of a double boiler over boiling water, melt half of the chocolate. Remove the pan from the heat, add the remaining chocolate, and stir until melted. Remove the top of the double boiler from the bottom and continue to stir for at least 10 minutes more, until the chocolate thickens and cools to room temperature.

Pour about ⅔ of the chocolate into the box. Rotate the box to evenly coat the bottom and up the sides to the rim, smoothing the chocolate with a rubber spatula. Coat the inside of the lid in the same way with the remaining chocolate.

Transfer the box and lid to the refrigerator and chill for about 30 minutes, until the chocolate has hardened. To unmold, place a plate on top of each and invert. Remove the cardboard frame and peel off the aluminum foil.

Yield = One 6 x 6 x 2-inch Chocolate Box with Cover

Dark & White Chocolate Lollipops

These marbleized chocolate lollipops, which make a striking accent in a gift basket, can literally be made in minutes. Plastic lollipop molds are available in many kitchenware stores in a variety of shapes—from roses to hearts emblazoned with Valentine's Day messages—as are lollipop sticks and wrapper bags.

- 4 ounces bittersweet chocolate, broken up
- 4 ounces white chocolate, broken up

Put the chocolates into separate 1-cup glass measuring cups. Melt the chocolate in a microwave oven for about 5 minutes at 50 percent power. Remove the measuring cups from the microwave and stir the chocolate a bit until completely melted and smooth.

Fill one side of each mold with bittersweet chocolate and the opposite side with white chocolate. Swirl together with a toothpick to create a marbleized effect. Take care to swirl the chocolate all the way into the mold and not just on the surface, so that both sides of the lollipop will be marbleized.

Insert a lollipop stick into each mold, pushing it about ¼ inch into the chocolate and smoothing chocolate over the stick so that it will be secure when hardened.

Refrigerate the lollipops for about 30 minutes, until hardened, and pop out of the molds. Wrap each in a lollipop bag.

Store the Chocolate Lollipops in an airtight container in the refrigerator for up to 3 months.

Yield = 4 lollipops

White Chocolate Cookie Bark

This cookies-and-cream concoction is intended to please the younger members of your household, but try to go easy on adults who get caught with a hand on the cookie bar.

> 8 ounces white chocolate, broken up
> 5 cream-filled chocolate sandwich cookies, broken into 4 pieces each

Line a baking sheet with wax paper and set it aside.

Melt half of the chocolate in the top of a double boiler over boiling water, stirring occasionally. Remove the pan from the heat. Add the rest of the chocolate and stir until melted. Remove the top part of the double boiler from the bottom and stir in the cookies.

Turn the mixture onto the wax paper and with a rubber spatula spread it into a thin, even layer about ¼-inch thick. Cool for about 10 minutes to room temperature. Place the sheet in the refrigerator for about 1 hour, until the bark is hard. Break it into chunks.

Store the bark in an airtight container in the refrigerator; it will keep for 2 to 3 weeks.

Yield = About 10 ounces

Chocolate-Covered Almond Butter Balls

One turn-of-the-century home economist, with an eye on augmenting the household budget, counsels: "There is a good market in all parts of the country for first class homemade candies. Even in cities where the large confectioners' shops seem capable of supplying every demand, good homemade candies are given preference at the highest prices; while in small towns and rural districts, where cheap candies are the rule, the homemade article, if of good quality, will always find a ready sale."

> ½ cup (1 stick) unsalted butter, at room temperature
> 1 cup almond butter
> 1½ cups confectioners' sugar
> 1 teaspoon vanilla extract
> 8 ounces bittersweet chocolate, broken up

Thoroughly combine the butter, almond butter, sugar, and

Edible Chocolate Centerpiece or Individual Serving Cups

Dessert is that much more of a treat when it's served in a luscious, edible chocolate receptacle. This recipe yields 6 individual chocolate serving baskets or a dramatic Chocolate Centerpiece. Fill the cups with ice cream, raspberries, or mousse, or with a few Chocolate-Covered Almond Butter Balls or Chocolate-Covered Sour Cherry Chews for a souvenir of the occasion. Heap a medley of fresh fruit or a selection of Home Made candies into the centerpiece.

> 12 ounces semisweet chocolate, broken up

Lay a sheet of wax paper on a countertop near the stove and coat it lightly with vegetable oil. Inflate a balloon to about a 7-inch diameter for a Centerpiece, or six balloons to a 3½-inch diameter for Serving Cups.

Melt half of the chocolate in the top of a double boiler over boiling water, stirring constantly. Remove the pan from the heat. Add the remaining chocolate and stir until melted.

Remove the top of the double boiler from the bottom. Dip the balloon(s) into the chocolate and swirl. Spread chocolate up onto the balloon(s) with a rubber spatula, smoothing evenly to coat the bottom ⅓ to ½ of the balloon(s).

Set the coated balloon(s) onto the prepared wax paper for 15 to 20 minutes, until the chocolate has cooled and hardened sufficiently so that the bottom of the balloon(s), when lifted, separates easily from the wax paper. Refrigerate for 30 minutes. If making serving cups, it may prove easier to transfer the balloons to the refrigerator if the sheet of wax paper is placed atop a baking sheet.

Deflate the balloon(s) by poking with a sharp knife and peeling it away, leaving the free-standing Chocolate Centerpiece or Serving Cups.

Yield = 1 Chocolate Centerpiece or 6 Individual Serving Cups

vanilla in a bowl with a wooden spoon until the mixture is as thick and smooth as cookie dough.

Roll the dough by the tablespoonful into balls and place on a baking sheet. Refrigerate for 15 minutes to harden.

Melt the chocolate in the top of a double boiler over boiling water, stirring occasionally.

Line another baking sheet with wax paper and place it next to the stove. Place an almond butter ball into the melted chocolate and rotate with a candy dipping spoon until completely coated, then drag it across the surface with a dipping fork to skim off excess chocolate. Transfer the ball to the wax paper and slide out the fork. Repeat until all balls have been coated. Transfer the sheet to the refrigerator and chill for 30 minutes.

The Chocolate-Covered Almond Balls should be stored in an airtight container in the refrigerator, where they will keep for about 1 month.

Yield = 30–32 pieces

Chocolate-Covered Candied Citrus Peel

If you have the willpower to save some of these heavenly chocolates for a purpose other than immediate gratification, they make wonderful cake decorations. Arrange on a cake with a dark chocolate frosting in a black-on-black pattern, mound atop a mocha-frosted cake, or use to provide a visual accent to an orange or lemon cheesecake.

We also like to scatter a few over citrus sorbets, or, for an extremely rich and intense dessert, over Home Made *Ann's White Chocolate Ice Cream (page 100).*

> 2 large navel oranges
> 1 large lemon
> 4½ cups water
> ½ teaspoon salt
> 1 cup plus 2 tablespoons sugar
> ¼ cup light corn syrup
> 6 ounces bittersweet chocolate, broken up

Peel the oranges and the lemon with a vegetable peeler and cut the peels into thin strips 1 inch long.

Combine the orange and lemon peel, 4 cups of water, and the salt in a medium saucepan. Cook for about 20 minutes over low heat, uncovered, until the peels are fork-tender.

Drain the peels in a colander and quarter each lengthwise into 1 x ¼-inch strips.

Rinse and dry the saucepan. Combine the sugar, corn syrup, and remaining water in it and bring to a boil over medium heat, stirring until the sugar dissolves. Stir in the peel and bring back to a boil. Reduce the heat to low. Simmer, uncovered, for 45 minutes. Remove the peel with a slotted spoon and drain it on paper toweling.

Melt the chocolate in the top of a double boiler over boiling water, stirring occasionally.

Line a baking sheet or cookie sheet with wax paper and place it next to the stove. Drop a peel into the melted chocolate, and, with a candy dipping fork, turn the peel until it is completely coated, then drag it across the surface to skim off excess chocolate. Transfer the peel to the wax paper and slide the fork from under it. Repeat until all peels have been coated. Transfer the sheet to the refrigerator and chill for 30 minutes.

The Chocolate-Covered Citrus Peels should be stored in an airtight container in the refrigerator, where they will keep for up to 3 months.

Yield = About 7 dozen pieces

Chocolate-Covered Sour Cherry Chews

These little candies make a nice gift in tandem with the milk-chocolate cashew clusters. If you don't have any Dried Sour Cherries on hand, substitute seedless raisins, dried cranberries, or chopped dried apricots.

> 4 ounces semisweet chocolate, broken up
> 7 teaspoons light corn syrup
> 2 teaspoons water
> ¾ cup *Home Made* Dried Sour Cherries (page 194)

Line a cookie sheet with wax paper, coat it lightly with vegetable oil, and set aside.

Combine half of the chocolate with all the corn syrup in the top

Chocolate Dipping

Chocolate Dipping is an easy way to add an elegant finishing touch to fresh or dried fruit, or, for that matter, to pretzels, whole coffee beans, or anything else that strikes your fancy. We prefer the assertive flavor of bittersweet chocolate, but semisweet, milk, or white chocolate can also be used.

Serve a mixture of these tasty morsels after dinner—perhaps, for variety, dipped in different chocolates—with a selection of Home Made liqueurs (pages 67–72).

> 8 ounces chocolate, broken up
> 2 tablespoons water and one of the following:
> 2 large navel oranges, peeled, pith removed, and sectioned
> 3 tangerines, peeled, pith removed, and sectioned
> 12–14 large strawberries, stems intact
> 6–8 hard, twisted cocktail pretzels
> ¼ pound whole French Roast coffee beans
> 2 bananas, peeled and thinly sliced crosswise
> ¼ pound seedless green grapes
> 6–8 large dried apricots

Line a baking sheet with wax paper and lightly grease the wax paper with vegetable oil. Set the sheet near the stove.

Combine half the chocolate with the water in the top of a double boiler. Heat over boiling water to melt the chocolate.

Remove the top of the double boiler from the heat. Add the remaining chocolate and stir until it is melted and smooth.

Dip each ingredient in the chocolate and transfer to the prepared sheet of wax paper. Most can be dipped easily with a chocolate dipping fork; for the grapes, dip each on a toothpick in order to coat without losing the grape in the chocolate pot, and dip the strawberries by hand, holding each by the stem. If you want an excuse to lick a little of the chocolate in the process, dip with your fingers as soon as the chocolate is cool enough.

Coat the grapes, coffee beans, and pretzels completely with chocolate. For visual effect, leave a little of the surface of the citrus, berries, bananas, or apricots uncoated.

Transfer the sheet to the refrigerator and chill for 30 minutes. Serve the dipped morsels at room temperature within 24 hours.

of a double boiler. Heat over boiling water, stirring occasionally, until the chocolate has melted.

Remove the pan from the heat. Add the remaining chocolate and the water, stirring constantly until the chocolate has melted. Stir in the cherries.

Drop the mixture by teaspoonfuls onto the wax paper. Put the baking sheet into the refrigerator for 1½ hours.

Store the clusters in an airtight container in the refrigerator for up to 3 months.

Yield = 18 pieces

Milk Chocolate Cashew Clusters

If you think these clusters taste a little like "turtles," you're right. In this version, we dispense with the caramel layer of the original, but add corn syrup to the chocolate to lend a similar texture.

3½ ounces milk chocolate, broken up
2 tablespoons light corn syrup
½ tablespoon water
1 cup whole salted cashews

Line a baking sheet with wax paper. Coat it lightly with vegetable oil and set it aside.

Combine the chocolate, corn syrup, and water in the top of a double boiler and heat over boiling water, stirring occasionally, until the chocolate has melted. Add the cashews and stir to mix.

Drop the mixture by teaspoonfuls onto the wax paper. Transfer the baking sheet to the refrigerator and chill for at least 45 minutes, until the chocolate coating on the nuts hardens.

Store the clusters in an airtight container in the refrigerator, where they will keep for up to 3 months.

Yield = 24 pieces

CHAPTER 7

Bread

Nothing in the whole range of domestic life more affects the health and happiness of the family than the quality of its daily bread. With good bread, the plainest meal is a feast in itself; without it, the most elaborately prepared and elegantly served menu is unsatisfactory," according to the author of one old cookbook we found. (And you know it's an *old* cookbook when scraps of newspaper tucked inside include a letter to the editor from a veteran recalling how he rallied to President Lincoln's call to arms.)

Another Victorian author advises, "There are many recipes for making good bread. Skeptics say it can't be made by rule. They are mistaken. It can. They put their material together any way it happens, have as good 'luck' as most of their neighbors and are content. The baking they lay upon the shoulders of the great god of chance. The deficiencies of the complacent cook, cheap flour and lazy housekeepers are at the bottom of more accidents in the bread . . . than in anything else."

Cheap flour and lazy housekeepers are seldom uppermost concerns for cooks today, and the complacent among us can all too easily find an adequate substitute for home-baked bread at a good bakery. There are, however, any number of otherwise accomplished and confident cooks who stop dead in their tracks at the prospect of bread making.

They needn't, nor must they depend upon the fickle shoulders of chance. Bread *can* be made by rule, and *Home Made* rules are easy and virtually foolproof. No one should be denied the visceral pleasure that comes from bread baking, nor the wonderful aromas that waft through the house, nor that first delicious bite of a warm slice of freshly made bread.

❈ ❈ ❈

The Basics

Yeast is the heart and soul of most *Home Made* breads, and "proofing" the yeast—sprinkling it over a water-and-sugar mixture and setting it aside for a few minutes until it bubbles—is an initial step in the recipes.

We call for quick-rise yeast, which considerably reduces the time needed for each rise of the bread. Lukewarm tap water that registers 110 to 115° F. on an instant-read thermometer provides just the right environment for quick-rise yeast to do its thing; hotter water can inhibit the action of the yeast, and colder water slows it down. Likewise, liquids that are cooked before being combined with the yeast must first be allowed to cool to 110 to 115° F.

Since even the most devoted bread bakers these days seldom have the time or energy for laborious mixing and kneading, the food processor does the work in most *Home Made* bread recipes. Besides, we've found that modern technology tends to transport bread making from the realm of mystery to that of precision and order, making it a lot easier to master without a mentor.

Essentially, food-processor bread making involves putting the dry ingredients into the bowl of the food processor and mixing briefly, then adding the proofed yeast (take care to scrape the proofing bowl thoroughly). A liquid is then drizzled through the feed tube while the machine is running, producing in a minute or less a ball of dough that requires at most a few seconds of additional kneading by hand.

Since the recipes for Old-Fashioned Raisin Pumpernickel and Multigrain Bread produce dough too thick for many food processors, they are prepared in a stationary electric mixer (which also does the lion's share of the work).

Here, the ingredients are added in reverse order: Most of the liquids go in first, then bread flour is added in increments until the dough reaches the desired consistency. Use the mixer's paddle attachment for the initial steps; attach the bread hook only after the first addition of flour has been mixed.

Once a dough ball has formed, set it aside in a warm, draft-free spot to double its size, then punch it down to release the air. The Old-Fashioned Raisin Pumpernickel and Multigrain Bread require a shorter, second rise at this time.

Converting Food Processor Recipes for Stationary Electric Mixers

Most of our yeast bread recipes use a food processor for two reasons: First, few sane people would choose to knead bread dough by hand when an appliance can do the work, and second, more people own food processors than stationary electric mixers with bread hooks.

Legions of bread bakers are devoted to both of these appliances. We were given our first food processor years ago as a Christmas gift by a friend who swore she used it to make the best breads possible, and received a stationary electric mixer on another Christmas from yet another friend who claimed that mixer breads were far superior to food-processor breads. We like them made both ways and intend to stay out of this particular line of fire.

Converting our recipes from the food processor to the stationary electric mixer is fairly easy. With the food processor, you start with the dry ingredients and add liquids until the dough forms a ball. When using the mixer, you start with the liquid ingredients and add flour until the dough reaches the desired consistency.

To prepare a food processor recipe in a stationary electric mixer, follow the recipe up to where dry ingredients are put into the food processor. Instead, put all of the liquid ingredients except the proofed yeast or those ingredients used to paint loaves into the bowl of the mixer. Add all of the dry ingredients but 1¼ cups of the bread flour (or 1¼ cups of the all-purpose flour in the Soft Pretzel recipe). Add the yeast, then affix the paddle attachment.

Turn to the recipe for Old-Fashioned Raisin Pumpernickel (page 162) and proceed with the stationary electric mixer steps that follow the first addition of flours through the last 10 minutes of mixing. Return to the original recipe for preparing the bowl for the first rise.

You're now ready to form the dough—into rectangles that will be put into loaf pans, ovals that will go on baking or cookie sheets, or into Soft Pretzels or Egg Bagels. The dough then goes back to the warm, draft-free spot for a final rise before baking (or boiling and baking, in the case of the bagels).

Chocolate Sour Cherry Bread and Maple Pecan Date Bread are quick breads that use baking soda and baking powder as leavening instead of yeast, and require no rise. These recipes take less than an hour from start to finish, as do those for Rye Parmesan Popovers and Gingerbread, a cake in bread clothing.

We also include directions for making a drier version of Gingerbread, fashioned into cookies or an edible serving bowl, and for Saltbread Dough, an inedible substance to craft into Christmas tree ornaments or into a breadbasket.

Ingredients

Most of the ingredients required for baking breads will be on hand in your pantry. Be sure to have *bread flour*, which has a higher gluten content than all-purpose flour (lending greater elasticity to the dough), and *quick-rise yeast*.

Several breads call for eggs; we recommend *Nest Eggs*® brand eggs (see Source Guide listing for chapter 4) or another brand of eggs from "uncaged" hens fed a drug-free diet.

Have a little extra butter or oil on hand, in addition to amounts specified in ingredient listings, as many recipes require greasing pans or cutting boards.

Equipment

An *instant-read thermometer* is crucial to determine the precise temperature of the proofing liquid for quick-rise yeast.

The workhorse of *Home Made* breads is the *food processor*, which does the mixing and kneading for you. A few recipes are written for a *stationary electric mixer*, and we provide directions for converting food processor recipes for the mixer.

It's best to put the dough in a *ceramic bowl* to rise. It is less susceptible to the chilling effects of drafts than metal or glass, which could slow down the rise. Plastic can become scratched, causing the dough to stick to the scratches.

In many cases, the *work surface* on which you shape and form dough can be a countertop. We call for acrylic cutting boards when the surface needs to be oiled, and for wood cutting boards in recipes where it's easier to work with a very sticky dough on a porous surface that will absorb a uniform coating of flour.

If you like very crusty bread, you may want to use a *baking stone*. We especially like to use one under pizza dough. The stone, which is preheated in the oven, becomes hotter than pans, creating the extra crustiness.

For authentic Classic French Bread, a *French bread pan* with double wells ensures the right shape and crustiness of 2 loaves.

TECHNIQUES

To *proof yeast*, mix lukewarm water (110 to 115° F. on an instant-read thermometer) with sugar. Sprinkle the yeast on top and set aside for 5 to 6 minutes, until the mixture is bubbly.

Most *Home Made* breads are *kneaded* in a food processor or a stationary electric mixer, but some require manual kneading. To knead by hand, put the dough on a work surface. Pat it down a bit, then draw the dough furthest away from you up toward the center with floured fingertips; press down firmly and push the dough away with the heel of your hand.

To *rise*, cover the dough with a damp or dry towel, as specified in the recipe, and set aside in a warm (75–85° F.), draft-free spot, until it has about doubled in size and no longer springs back to the touch.

"Yeast is a minute plant, and like other plants must have the right conditions of heat, moisture, and nourishment in order to live or to flourish," a late nineteenth-century cook advises. "It will be killed if scalded, or if frozen, as any other plant would be; therefore, as we depend upon the growth of this little plant for raising our bread, we must give its requirements as much care as we do our geraniums or our roses."

Amongst all but the most diehard bread bakers, fear of yeast is an insecurity far more widespread than fear of heights or fear of flying. We admit to a few jitters ourselves when we first dove into this chapter, only to emerge triumphant, with grins as wide as kids who just made the family breakfast.

Follow these recipes closely, but with confidence: We've tried to write them to be simple and mistake-proof. For starters, we add sugar to the water the yeast is proofed in. Yeast loves sugar and reacts to its presence almost without fail. Proof the yeast in lukewarm water (lest the yeast be "scalded or frozen"); for quick-rise yeast, 110–115° F. is a foolproof range.

Home Made yeast breads rise at least twice. The first rise usually takes between 1¼ and 1½ hours. The second rise, which usually takes place after the dough has been shaped, usually takes from 45 to 60 minutes. The Old-Fashioned Raisin Pumpernickel and the Multigrain Bread rise a third time, for about 30 to 40 minutes.

Set the dough aside in a warm (ideally 75–85° F.), draft-free spot to rise. In addition to sugar, yeast loves humidity; the higher the humidity, the more active the yeast. We tested these recipes during the summer and found an enclosed, non-air-conditioned back porch to be a perfect environment. Other ideal spots include the top of a running clothes dryer, the top of a refrigerator, or the top of an older gas range with a perpetual burner pilot light.

If you have a gas oven, you can reduce the rising time by about 25 percent (facilitated by heat generated by the oven's pilot light) by putting the dough on the middle rack with the oven door closed.

We've also discovered a quick trick for cutting the rising time by a third to a half in an electric oven. Fill a 9 x 12-inch cake pan halfway with very hot tap water and set it on the bottom-most rack. Put the dough directly above it on the middle rack. Close the oven and turn it on to 400° F. for exactly 1 minute. Turn the oven off and leave the dough inside until it rises.

Stovetop and oven-rising techniques are best used with the first rise, since recipes often call for preheating the oven during subsequent rises. When setting the dough into a gas or electric oven to rise, always cover it with a dry towel, even if

Semolina Challah

We've varied the standard formula for this gorgeous braided egg bread by adding semolina, a grain most commonly used in pasta and couscous.

> ¼ cup lukewarm water (110–115° F.)
> ½ tablespoon sugar
> ¼ ounce (1 packet) quick-rise yeast
> 2 cups bread flour
> 1 cup plus 2 teaspoons semolina
> ½ teaspoon salt
> 2 tablespoons vegetable oil
> 2 large eggs
> 3 to 3½ tablespoons cold water
> 1 large egg yolk
> 1 tablespoon sesame seeds

Combine the lukewarm water and the sugar in a small bowl. Sprinkle the yeast on top and set aside for 5 to 6 minutes to proof, until bubbly.

Put the flour, 1 cup of the semolina, and the salt into the bowl of a food processor and process for 1 minute. Scrape in all of the yeast mixture, add the vegetable oil and the whole eggs. Turn the machine on and process for 1 minute. While the machine is still running, add 1 to 1½ tablespoons of the cold water through the feed tube, until the dough forms a ball. Continue to process for 2 more minutes, then turn off the machine and let the dough sit for another 2 minutes.

Lightly grease a ceramic bowl with vegetable oil. Transfer the dough to the bowl and roll it around to coat with oil. Cover the bowl with a damp towel and put it in a warm, draft-free spot for 1¼ to 1½ hours, until the dough has doubled in size and does not spring back when pressed with a finger. Punch the dough down and fold the edges toward the center.

Re-cover with the damp towel and return the bowl to the draft-free spot for 45 minutes to let the dough rise a second time. Punch the dough down again, fold it over, and press down.

Remove the dough to a work surface, form it into a 15 x 9-inch rectangle, and cut it lengthwise into 3 strips. Roll each strip into an evenly shaped 15-inch rope about 1 inch thick.

Lightly grease a cookie sheet with vegetable oil and dust with the 2 teaspoons of semolina.

Place the dough strips on the cookie sheet about ½ inch apart. Crimp the ropes together at one end, braid them together, and crimp at the other end.

Cover the cookie sheet with a dry towel and place it in the draft-free spot for 45 minutes to rise for a third time.

After about 30 minutes, preheat the oven to 350° F.

Mix the egg yolk and the remaining 2 tablespoons cold water in a small bowl and paint the bread. Sprinkle with the sesame seeds.

Bake for 30 to 35 minutes, until the bread is golden brown and sounds hollow when tapped. Transfer the bread to a wire rack to cool.

The Semolina Challah has a shelf life of 3 to 5 days; wrap the bread loosely in aluminum foil to store.

Yield = One 15-inch loaf

the original recipe calls for a damp towel.

The fastest technique for the first rise involves a microwave oven (subsequent rises are usually after the dough has been transferred to metal loaf pans, baking sheets, or cookie sheets, which cannot be put into a microwave).

After the dough has been processed, remove it from the food processor, knead 2 or 3 times, form it into a large doughnut and refit it around the center of the food processor bowl. Cover with a dry towel. Fill a 1-cup glass measuring cup with water and set it into a back corner of the microwave with the covered food processor bowl in front.

Set a 500-watt microwave oven at 90 percent power, a 600-watt oven at 70 percent power, or a 700-watt oven at 60 percent power. Turn the microwave on for 3 minutes, leave it off for 3 minutes without opening the door, turn it on for 3 minutes more, and leave it off undisturbed for an additional 6 minutes.

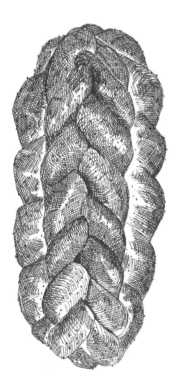

◇ ◇ ◇ *Variation*: For Cinnamon Raisin Swirl—a perfect breakfast bread—cut the dough in half after the first rise and shape each half into an 8-inch square. Mix ½ cup sugar and 2 tablespoons ground cinnamon in a small bowl and cover each piece of dough with half of the mixture. Scatter ½ cup raisins over each. Roll each square of dough up like a jelly roll, place in the prepared loaf pans, and proceed as with the original recipe. ◇ ◇ ◇

◇ ◇ ◇ *F*or Hot Cross Buns to grace your Easter brunch spread, follow the directions for preparing Cinnamon Raisin Swirl up to forming the dough into two 8-inch squares. Melt ½ cup (1 stick) unsalted butter. When it has cooled to room temperature, brush over the dough. Cover each square with the sugar-and-cinnamon mixture, ½ cup raisins, and 3 tablespoons chopped candied citron. Roll the squares up and slice each roll into 8 circles.

Grease the bottom and sides of a large baking sheet with vegetable oil. Put the circles onto the baking sheet, cover with the damp towel, and place it in the draft-free spot to rise again.

After about 30 minutes, preheat the oven to 375° F.

Mix 1 large egg white with 1 tablespoon cold water and brush the mixture over the dough. Bake for 12 to 15 minutes, until the buns are golden brown. Transfer the baking sheet to a

Country White Bread

"It is not pleasant to think or write about, but upon thousands of tables in otherwise comfortable homes good bread is an unknown phenomenon," one observer noted in 1891. *"There are homes in which the bakery sponges {are served}, which are flavorless and 'dry as a chip' when a day old."*

Country White Bread is good, old-fashioned, and hearty; it bears little resemblance to the spongy derivative that has given white bread in particular a bad name.

    1 cup milk
    2 tablespoons unsalted butter
    ½ cup cold water
    ¼ cup lukewarm water (110–115° F.)
    2 tablespoons plus ½ teaspoon sugar
    ¼ ounce (1 packet) quick-rise yeast
    4½ cups bread flour
    2 teaspoons salt

Scald the milk in a small saucepan over medium heat, just until bubbles begin to form around the edge of the pan. Remove from the heat, add the butter, and allow it to melt. Add the cold water and set the pan aside until the contents have cooled to lukewarm (110–115° F.), about 5 minutes.

Meanwhile, combine the lukewarm water and ½ teaspoon of the sugar in a small bowl. Sprinkle the yeast on top. Let the mixture proof for 5 to 6 minutes, until bubbly.

Put the flour, salt, and the remaining sugar into a food processor and process for 30 seconds. Add the yeast, taking care to scrape the proofing bowl well. Turn the machine on and slowly add the cooled milk through the feed tube until a ball forms, about 1 minute. Discard any remaining milk and continue to process for 2 minutes more.

Transfer the dough to a work surface and knead 2 or 3 times, until the dough is elastic and glossy.

Grease a large ceramic bowl with vegetable oil. Put the dough into the bowl and rotate to coat it with the oil. Cover the bowl loosely with a damp towel and set it aside in a warm, draft-free spot for 1¼ to 1½ hours, until the dough has doubled in size and does not spring back to the touch.

Punch the dough with your fist and fold the outer edges of the dough toward the center.

Lightly grease two 8-inch loaf pans.

Transfer the dough to a work surface. Flatten the dough and shape it into an 8-inch square. Cut the square in half. Place each rectangle into a loaf pan and pat it so that the dough touches the sides of the pan. Return the loaf pans to the draft-free spot, cover with the damp towel, and allow them to sit for 45 to 60 minutes, until the dough has again doubled in size.

After about 30 minutes, preheat the oven to 425° F.

Bake the loaves for 15 minutes, turn the oven down to 375° F., and bake for about 20 minutes longer, until the bread is brown on top and sounds hollow when tapped. Remove the loaves from the pans and set them on a wire rack to cool.

The Country White Bread has a shelf life of 3 to 5 days; wrap the bread loosely in aluminum foil to store.

Yield = Two 8-inch loaves

wire rack and let the buns cool for 15 to 20 minutes.

Meanwhile, stir ¾ cup confectioners' sugar with 1 teaspoon light corn syrup and 1½ tablespoons milk until thick. Spoon or pour onto each bun in the shape of a cross.

Serve warm or room temperature. The Hot Cross Buns have a shelf life of 3 to 5 days.

Yield = 16 buns ◇ ◇ ◇

Harry's Long-Awaited Corn Rye

Twenty-odd years ago, Barry's brother Harry left New York for California. Ever since, he's been pining for a hearty peasant corn rye, the kind sold in every neighborhood Jewish bakery in the Big Apple. For most of that time, Barry's been promising to come up with a recipe that approximates the bread of their childhood memories. He finally made good.

> 1 cup boiling water
> 1 cup plus 2 tablespoons finely ground yellow cornmeal
> ⅓ cup lukewarm water (110–115° F.)
> 2½ tablespoons sugar
> ¼ ounce (1 packet) quick-rise yeast
> 1¼ cups rye flour
> 4 to 4¼ cups bread flour
> 1½ teaspoons salt
> 6 tablespoons vegetable oil, plus extra for greasing
> 1 tablespoon cider vinegar
> 1⅛ cups plus 2 tablespoons cold water
> 1 large egg white

Combine the boiling water and 1 cup of the cornmeal in a medium bowl, stir, and set aside.

In a small bowl, combine the lukewarm water and the sugar. Sprinkle the yeast on top and let the mixture proof for 5 to 6 minutes, until bubbly.

In a food processor, process the rye flour, 4 cups of the bread flour, and the salt for 1 minute. Add the soaked cornmeal and the yeast, scraping the proofing bowl thoroughly. Process for 30 seconds, then add 4 tablespoons of the vegetable oil and the vinegar through the feed tube. Begin to drizzle in the cold water. Add up to 1⅛ cups to form a ball, which should take about 1 minute. Continue to process for 2 minutes more.

Remove the dough from the food processor. If the dough sticks to your fingers, sprinkle the remaining ¼ cup bread flour onto the work surface before working the dough. Knead the dough for 1 to 2 minutes, until glossy and elastic.

Grease a ceramic bowl lightly with vegetable oil. Put the dough into the bowl and rotate it to coat with oil. Cover the bowl with a damp towel and place it in a warm, draft-free spot for 1¼ to 1½ hours, until the ball has doubled in size and the dough no longer springs back to the touch.

Release the air inside the dough by punching it with your fist and fold the edges of the dough toward the center. Transfer the dough to a work surface. Cut it in half and form each half into an oval about 9 inches long and 4 inches across at the widest point.

Lightly grease a baking sheet with vegetable oil and dust with the remaining 2 tablespoons cornmeal. Put the dough onto the baking sheet and rub each oval with a tablespoon of vegetable oil. Re-cover with the damp towel and put the baking sheet in the draft-free spot for 45 to 60 minutes, until the dough has again doubled in size.

After about 30 minutes, preheat the oven to 375° F.

Mix the egg white and 2 tablespoons of the cold water and brush over the loaves. With a very sharp knife, make 3 diagonal slashes across the top of each loaf. Bake for 35 to 40 minutes, until the bread has browned and sounds hollow when tapped. Transfer the bread to a wire rack to cool.

The Corn Rye has a shelf life of 3 to 5 days; to store, wrap the loaf loosely in aluminum foil.

Yield = Two 9-inch loaves

Classic French Bread

One bite of this bread conjures up turn-of-the-century Parisians toting their beloved baguettes in the shadow of the newly erected Eiffel Tower; listen closely and you can almost hear faint strains of the Marseillaise *in the background. For a modern twist on the classic, we add just a bit of whole wheat flour.*

A French bread pan produces the perfect shape and degree of crustiness, but a cookie sheet, greased with a little vegetable oil and dusted with cornmeal, makes a close approximation.

> ¼ cup lukewarm water (110–115° F.)
> 1 teaspoon sugar
> ¼ ounce (1 packet) quick-rise yeast
> 2½ cups bread flour
> ⅓ cup whole wheat flour
> 1 teaspoon salt
> 1 cup less 1 tablespoon room-temperature water
> ¼ teaspoon vegetable oil, plus extra for greasing
> ½ teaspoon cornmeal (if using a cookie sheet)
> 2 teaspoons all-purpose flour
> 3 ice cubes

Combine the lukewarm water and the sugar in a small bowl. Sprinkle the yeast on top. Allow the yeast mixture to proof for 5 to 6 minutes, until bubbly.

Process the bread flour, whole wheat flour, and salt in a food processor for 1 minute. Add the yeast, scraping the proofing bowl well.

Turn the machine on and slowly add the room-temperature water in a thin stream through the feed tube for about 1 minute, until a ball forms. Discard any remaining water and continue to process until the dough has made 30 revolutions in the food processor.

Lightly grease a ceramic bowl with vegetable oil. Roll the dough around in the bowl until coated with the oil. Cover the bowl loosely with a damp towel and set it aside in a warm, draft-free spot for 1¼ to 1½ hours, until the dough has doubled in size and does not spring back when pressed.

Release the air inside the dough by punching it with your fist, then fold the outer edges toward the center and push down.

❖ ❖ ❖ *T*o make 2 thin baguettes instead of 1 thick loaf, flatten and shape the dough into an 18 x 14-inch rectangle after the first rise. Cut the dough into two 14 x 9-inch pieces. Roll each into a 14-inch loaf and place in a well of a French bread pan or onto the prepared cookie sheet. Bake for 15 to 20 minutes, until the tops of the loaves are brown and they sound hollow when tapped. ❖ ❖ ❖

Stuffed French Bread

The quick addition of a few ingredients can turn Home Made Classic French Bread *into a meal. Stuffed French Bread is just the thing to prepare on weekends before busy weeks, when you'll be too busy to make even a sandwich (the sandwich, as it were, being already in the bread); it also makes a perfect buffet item or quick snack.*

Just sprinkle any of the following combinations (or any others that strike your fancy) onto the dough before rolling it up. Since the dough will be rising at room temperature for up to an hour, avoid highly perishable ingredients like fresh meat or fish, or soft cheese.

These proportions are for one large French bread loaf or for two thin baguettes.

> ⅔ cup chopped Greek or calamata olives
> ½ cup grated Parmesan cheese

½ cup grated Romano
cheese

or

4–6 thin slices *Home Made*
Honey-Basted Hickory-
Smoked Ham (page 108)

1 cup shredded Swiss
cheese

or

1 cup shredded provolone
cheese

¼ teaspoon crushed red
pepper flakes

1 tablespoon freshly
ground black pepper

or

1 cup grated cheddar
cheese

1 tablespoon dried dill

Transfer the dough to a work surface. Flatten and shape it into a
15 x 10-inch rectangle, then roll it into a 15-inch loaf.

Place the loaf in one well of a nonstick French bread pan or onto
a greased nonstick cookie sheet dusted with the cornmeal. Rub the
vegetable oil lightly over the loaf. Cover with a damp towel and return the loaf to the draft-free spot for 45 to 60 minutes, until it has
again doubled in size.

After about 30 minutes, preheat the oven to 425° F.

With a very sharp knife, make 6 diagonal slashes in the top of the
loaf. Sprinkle with the all-purpose flour.

Put 2 of the ice cubes directly onto the bottom of the oven. Bake
the bread for 5 minutes, add the remaining ice cube, and bake for
about 25 minutes more, until the bread has browned and sounds
hollow when tapped. Transfer the loaf to a wire rack to cool.

The French Bread has a shelf life of 2 to 3 days; wrap the loaf
loosely in aluminum foil to store.

Yield = One thick 15-inch loaf

Egg Bagels

We find Egg Bagels richer in texture and more flavorful than plain. The final stage lends itself readily to participation by an informal brunch crowd, who will most likely be camped out in the kitchen near the cof-feepot or the pitcher of Bloody Marias anyway. Let everyone garnish his or her own bagels.

> ¾ cup milk
> ¼ cup (½ stick) unsalted butter
> ⅓ cup lukewarm water (110–115° F.)
> 3½ tablespoons sugar
> ¼ ounce (1 packet) quick-rise yeast
> 3¾ cups bread flour
> 1 teaspoon salt
> 1 large egg
> 8 cups water
> 1 large egg white
> 2 tablespoons cold water
> Coarse kosher salt, poppy seed, sesame seed, or finely minced white onion

Scald the milk in a small saucepan over medium heat, just until bubbles begin to form around the edge. Remove the pan from the heat and add the butter. Set the pan aside for about 10 minutes, un-til the milk cools to 110 to 115° F.

Meanwhile, combine the lukewarm water and ½ tablespoon of the sugar in a small bowl. Sprinkle the yeast on top and set the mixture aside for 5 to 6 minutes to proof, until bubbly.

Put the flour, salt, and 1 tablespoon of sugar into a food proces-sor. Pulse for 5 seconds. Add the egg and pulse for 5 seconds more. Scrape in all the proofed yeast and pulse for another 5 seconds. With the machine on, slowly add just enough lukewarm milk through the feed tube to form a ball, about 1 minute. Process for 1 minute more.

Grease a ceramic bowl with vegetable oil and roll the dough in the oil to coat. Cover the bowl with a damp towel and set it aside in a warm, draft-free spot for 1¼ to 1½ hours, until the dough has doubled in size and no longer springs back to the touch.

Punch the dough with your fist and fold the edges toward the center.

❖ ❖ ❖ *F*or 18 Mini-Bagels, flatten and shape the dough into a 6 x 3-inch rectangle after the first rise. Cut it into eighteen 1-inch squares and roll each into an evenly shaped 6-inch rope. After the bagels have been boiled and brushed with the egg wash, top each, if desired, with ¼ teaspoon salt, ¼ teaspoon poppy seed, ½ teaspoon sesame seed, or ½ teaspoon minced onion. Bake for 12 to 15 minutes, until they are golden brown and sound hollow when tapped.
❖ ❖ ❖

Transfer the dough to a work surface. Flatten and shape the dough into a 4 x 3-inch rectangle and cut it into twelve 1-inch squares. Roll each square into an evenly shaped 10-inch rope. Transfer the ropes to a large nonstick cookie sheet; moisten the ends of each with a few drops of cold water and crimp them together to form a circle. Cover the sheet with a dry towel and place it in the draft-free spot for 45 to 60 minutes, until the bagels have about doubled in size.

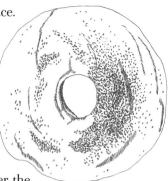

Preheat the oven to 400° F.

Combine the 8 cups water and the remaining 2 tablespoons sugar in a Dutch oven and bring to a boil over medium-high heat. Reduce the heat to low. Cook the bagels, 2 or 3 at a time, for 3 minutes, then flip and cook for 1 minute on the other side. Return the bagels to the cookie sheet. Repeat the process until all the bagels have been cooked.

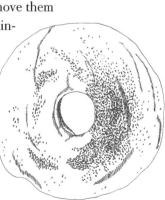

Mix the egg white and the cold water in a small bowl and brush on the bagels. According to preference, top each bagel with ⅜ teaspoon coarse kosher salt, ⅜ teaspoon poppy seed, ¾ teaspoon sesame seed, or ¾ teaspoon finely minced white onion.

Bake the bagels for 15 to 18 minutes, until they are golden brown and sound hollow when tapped. Remove them to a wire rack and cool for 20 to 30 minutes.

The bagels have a shelf life of 2 to 3 days; store in a tightly sealed plastic bag.

Yield = 12 bagels

Soft Pretzels

Although they originated in Philadelphia, Soft Pretzels are probably most associated with New York, where countless street vendors dish them up hot, laden with salt, and slathered with yellow mustard.

1	cup lukewarm water (110–115° F.)
1½	tablespoons sugar
¼	ounce (1 packet) quick-rise yeast
2⅔	cups all-purpose flour
¾	teaspoon salt
2	tablespoons unsalted butter, cut into small pieces
1	large egg white
2	tablespoons cold water
2	tablespoons coarse kosher salt

Combine the lukewarm water and the sugar in a 2- or 4-cup measuring cup. Sprinkle the yeast on top. Set the mixture aside to proof for 5 to 6 minutes, until bubbly.

Process the flour and plain salt in a food processor for 1 minute. Add the butter and process for 30 seconds more.

With the machine on, drizzle the yeast in through the feed tube, taking care to add it all. After about 1 minute, a ball will form; continue to process until the dough has made 30 revolutions.

Grease a ceramic bowl lightly with vegetable oil. Transfer the dough to the bowl and roll it around to coat with the oil. Cover the bowl with a damp towel and place it in a warm, draft-free spot for 1¼ to 1½ hours, until the dough has doubled in size and no longer springs back to the touch.

Lightly coat a large cookie sheet with vegetable oil and set it aside.

Punch the dough down and fold the edges toward the center.

Transfer the dough to a work surface and form it into an 8 x 6-inch rectangle, then cut it into twelve 2-inch squares. One at a time, roll each square into a thin, evenly shaped rope about 15 inches long. Form it into an upside-down U, with 7¼-inch-long sides. Cross the ends about a third of the way from the curve of the U, then fold the ends up at about a 45-degree angle so they touch the circle in a "10 o'clock" and "2 o'clock" position. Repeat the process until you have formed 12 pretzels. Place the pretzels at least 1 inch apart on the prepared cookie sheet.

Saltbread Christmas Ornaments and Breadbasket

Saltbread (an inedible flour, salt, and water mixture) has been used to illustrate themes from folklore and religion since ancient Greece and Rome. When Christmas trees became popular in Europe during the nineteenth century, saltbread ornaments soon followed. We first discovered them in South America, where they remain popular today.

Christmas tree ornaments are cut with cookie cutters from white saltbread dough and then painted—a perfect family project for the day (or the weekend) before trimming the tree.

We also provide directions for fashioning a handsome scalloped breadbasket that can grace your dinner table all year round. Its earthen shade comes from rye and wheat flour.

Our directions yield either sufficient earthen dough for 1 breadbasket or white dough for 18 to 36 ornaments, depending upon their size. Since the dough dries out very quickly, it must be used within 5 or 6 hours, or stored in an airtight plastic bag to seal in moisture.

Acrylic paints for decorating the ornaments and shellac for sealing the breadbasket or the ornaments are available from crafts shops. Polyurethane, which makes either more durable, can be purchased at a hardware store.

CHRISTMAS TREE
ORNAMENTS

    2 cups all-purpose flour
    ¾ cup salt
    ¾ cup water

Process the flour and salt in the bowl of a food processor for about 15 seconds, then drizzle the water through the feed tube. Once a ball has formed, continue to process for 3 minutes more.

Transfer the dough to a work surface and knead it 5 or 6 times, until it is no longer sticky to the touch. Put the dough in a plastic bag to keep it moist while you are shaping the ornaments.

Preheat the oven to 200° F.

Remove a bit (about ¹⁄₁₀) of dough at a time from the plastic bag, and roll it out ¼ inch thick. Cut ornaments in festive holiday shapes with cookie cutters or by hand with a sharp knife.

Transfer the ornaments to an ungreased, nonstick baking sheet and make a small hole (for hanging) at the center of the top of each with a chopstick, skewer, or pencil. When all of the dough has been shaped into ornaments, bake for about 1 hour, until the ornaments are as stiff and dry as ceramic. (They will be ivory to light tan in color.)

Remove the sheet from the oven and set it aside for about 1 hour to allow the ornaments to cool.

Decorate the ornaments with acrylic paints and let them dry thoroughly for 15 to 20 minutes. Coat one side of the ornaments with shellac to seal and set them aside for 2 to 3 hours until thoroughly dry and no longer

Mix the egg white with the cold water and brush over the pretzels. Sprinkle ½ teaspoon of kosher salt atop each pretzel. Cover the cookie sheet with a dry towel and set it in the draft-free spot for 45 to 60 minutes, until the pretzels rise to about double their original size.

After about 30 minutes, preheat the oven to 400° F.

Bake the pretzels for about 20 minutes, until they have browned and sound hollow when tapped. Let the pretzels cool for 15 minutes on the cookie sheet and serve immediately.

Yield = 12 soft pretzels

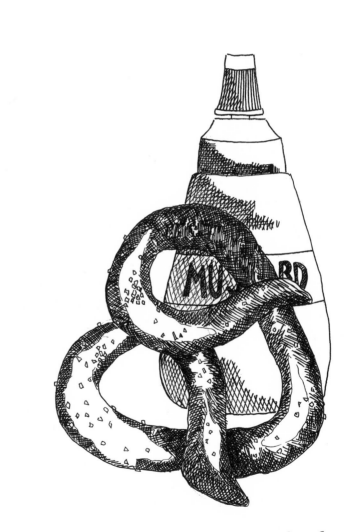

Old-Fashioned Raisin Pumpernickel

This is one of the recipes that calls for a stationary electric mixer instead of a food processor. Many food processors come with only a steel blade, which would rip the raisins to bits, and none but the most heavy-duty models have a motor capable of processing a dough this thick and heavy.

If you must, borrow a neighbor's mixer, using as a bribe a few slices of the dense and dark end result, preferably coated with Home Made Cream Cheese (page 94).

Execute all the steps on the second to lowest setting of the mixer.

> 2 cups seedless raisins
> 1 cup boiling water
> ⅓ cup lukewarm water (110–115° F.)
> 1 teaspoon sugar
> ¼ ounce (1 packet) quick-rise yeast
> 3 tablespoons blackstrap molasses
> 1 tablespoon cider vinegar
> 2 tablespoons vegetable oil
> ½ cup plus 2 tablespoons cold water
> 1½ cups rye flour
> 2½ to 2¾ cups bread flour
> 1 teaspoon salt
> 1½ tablespoons cornmeal
> 1 large egg yolk

Put the raisins and the boiling water into a small bowl and set aside.

In another small bowl, combine the lukewarm water with the sugar. Sprinkle the yeast on top and let it proof for 5 to 6 minutes, until bubbly.

Put the molasses, vinegar, vegetable oil, and ½ cup of the cold water in the bowl of a stationary electric mixer. Fit the mixer with the paddle attachment and mix for 30 seconds. Add the raisins with their soaking water and scrape in the proofed yeast. Mix for 10 seconds and turn the machine off.

Add the rye flour, 1½ cups of the bread flour, and the salt. Turn the machine back on and add ¾ cup more of the bread flour, ¼ cup at a time. At this stage, the dough should be gathered around the paddle. Turn the machine off and scrape the dough from the paddle back into the bowl.

tacky. Flip the ornaments, shellac the other side, and allow to dry for another 2 to 3 hours.

For a protective coating that will last for years, apply two coats of polyurethane to each side of the ornaments, allowing 2 to 3 hours drying time for each coat, and for each side.

To hang the ornaments, thread lengths of decorative ribbon through the holes at the top of each ornament and tie.

BREADBASKET

> 1 cup rye flour
> 1 cup whole wheat flour
> ¾ cup salt
> ¾ cup water

Process the flours and salt in the bowl of a food processor for about 15 seconds, then drizzle the water through the feed tube. Once the dough has formed a ball, continue to process for 3 minutes more.

Transfer the dough to a work surface and knead it 5 or 6 times, until no longer sticky to the touch.

Preheat the oven to 200° F.

With a rolling pin, roll the dough into a circle ¼ inch thick and about 13 inches in diameter.

Cover the outside of an oven-proof, round 2-quart casserole with aluminum foil, tucking the foil into the inside. Place the casserole upside down on a cookie sheet.

Carefully lift the dough (it should be thick enough to hold its shape) and drape it evenly over the casserole. Bake for about 1½ hours, until the breadbasket is as stiff and dry as ceramic.

Remove the sheet from the oven and allow the breadbasket to cool for 20 minutes undisturbed.

Gently slide the casserole off the sheet and place it upright onto a towel placed on a countertop. Open the foil, carefully remove the casserole, and slowly peel the foil from the saltbread. Let the breadbasket cool for another 30 minutes.

Spray one side of the breadbasket with shellac to seal and set it aside for 2 to 3 hours, until thoroughly dry and no longer tacky. Turn the basket over, spray the other side, and allow it to dry for another 2 to 3 hours.

For a protective coating that will last for years, apply a coat of polyurethane to each side of the breadbasket, allowing 2 to 3 hours drying time for each side. Repeat the process to apply a second coat of polyurethane.

Replace the paddle with the dough hook and turn the machine back on. Add $1/4$ to $1/2$ cup of the remaining bread flour, 2 tablespoons at a time as needed, until the dough is no longer sticky to the touch. Continue to mix for 10 minutes more.

Grease a ceramic bowl with vegetable oil. Transfer the dough to the bowl and roll it around to coat with oil. Cover the bowl with a damp towel and put it in a warm, draft-free spot for $1\frac{1}{4}$ to $1\frac{1}{2}$ hours, until the dough has doubled in size and no longer springs back when poked with a finger.

Punch the dough down and fold the edges toward the center. Re-cover with the damp towel and return the bowl to the draft-free spot for another 45 to 60 minutes, until the dough has again doubled in size.

Lightly grease a large baking sheet with vegetable oil and dust it with the cornmeal.

Punch and fold the dough down again. Transfer the dough to a work surface and cut it in half. Form each half into an oval 8 inches long and 6 inches across. Place the ovals onto the baking sheet; they should be at least 3 inches apart, and also not touch the sides. Cover with a dry towel and put the dough back in the draft-free spot for 30 to 40 minutes more to rise one last time.

After about 15 minutes, preheat the oven to 350° F.

Make 2 diagonal slashes across the top of each loaf with a very sharp knife. Mix the egg yolk and the remaining cold water and brush over the loaves. Bake for 1 hour to 1 hour and 10 minutes, until the bread is crusty and hollow-sounding when tapped. Remove the loaves to a wire rack to cool.

The Raisin Pumpernickel has a shelf life of 3 to 5 days; wrap it loosely with aluminum foil to store.

Yield = Two 8-inch long oval loaves

Gingerbread

From London street stalls to Midwestern kitchens, gingerbread was dispensed in great quantity around the last turn of the century. In addition to ingredients so prized by cooks of the period—molasses, ginger, and nutmeg—we include a little applesauce for extra moisture.

This most Victorian of desserts pairs well with Home Made *Vanilla Ice Cream (page 98) or with* Home Made *Cream Cheese (page 94).*

⅓ cup (5 tablespoons) unsalted butter
1 cup blackstrap molasses
1 egg, beaten
2 cups all-purpose flour
½ tablespoon baking soda
¼ teaspoon salt
½ tablespoon ground ginger
½ tablespoon ground cinnamon
¼ teaspoon ground nutmeg
1 cup applesauce

Preheat the oven to 350° F.

Cream the butter in a large bowl with an electric mixer set at medium speed. While beating, slowly add the molasses. Add the egg and continue to beat until well blended.

Combine the flour, baking soda, salt, and spices in a sifter. Sift into the creamed mixture. Add the applesauce, then beat at medium speed until smooth and thoroughly blended.

Lightly grease an 8-inch square cake pan with vegetable oil and pour the batter into the pan. Bake for 35 to 40 minutes, until the gingerbread begins to separate from the sides of the pan and a tester inserted into the center comes out clean. Transfer the pan to a wire rack and let the gingerbread cool in the pan.

The Gingerbread has a shelf life of 3 to 5 days; store in a tightly sealed plastic bag.

Yield = One 8-inch square loaf

Gingerbread Cookies and Edible Bowl

Gingerbread Cookies are a perennial Christmastime treat, and what better way to serve them—or a host of other holiday goodies—than in an edible Gingerbread Bowl? While our Gingerbread recipe makes a cakelike dessert, this ingredient mixture produces a drier, crisper Gingerbread.

The recipe yields enough dough for either a serving bowl or 12 to 24 cookies, depending upon their size. For either, follow the same initial steps for preparing the dough. Both have a shelf life of 3 to 5 days stored in a tightly sealed plastic bag.

½ tablespoon ground ginger
½ tablespoon ground cinnamon
½ teaspoon ground nutmeg
½ teaspoon baking soda
¾ cup sugar
½ cup blackstrap molasses
½ cup (1 stick) unsalted butter, at room temperature
1 large egg
3½ cups all-purpose flour

Combine the ginger, cinnamon, nutmeg, and baking soda in a small bowl and set it aside.

Put the sugar and the molasses into a small saucepan. Cook over medium-low heat for 3 to 4 minutes, stirring constantly, until the sugar has dissolved. Add the spices and baking soda. While stirring, continue to cook for a few seconds more, until bubbly. Remove the pan from the heat, stir in the butter, and let cool to room temperature.

In a large bowl, beat the egg with an electric mixer set at medium speed for about 10 seconds, or until pale. Add the cooled sugar and molasses and beat for a few seconds more to blend. Beat in 3¼ cups of the flour, adding it in increments. Continue beating for about 1 minute, until a stiff dough forms.

Turn the dough out onto a sheet of wax paper. Form into a ball, wrap it in the wax paper, and refrigerate for 1 hour.

Preheat the oven to 325° F.

Dust a large wood cutting board with the remaining flour and transfer the dough to the board.

To make cookies, roll the dough out so it's ⅛ to ¼ inch thick and about 15 inches around. Cut out people, animals, houses, or other shapes with cookie cutters. Line a baking sheet with parchment paper. Put the cookies onto the paper and bake for 10 to 12 minutes, or until firm to the touch. Transfer the cookies to a wire rack to cool.

When they have cooled a bit, the cookies can be decorated.

To make a bowl, cover the outside of a ceramic or oven-proof glass bowl that is about 8 inches in diameter and 4 inches deep with aluminum foil, tucking the foil into the inside of the bowl. Grease the foil on the outside of the bowl with vegetable shortening, coating thoroughly all over.

Rye Parmesan Popovers

Rye flour makes these popovers heartier than most, and Parmesan cheese lends an unexpected nuance. They're superb any time of day fresh from the oven, topped with a little sweet, creamy Home Made *Butter (page 96). We also like to serve them for breakfast with a few* Home Made *preserves (pages 20–24) and for dinner with a selection of* Home Made *soft cheeses (pages 87–94).*

> ½ cup rye flour
> ½ cup bread flour
> ½ teaspoon salt
> ¼ cup freshly grated Parmesan cheese
> 6 teaspoons olive oil
> 2 large eggs
> 1 cup milk
> 2 tablespoons unsalted butter, melted

Preheat the oven to 425° F.

Combine the flours, salt, and Parmesan in a sifter and set it aside.

Put ½ teaspoon olive oil into each well of a 12-well muffin tin (don't coat yet). Put the tin into the oven for 15 minutes.

Meanwhile, beat the eggs until frothy in a large bowl with an electric mixer set at medium speed. While continuing to beat, pour in the milk, sift in the flour mixture, and add the melted butter.

Remove the muffin tin from the oven and rotate it to coat the wells with the hot oil. Quickly pour the batter into the wells, filling each about ⅔ full.

Bake for 15 minutes, then lower the oven temperature to 375° F. and bake for 20 minutes more. Serve immediately.

Yield = 12 popovers

Multigrain Bread

This hearty, healthy bread is moister than many multigrain breads—the secret ingredient is buttermilk. It's a great sandwich bread, especially toasted. To store for sandwiches, slice a loaf as soon as it cools. Put pieces of wax paper between each slice and freeze the bread in an airtight freezer storage bag.

Like the Old-Fashioned Raisin Pumpernickel, this dough is a bit too thick for most food processors to handle, so we've written the recipe for a stationary electric mixer. Again, the mixer should be on the second to lowest setting.

1 teaspoon sugar
¼ cup lukewarm water (110–115° F.)
¼ ounce (1 packet) quick-rise yeast
1 cup buttermilk
1¼ cup very hot tap water
2 tablespoons honey
2 tablespoons distilled white vinegar
2 tablespoons vegetable oil
1¼ cups rye flour
1½ cups whole wheat flour
3¾ to 4 cups bread flour
1 tablespoon coarse kosher salt
1½ tablespoons caraway seed
1 large egg white
1 tablespoon cold water

Combine the sugar and the lukewarm water in a small bowl. Sprinkle the yeast on top and set it aside for 5 to 6 minutes to proof, until bubbly.

Put the buttermilk into the bowl of a stationary electric mixer fitted with the paddle attachment.

Combine the hot tap water and the honey in a 2-cup measuring cup, stir until the honey has dissolved, and add to the mixer bowl. Add the vinegar, vegetable oil, rye flour, whole wheat flour, 1½ cups of the bread flour, salt, and caraway seed, and mix for about 30 seconds, until the flour is completely incorporated. Add another 1¾ cups of bread flour and all of the yeast mixture and mix for 1 minute. Add ¼ cup bread flour and continue to mix until the dough gathers around the paddle, about 30 seconds.

Line a cookie sheet with parchment paper and place the bowl upside down on the paper.

Roll the dough into a ¼-inch-thick circle with a diameter of about 12 inches. Roll the dough around the rolling pin as you would a piecrust, and unroll over the upside-down bowl. Shape it onto the bowl, trimming any excess and brushing off any remaining bits of flour.

Bake for 12 to 14 minutes, until the Gingerbread is firm to the touch. Remove the cookie sheet from the oven and allow the Gingerbread to cool undisturbed for 10 minutes.

Gently slide the bowl off the sheet and set it upright onto a towel placed on a countertop. Open the foil, carefully remove the bowl, and slowly peel the foil from the Gingerbread Bowl. Let the Gingerbread cool for another 15 to 20 minutes before using.

Turn the machine off and scrape the dough off the paddle into the bowl.

Add ¼ cup more bread flour. Replace the paddle with the dough hook and mix for about 1 minute, until the flour is completely incorporated. With the machine running, add as much of the remaining ¼ cup bread flour as needed, 1 tablespoon at a time, until the dough no longer sticks to your fingers when touched. Continue to mix for 7 minutes more.

Dust a work surface with bread flour. Transfer the dough to the floured surface and form it into a ball.

Lightly grease a ceramic bowl with vegetable oil. Put the dough into the bowl and cover it with a damp towel. Set the bowl aside in a warm, draft-free spot for 1 to 1¼ hours, until the dough has doubled in size and no longer springs back to the touch.

Punch the dough down to release as much air as possible. Re-cover the bowl and return it to the draft-free spot for 35 to 45 minutes more, until the dough has once more doubled in size.

Punch the dough down again. Transfer it to a work surface and form the dough into a 10 x 9-inch rectangle, then cut it in half crosswise. Mix the egg white and cold water in a small bowl and brush it over the dough.

Lightly grease two 9¼-inch loaf pans with vegetable oil. Put the dough into the loaf pans, spreading it so the dough touches the sides of the pans. Return the loaves to the draft-free spot, recover with the damp towel, and let sit for 30 to 40 minutes, until they double in size again.

After about 15 minutes, preheat the oven to 375° F.

Bake the loaves for 30 to 40 minutes, until the bread is golden brown and sounds hollow when tapped. Remove the loaves to a wire rack to cool.

The Multigrain Bread has a shelf life of 3 to 5 days; wrap loosely in aluminum foil to store.

Yield = Two 9¼-inch loaves

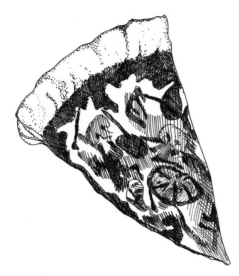

Pizza Dough

Pizza is a relatively modern concoction that benefits from old-time bread-baking skills. Made at home from scratch, pizza just seems to taste better—at least in part because it's fun to make, a process the whole household can take part in.

This crispy dough is easy and versatile. We use it for Oven-Baked Pizza, for Grilled or Broiled Pizzas, and for Focaccia, an Italian specialty with a thicker crust.

> ¼ cup lukewarm water (110–115° F.)
> ½ teaspoon sugar
> ¼ ounce (1 packet) quick-rise yeast
> 2¾ cups all-purpose flour
> ½ cup semolina
> 1 tablespoon coarse kosher salt
> 1½ tablespoons olive oil
> 1 cup cold water

Combine the lukewarm water and sugar in a small bowl. Sprinkle the yeast on top and set it aside for 5 to 6 minutes to proof, until bubbly.

Put the flour, semolina, salt, and olive oil in a food processor and

Home Made *Pizza*

Pizza night is a happening! Gather the troops, assign jobs, crack a bottle of robust wine, and let the games begin.

Each recipe of *Home Made* dough will make four 12-inch round pizzas—but it's up to you whether it will be a traditional sausage-and-cheese oven-baked rendition or a light, elegant variation to be grilled or broiled. We also use this dough to make four 8-inch square Focacce, which juxtaposes a thick, garlicky crust with a thin layer of "Sun-Dried" Tomatoes and fresh basil.

Serve each *Home Made* Pizza or Focaccia as a generous individual portion, or cut them up for appetizers or pizza grazing.

OVEN-BAKED PIZZA

> 1 cup *Home Made* Italian Sausage (page 125)
> 1 tablespoon cornmeal
> 1 chunk *Home Made* Pizza Dough (¼ recipe)
> ¼ cup pizza sauce
> 1 garlic clove, minced
> 2 tablespoons chopped red bell pepper
> 2 tablespoons chopped green bell pepper
> ¼ cup sliced mushrooms
> 1 tablespoon sliced pitted black olives
> 1 tablespoon chopped white onion
> ½ cup shredded *Home Made* Mozzarella (page 89)

Preheat the oven to 500° F. If using a baking stone for a crisper crust, put the stone into the oven when you turn it on to preheat.

In a heavy fry pan, cook the sausage over medium heat for about 10 minutes, until browned, breaking the meat up a bit as it cooks. With a slotted spoon, transfer the sausage to paper toweling to drain.

Scatter the cornmeal onto a large cookie sheet; set it aside.

Place a chunk of Pizza Dough on a work surface. Taking care not to rip the dough, stretch and shape it by hand into a 12-inch circle about 1/8 inch thick.

Transfer the dough to the prepared cookie sheet and coat it evenly with the pizza sauce. Scatter the garlic and Italian Sausage over the sauce. Layer with any or all of the bell peppers, mushrooms, olives, and onion. Top with the mozzarella.

Place the cookie sheet in the oven, or slide the pizza from the sheet onto the baking stone. Bake for about 15 minutes, until the crust is brown and the cheese is bubbly.

GRILLED OR BROILED PIZZA

1 chunk *Home Made* Pizza Dough (1/4 recipe)
3 teaspoons olive oil
1 garlic clove, peeled and minced
3 ounces *Home Made* Honey-Basted, Hickory-Smoked Ham (page 108), julienned
2 Italian plum tomatoes, cored and thinly sliced
2 tablespoons chopped fresh basil
3 tablespoons grated Parmesan cheese

or:

process for 1 minute. Scrape in the proofed yeast. Turn the machine on and drizzle the cold water through the feed tube. A ball should form in less than a minute; process for 1 minute more.

Transfer the dough to a work surface, incorporating any bits of loose dough from the food-processor bowl into the ball, and knead it 10 times.

Grease a ceramic bowl with vegetable oil. Put the dough into the bowl and roll it around in the oil to coat. Cover with a damp towel and place the bowl in a warm, draft-free spot for 1¼ to 1½ hours, until it doubles in size and no longer springs back to the touch.

Punch the dough down and fold the edges toward the center. Turn the dough upside down, re-cover the bowl, and return it to the draft-free spot for 45 to 60 minutes more until it has again doubled in size.

Punch the dough down a second time, then cut it into 4 chunks.

If you are not going to use the dough immediately, wrap each in plastic wrap and store in the refrigerator, where they will keep for up to 2 days. Let the dough warm for about 20 minutes to room temperature before using it.

Yield = Four 12-inch pizza crusts

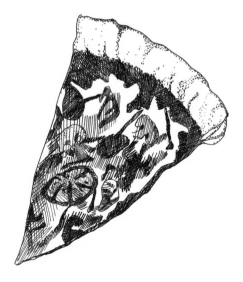

Maple Pecan Date Bread

"Bread-making should be regarded as one of the highest accomplishments," according to a period critic who goes on to lament that bread receives less than "one tenth part of the interest, time, and thought which are devoted to cake and pastry."

Perhaps this quick comfort bread (or comforting "quick" bread) will solve the dilemma, since it can serve equally well as a dessert. It's our updated version of the date nut bread moms used to ship en masse to college dorms across the country.

1 large egg
½ cup milk
½ cup pure maple syrup
¼ cup (½ stick) unsalted butter, melted
2 cups all-purpose flour
2 teaspoons baking powder
½ teaspoon baking soda
½ teaspoon salt
½ cup chopped pecans
¾ cup roughly chopped pitted dates

Preheat the oven to 375° F.

In a large bowl, beat the egg with an electric mixer set at medium speed until frothy. Add the milk, maple syrup, and melted butter, and beat at medium speed until thoroughly mixed.

Sift the flour, baking powder, baking soda, and salt into the bowl. Stir with a wooden spoon just until blended, then stir in the pecans and dates.

Grease a 9¼-inch loaf pan with vegetable oil and pour in the batter. Bake for 40 to 50 minutes, until the bread begins to pull away from the edges of the pan and a tester inserted into the loaf comes out clean. Remove the loaf to a wire rack to cool.

The Maple Pecan Date Bread has a shelf life of 3 to 5 days; loosely wrap in aluminum foil to store.

Yield = One 9¼-inch loaf

1 chunk *Home Made* Pizza Dough (¼ recipe)
2 teaspoons olive oil
¼ cup *Home Made* Barbecue Sauce (page 54)
½ cup cubed *Home Made* Lemon Tea-Smoked Chicken (page 116)
6 red onion rings (1 slice, separated)
3 tablespoons chopped fresh spinach
⅓ cup shredded *Home Made* Mozzarella (page 89)

Preheat a broiler or a gas grill set at high, or prepare a charcoal grill by lighting a mound of charcoal briquets and letting them burn for about 20 minutes, until ashen and glowing.

Grease an acrylic cutting board or the back of a baking or cookie sheet with olive oil. Put a chunk of Pizza Dough onto the prepared surface. Stretch and shape it into a 12-inch circle about ⅛ inch thick, taking care not to rip the dough. Brush the top of the dough with 1 teaspoon of the oil.

Place the dough, oiled side down, on the grill or oiled side up under the broiler. Cook for 1½ to 2 minutes, checking frequently, until grill marks form on the bottom or, in the broiler, brown spots are visible on the top.

Transfer the crust to a work surface and brush the unoiled side with another teaspoon of olive oil. Layer with the garlic, ham, tomatoes, basil, Parmesan, and remaining teaspoon of oil, or with the barbecue sauce, chicken, onion rings, spinach, and mozzarella.

Return the pizza to the grill or the broiler and cook for 2 to 3 minutes, until the crust is lightly browned and the cheese has melted.

FOCACCIA

- 1 chunk *Home Made* Pizza Dough (¼ recipe)
- ½ tablespoon *Home Made* Garlic Oil (page 38)
- 6 *Home Made* "Sun-Dried" Tomatoes (page 194), reconstituted and thinly sliced
- 2 tablespoons chopped fresh basil
- 1 teaspoon coarse kosher salt
- 1 teaspoon olive oil

Thoroughly coat the bottom and sides of an 8 x 8 x 2-inch cake pan with olive oil. Put the chunk of pizza dough into the pan, and spread it by hand until it covers the bottom, making sure to push it into the corners.

Brush the top of the dough with the garlic oil. Scatter the tomatoes over the surface and top with the basil and the salt. Drizzle the olive oil over all.

Cover the pan with a dry towel and set it aside in a warm, draft-free spot for about 30 minutes, until the dough has doubled in size and no longer springs back to the touch.

After about 15 minutes, preheat the oven to 400° F.

Bake the Focaccia for about 15 minutes, until golden brown.

Chocolate Sour Cherry Bread

Here we combine two all-time favorite flavors, sour cherry and chocolate. If you don't have access to the farmstands in New England and the upper Midwest, where succulent sour cherries abound in early to midsummer, you can buy them frozen or canned in most supermarkets.

- 3 ounces unsweetened baking chocolate, broken up
- ¼ cup (½ stick) unsalted butter
- ½ cup sugar
- 1 large egg, beaten
- ¾ cup buttermilk
- 2 cups all-purpose flour
- ½ tablespoon baking powder
- ¼ teaspoon salt
- ½ cup pitted sour cherries
- 1 tablespoon unsweetened cocoa powder

Preheat the oven to 350° F.

Melt the chocolate and butter in the top of a double boiler over boiling water, stirring constantly. Remove the pot from the heat and stir in the sugar until incorporated.

In a large bowl, whisk the beaten egg with the buttermilk until pale yellow. Stir in the melted chocolate. Sift in the flour, baking powder, and salt, then add the sour cherries and stir until well blended.

Grease a 9¼-inch loaf pan with vegetable oil and dust it with the cocoa powder. Pour in the batter. Bake for 45 to 55 minutes, until the bread begins to separate from the edges of the pan and a tester inserted into the center comes out clean. Transfer the loaf to a wire rack to cool.

The Chocolate Sour Cherry Bread has a shelf life of 3 to 5 days; to store, wrap loosely in aluminum foil.

Yield = One 9¼-inch loaf

CHAPTER 8

Kitchen Growing & Drying

Self-sufficiency and economy were the values held dearest by our turn-of-the-century forebears. Producing as many of their own foods as circumstances allowed was a part of everyday life. The bounty of their efforts was a precious commodity, when ties to the land and the cycles of the seasons were still very powerful. Rural dwellers and those of modest means stored foods for the coming months out of necessity; even the emerging urban elite shipped back the produce from their summer homes' gardens for economy, and to make sure these goods would be available year-round.

Despite the vast differences between then and now, one can't help but sense a resurgence of this ethic as the once-bright glow of a seemingly limitless marketplace has begun to dim. Few of us will ever be in a position to grow any significant portion of our own food, but with every pot of herbs or crop of sprouts we cultivate, we reestablish a link to the land.

❖ ❖ ❖

The Basics

Those lucky souls with outdoor gardens will no doubt use them to their fullest potential. We developed the growing directions in this chapter to meet what we consider the real challenges—how to do a bit of kitchen gardening without outdoor space, and how to do it year-round, which in most climates means indoors for several months of the year.

Many herbs can thrive indoors, given sufficient sunlight (or a grow light) and a little loving care. If you plant an outdoor herb garden, save a few seeds to start another crop indoors after the season; we give instructions on page 181.

Or you may find it easier to skip a few steps and start with the seedlings available from nurseries and many supermarkets. These can be snipped and used almost as soon as transplanted, and with a little patience and nurturing will provide a steady supply of fresh herbs for 3 to 6 months.

We provide directions for growing a variety of sprouts from seeds or beans, which sprout within 3 to 6 days.

We also include a farrago of rainy-day kitchen gardening projects that transform pantry scraps into everything from delicate seasonings to bushy house plants—one of which, with a little luck, will bear fruit when you least expect it.

A dehydrator or a microwave may have replaced the Victorian root cellar, but we can still save a bit of the harvest—be it home-grown herbs or farmer's market produce—for the seasons to come.

Herbs are dried by any of three methods. In traditional air drying, sprigs are hung freestanding or in a paper bag for 7 to 10 days. Microwave drying accomplishes the task in a few minutes, retaining much of the color and taste of the fresh herb in the process. We also note flowers that survive both of these drying methods well.

Freezer drying extends the life, look, and aroma of fresh herbs for months. In addition to the usual chopped form of dried herbs, this method allows you to preserve whole sprigs. We also use it to dry chopped herbs in ice cubes that can be conveniently added to season soups and stews.

Produce is dried either in the oven or in a dehydrator, a versatile appliance we find well worth its modest cost and then some. In addition to drying a variety of food at once, a dehydrator can be turned on and left unattended through the workday or overnight to do its thing.

After considerable experimentation with both methods, we call for drying tomatoes, sour cherries, and blueberries in the oven and leave the choice of drying medium to you in the case of most mushrooms. We employ the dehydrator to dry the components of a hearty trail mix, a teriyaki turkey version of jerky, and corn. (Before going into the dehydrator or oven, fruit and tomatoes *must* first be washed and thoroughly dried.)

Food drying times are approximate, and they'll vary according to size and moisture content, so it's a good idea to start checking an hour or two before the specified time is up.

Dried herbs and foods should keep for at least 6 months if stored in airtight containers; store the herbs in opaque vials.

Growing

Sprouting

From good old Alfalfa Sprouts to the newly popular varieties like Radish and Onion, sprouts are a healthy means of adding flavor and texture to a variety of dishes.

They are best used dry and crisp. It's great that they are now widely available, but by the time the sprouts show up on the grocer's shelf they are usually well past the prime of their short and highly perishable existence. Within a day or two, you're often left with slightly soggy sprouts that are already losing their characteristic texture. Growing your own assures a constant supply of wonderful fresh sprouts.

Alfalfa, Radish, and Onion Sprouts derive from varieties of grass seeds, Mung and Lentil Sprouts from beans, and Wheat and Rye Sprouts from grain seeds. Use seeds or beans that are specifically designated for sprouting; they can be obtained from natural or health food stores or from seed catalogs. Take care not to use seeds intended for gardening (i.e., you want "radish sprouting seeds," not seeds for growing radishes), since garden seeds are frequently

Cooking with Sprouts

Beyond the obvious raw sandwich and salad applications, many sprouts are good cooked: Steam 2 cups Onion, Lentil, or Mung Bean Sprouts for about 20 minutes, until tender, then toss them in 1 tablespoon *Home Made* Oriental Vinegar (page 46) for an interesting side dish.

Wheat and Rye Sprouts add a nutritious crunch to baked goods; we sometimes add about 2 cups, at the same time as the flour, to *Home Made* Multigrain Bread (page 166).

Mung Bean Sprouts are a staple in Chinese cooking.

treated with poisonous chemicals, pesticides, and fungicides.

Combine the correct amount of seeds or beans and lukewarm water (see the chart at right) in a 1-quart Mason jar. Top the jar with a sprouting screen, available from health food stores and from many hardware stores, or with a piece of cheesecloth, and screw the ring on; don't use the jar's flat metal seal. Set the jar aside overnight in a cool, dark place (in a cabinet or closet with a temperature of about 70° F.; don't refrigerate).

Dump the soaking water out through the sprouting screen or cheesecloth. Add lukewarm water, swirl the jar a bit, and pour the water out twice. Roll the jar on its side so that the seeds or beans, which are moist and will adhere to the glass readily, coat the surface of the jar in a single layer. Rest the jar on its side in the cool, dark place to sprout, for the approximate number of days noted below, until the sprouts have reached their desired length.

The temperature and brightness of the spot used for sprouting is important. Too much heat encourages mold, too much cold air discourages sprouting, and too much light causes the seeds or beans to dry too quickly.

Two to three times a day, rinse the jar with lukewarm water and discard the water. Before resting the jar again on its side, rock it a bit to distribute the new sprouts, which will have begun to fall from the top side of the jar, over the bottom side.

When the sprouts reach the desired length (for some, this is a range, and the sprouts can be "picked" at any point through the range), rinse them again, remove them from the jar, and store for up to 1 week in an airtight plastic bag in the refrigerator. Lentil Sprouts, by the way, are crunchier and more flavorful when they are allowed to grow to 1 inch in length, but are most nutritous at ½ inch.

For Alfalfa or Radish Sprouts only, place the jar in direct sunlight or bright light for 4 to 6 hours before rinsing and removing the sprouts, which will encourage edible leaves to form.

Sprout	Combine	Days	Length	Yield
Alfalfa	1½ tablespoons seeds & ¼ cup water	3–5	1–2 inches	2 cups
Radish	1 tablespoon seeds & ¼ cup water	3–6	1–1½ inches	1 cup
Onion	2 tablespoons seeds & ½ cup water	3–5	½–1½ inches	2 cups
Mung	½ cup beans & 2 cups water	3–4	2 inches	2–2½ cups
Lentil	½ cup beans & 2 cups water	2–4	½–1 inch	3–4 cups
Wheat	½ cup seeds & 2 cups water	2–4	½ inch	2 cups
Rye	½ cup seeds & 2 cups water	3–4	½ inch	2 cups

Pantry Flora

Our vigilant pursuit of innovative ways to use odds and ends from the pantry has spawned an avocation some friends irreverently refer to as our kitchen garbage gardening. Let them scoff—*we're* producing delicately flavored edible flora from surplus bits of garlic and onion, and unique house-plants from avocado pits and potatoes a bit past their prime.

Pantry gardening's also a great way to engage the interest of the future gardeners in your house-hold. We guarantee that they'll check the pineapple plant regularly for signs of progress and squeal in long-awaited delight if it takes and gives off a new pineapple.

Minimal gardening accoutrement is required. Start with a 6-inch-tall clay pot with a saucer. Layer the bottom with stones or a few pieces of broken pot to raise the soil and facilitate drainage. We use the usually all too plentiful Styrofoam packing bits, which are absorbent and thus have the added advantage of maintaining moisture in the pot. Fill the pot almost to the top with commercial potting soil and water.

To grow a garlic plant, push 2 or 3 unpeeled garlic cloves, evenly spaced, into wet soil, flat side down and pointed side up, just to bury. Place the pot out of direct sunlight for about 10 days, until the cloves sprout. Water sparingly only to keep the soil moist, taking care to neither let the soil dry out nor drench it.

Once it has sprouted, transfer the plant to a sunny windowsill and begin to water it every 2 or 3 days, as needed, until the water flows through into the saucer.

In 10 days to 2 weeks, the garlic plant should give off long, thin green stalks that taste a bit like chives, with a slight garlicky undertone. Snip and use them as you would chives, raw or in cooking.

To grow an onion plant, bury an unpeeled, small yellow onion about halfway in wet soil, root end down. Place the pot out of direct sunlight for about 10 days, until it sprouts. During this time, water sparingly only to keep the soil moist; take care to neither let the soil dry out nor drench it.

Transfer the plant to a sunny windowsill and begin to water every 2 or 3 days, as needed, until the water flows through into the saucer.

Within 2 weeks, the onion plant should bear stalks with buds that will flower within the next 2 weeks. Snip both the stalks and the flowers to add a delicate onion taste and an elegant touch to salads.

To grow a pineapple plant, you may need to use a slightly larger pot, depending on the size of the leafy crown atop the pineapple.

Slice the pineapple ¾ inch to 1 inch beneath the crown. Bury in wet soil just up to the bottom of the leaves. Place the plant immediately into direct sunlight and water every few days, as needed.

If the plant continues to thrive, it will give off a new pineapple 6 months to 1 year later.

To grow an avocado plant, stick toothpicks into the avocado pit to suspend it over a glass of water, large end down, with about half of the pit submerged. Set the glass out of direct sunlight for about 3 weeks, until a root about 1½ to 2 inches long forms.

Bury the pit, root side down, in wet soil and transfer the pot to direct sunlight. Water it as you would any houseplant. Leaves will begin to pop up; once a cluster of 3 leaves emerges, pinch off the center leaf.

The leaves should continue to grow into a thick, full houseplant.

To grow a potato plant, take a white baking potato that is still firm but that has begun to form roots in the eyes. Slice the potato 1 to 1½ inches below a root. Using toothpicks, suspend the potato over a glass of water, making sure that the root is submerged in the water. Place the glass out of direct sunlight for 1 week to 10 days, until a root ball forms.

Bury the potato just below the surface in wet soil, root side down. Transfer to a sunny windowsill and water every few days as needed, until the water flows through into the saucer.

The potato plant should soon begin to spawn leaves that will grow into a bushy houseplant.

Indoor Herb Growing

Herbs have been cultivated since ancient times, when they were first used for medicinal purposes. In the Middle Ages, peasants grew them to flavor their rather meager culinary fare and sorcer-

ers, legend has it, used them to cast spells. Later, their purely aesthetic merits came to be appreciated in gardening and decorating.

Victorians cultivated herbs more for their medicinal and aesthetic applications than for their culinary value. Cooking with herbs derived a certain cachet from its association with French cuisine, but the everyday tastes of the time leaned more toward the sometimes heavy-handed use of the likes of nutmeg and cinnamon.

Today, it's hard to imagine spending much time in the kitchen without a wide array of herbs close at hand. Lack of garden space is no excuse for not maintaining a fragrant crop of fresh herbs in your home—particularly if you cheat a bit by starting with seedlings.

Of the herbs that we dry (pages 184–189), only dill, a weed that just doesn't thrive indoors, and lavender, which requires specialized lighting, fail the test of indoor growing.

Herbs that do grow well indoors include basil, chive, marjoram, mint, oregano, rosemary, sage, tarragon, thyme (all of which dry well, too), and bay leaf, borage, chervil, lemon balm, parsley, and summer savory.

Transplant the seedlings to a 6-inch-tall clay pot with a saucer. Layer about an inch of Styrofoam packing bits, stones, or pieces of broken pot on the bottom of the pot and add a layer of commercial potting soil halfway up the pot. Gently break away the original potting soil from the roots of the seedling, bury it to the original soil line, and water immediately.

Place the pot on a windowsill where it will get 6 to 7 hours of direct sunlight a day, or expose it to a grow light, fitted into a gooseneck lamp and positioned 10 to 12 inches above the plant, for 6 to 7 hours a day. (Grow lights are available from any hardware store or supermarket that has a well-stocked selection of lightbulbs.)

Water the plant until the water flows into the saucer below every 2 to 3 days, as needed. Rosemary and thyme must be misted daily.

The herbs can be used almost immediately, but you may want to leave them for 2 or 3 weeks to grow enough to produce a readily replenishing supply.

A word of caution: Seedlings often harbor a common parasite known as white flies. They won't spread beyond the immediate vicinity of the plants, but will kill the herbs if not treated. To treat, mist with a solution of 1 tablespoon dishwashing detergent and

1 cup water; one or two applications should do. Be sure to rinse the herbs thoroughly before using.

To start your indoor herb garden from seed, soak one peat pot disc—available from nurseries—per seed in water for about 5 minutes until it expands into a little pot. Drop a seed into the hole in the top of each pot and place all of the pots into a baking dish.

Put the baking dish in a bright spot, but out of direct sunlight, and loosely drape with a sheet of plastic wrap. Pour water into the baking dish as needed to keep the pots from drying out. Once seedlings begin to appear, feed the plants about every third watering with a mixture of ⅛ teaspoon all-purpose plant food to 2 cups water.

When the seedlings are 3 to 4 inches tall and seem sturdy, plant them (peat pot intact) and proceed as you would for raising baby herb plants.

Herbal Candles

Making candles at home is an easy and entertaining way to keep a supply on hand for relaxing candlelit evenings or to add just the right finishing touch to a gift basket.

Floating herb-flecked candles, for which we provide directions below, add an elegant air to the dinner table when placed in a water-filled cut glass centerpiece. They give off subtle wisps of fragrance as they burn.

Variations on this candle-making theme are almost too numerous to mention. Candles can be colored simply by adding chopped crayon to the wax before pouring it into the mold. We use tart tins to mold our floating candles, but they can also be formed in miniature pastry and petits fours tins or individual metal chocolate molds, all of which come in an array of decorative shapes.

Freestanding pillar candles can be made in clean and dry milk cartons from which the top has been trimmed, heat-resistant wax paper cups, or straight-sided (nonridged) aluminum cans. For any candles that are to be unmolded after hardening, be sure to lightly but thoroughly grease the inside of the mold first with vegetable oil.

The greater height of pillar candles means you can add whole sprigs of herbs or bay leaves, rather than the chopped herbs more appropriate for scenting shallow floating candles. To position whole herbs or bay leaves, initially pour just enough hot wax into the mold so that when swirled it will coat the surface of the mold. Carefully arrange the sprigs or leaves around the perimeter, holding each in place briefly with a skewer until anchored in the wax; then pour the remaining wax into the mold.

Votive candles can be made in the votive glass containers, available from many gift shops; in this case, greasing the container is unnecessary since the candle won't be unmolded.

To make our candles, we use supermarket-variety household paraffin wax. The stearic acid that is added to the wax, the wick, and the wick bases are available from crafts shops or candle-making supply houses (see Source Guide). In a pinch, everyday string can be substituted for wick. Beeswax, which doesn't require acid, is stocked by many crafts shops.

For those who decide to pursue this new hobby with a vengeance, candle-making supply houses dispense professional candle-making wax that comes premixed with acid, oil-based candle perfumes in a range of scents, all sorts of molds, and other sophisticated paraphernalia.

For *floating herbal candles,* you will need:

- ½ pound household paraffin wax
- ½ tablespoon stearic acid
- 13½ inches flat-braided candlewick, cut into three 4½-inch lengths
- 3 wick bases
- A clean and dry 24- or 26-ounce coffee can or an old 1-quart saucepan not intended for future cooking use
- Three 4-ounce tart tins (about 4 inches wide and 1½ inches deep)
- 1½ teaspoons chopped fresh bay leaf, lavender, lemon balm, marjoram, mint (spearmint, peppermint, or orange mint), or rosemary to scent the candles
- Optional: 1 crayon, coarsely chopped, to color the candles
- 1½ teaspoons vegetable oil to grease the molds

Fill a large saucepan halfway with water. Put the wax into the coffee can or 1-quart saucepan and float the smaller container in the large saucepan. Melt the wax over low heat, about 15 to 20 minutes. Meanwhile, grease each tart tin with ½ teaspoon of the vegetable oil. Tape one end of each 4½-inch length of wick to a pencil or a wooden chopstick. (If using a different size mold, cut wick to a length equal to the depth of the mold plus about 3 inches.) Thread the other end down through the raised center of a wick base and secure the wick in place by bending the raised tip down over the wick.

Suspend the pencil or chopstick across the top of the tin so that the wick extends down through the center of the tin and the base touches the bottom. Roll the wick up around the pencil until it is almost taut. If you don't have a base to weight the wick down, carefully dip the free end into the hot wax to moisten and press it down in the center of the bottom of the tin until affixed.

Remove the large saucepan and its contents from the heat. Dissolve the acid in the hot wax, using a disposable stirrer or chopstick. If you are making colored candles, stir in the crayon.

Carefully pour the wax into the molds, filling to within ½ inch of the top. Sprinkle ½ teaspoon of chopped herb into each mold. Let the candles cool for 1½ to 2 hours, until completely hardened.

Cut the wick on each candle beneath the pencil to the desired length. Unmold the candles by turning them over and tapping the molds upside down to loosen and free the candles.

Yield = Three 4-inch-wide floating herbal candles

To make unique little *wax Christmas tree ornaments,* use appropriately shaped miniature molds. Follow the directions above—varying quantities as dictated by the number and size of molds used—except for those steps pertaining to preparing and positioning the wick.

Instead, cut a 4-inch length of wick to serve as a hanger for each ornament. Carefully dip one end into the hot wax and press the ends together to form a loop. Pour the wax into the mold and prop the loop so that the ends are suspended into the wax at the point from which you want the ornament to hang.

When it's time for the tree to come down, the hanger can be cut open and the ornament takes on new life as a floating candle.

Drying

Air-Dried Herbs and Flowers

"Herbs should be gathered in dry weather, carefully picked over and dried...under a hotbed sash," advises a nineteenth-century expert. "Fresh herbs are, of course, to be preferred, but as they are not obtainable in winter it is necessary to preserve them by drying... Herbs will be found useful condiments in cookery, and several of them have medicinal qualities."

Air drying (no hotbed sash required) produces the intense and slightly bitter concentrated flavor commonly associated with dried herbs; use only about ⅓ as much of herbs dried this way as you would of fresh.

Several varieties of flowers can also be air dried.

To air dry lavender, marjoram, mint, oregano, rosemary, sage, tarragon, and thyme, first gather 6 to 8 sprigs of each herb loosely together at the stem end. Attach with a rubber band to a hook (such as a small hook from a pot rack, a drapery hook, or a sturdy paper clip opened into a hook) and hang in a dry place, out of direct sunlight, for 7 to 10 days.

An alternative method is to suspend the sprigs upside down in a paper bag, gather the top of the bag around the stems, and secure closed with a rubber band. Place the bag in a dry place, out of direct sunlight, for 7 to 10 days.

When the herbs have dried, remove the leaves from the stems and store in an opaque, airtight container. If the herbs have been dried in a paper bag, give the bag a few vigorous shakes before opening and the leaves should fall free.

To air dry bachelor's buttons, black-eyed Susans, cornflowers, Job's tears, everlastings, tea roses, statices, strawflowers, and yarrows (yellow or white), first remove most of the leaves from the stems, leaving only a few at the top. Gather 6 to 8 stems loosely together, attach with a rubber band to a hook (such as a small hook from a pot rack, a drapery hook, or a sturdy paper clip opened into a hook), and hang in a dry place, out of direct sunlight, for 7 to 10 days.

Spray each flower lightly from a distance of about 10 inches with hair spray or spray shellac to preserve. If you wish, break off the stems entirely, or to a shorter length.

Microwave-Dried Herbs and Flowers

Microwave drying is quicker than air drying herbs or flowers.

Many cooks prefer it because herbs dried this way retain more of their original color and a closer approximation of fresh taste. Like air drying, however, microwave drying concentrates the flavor; use only about ⅓ as much of a dried herb as you would fresh.

To dry lavender, marjoram, mint, oregano, rosemary, sage, tarragon, and thyme in a microwave, first wash and dry the herbs thoroughly and remove the leaves from the stems.

Lay paper towels in the microwave. Spread the herbs on the paper in a single layer and lay 1 paper towel loosely on top. In a 700-watt oven, microwave the herbs at full power for 3 minutes; in a 500- or 600-watt oven, microwave at full power for 4 minutes. If the herbs require additional drying, do so in 30-second intervals at full power.

Remove the herbs from the oven and let them cool for about 10 minutes. Store in an airtight container.

To dry bachelor's buttons, black-eyed Susans, cornflowers, Job's tears, everlastings, tea roses, statices, strawflowers, and yarrows (yellow or white) in the microwave, spread a thin layer of silica gel on the bottom of a glass baking dish. Lay the flowers on top so that they do not touch each other. Cover them completely with silica gel.

Microwave (in any size oven) at 50 percent power for about 2 to 3 minutes, until a glass (dairy or candy) thermometer inserted into the gel registers a temperature of 160° F. Leave the baking dish in the oven undisturbed for 30 to 45 minutes, until the gel has cooled enough to handle.

Remove the flowers gently and brush away any granules of gel that remain between petals with a small, fine-bristled paintbrush.

◇ ◇ ◇ *You* **can preserve more of the fresh color and extend the life of dried flowers by dipping them in silica gel before drying, which is available from nurseries.** ◇ ◇ ◇

Recycled Blender Paper

You can turn scraps of construction paper, artist's paper, or even surplus grocery bags into parchment sheets elegantly flecked with dried herbs, strips of citrus zest, or dried floral petals.

You will need:

- One 10-pound recycled brown paper bag (this size bag stands a little over a foot tall when opened), ripped into 1-inch squares; *or*

  Two 8½ x 11-inch sheets pale-colored construction paper, ripped into 1-inch squares; *or*

  One 14 x 20-inch sheet artist's watercolor paper (this paper has a high fiber content) ripped into 1-inch squares; *or*

  1¼ cups any combination of the above

- 1 tablespoon any variety *Home Made* air- *or* microwave-dried herb; *or*

  1 tablespoon any variety *Home Made* dried flower petals; *or*

  1 tablespoon thin strips orange or lemon zest, left to dry for 2 to 3 hours

- A portable window screen, about 9 x 12 inches
- An 11 x 17-inch roasting pan
- A large baking sheet
- Two 14 x 20-inch sheets of cheesecloth, folded in half to 10 x 14 inches
- A clean sponge

Place the pieces of paper into a blender. Add 4 cups water and let the paper soak for about 30 minutes.

Add the dried herbs, flowers, or zest. Run the blender at the highest speed for 1 minute.

Fit the screen into the roasting pan. Pour the contents of the blender onto the screen. Pick up the screen and shake and rock it to distribute the pulp evenly over the entire surface while the water drains into the roasting pan.

Place the screen onto a towel-lined countertop or suspend it securely over the sink. Cover the pulp completely with one folded sheet of cheesecloth and press down firmly to force excess water through the screen. Lay the baking sheet over the cheesecloth, carefully flip the whole assemblage over, and lift off the screen,

leaving a thin layer of pulp atop the cheesecloth in the baking sheet.

Pat the pulp firmly all over with a sponge to compress the fibers and absorb remaining moisture. Lay the second folded piece of cheesecloth over the pulp to cover completely and pat down again. Set the baking sheet aside for at least 24 hours to dry.

When the paper is dry, remove the top layer of cheesecloth and peel the paper off the bottom layer.

Yield = One 9 x 12-inch sheet of paper

Freezer-Dried Herbs

"Freezer drying" herbs is not really drying in the classic sense, but rather a means of extending the shelf life of fresh herbs from a matter of days to months. Once thawed, the texture of herbs preserved this way is moist and supple, so freezer drying also enables you to preserve the herbs whole. Freezer-dried herbs retain much of their fresh flavor, aroma, and appearance; use in the same proportions as fresh herbs.

There are several methods of freezer drying herbs. We've organized directions by which method works best for various herbs, and by whether they are commonly used whole or chopped. Herbs that are often used in soups and stews can be conveniently dried in ice cube trays and the cubes added as needed directly to the stock.

To freezer dry whole sprigs of basil, mint, and sage, fill a saucepan ¾ full with water and bring to a boil over high heat. Using tongs, grasp 2 to 3 sprigs of herb at a time, immerse them in the boiling water for 3 seconds to blanch, then immediately hold them under cold running water for 10 seconds.

Set the herbs between sheets of paper towels for a few minutes to dry.

Put a sheet of wax paper on a countertop. Lay 2 sprigs of herbs at one end of the sheet and fold over to enclose the herbs; continue to fold up the wax paper, with 2 sprigs of herbs between each layer. Insert the wrapped herbs into an airtight plastic bag, push out excess air, seal, and freeze.

To freezer dry chopped basil, chives, dill, mint, and sage, fill a saucepan ¾ full with water and bring to a boil over high heat. Using tongs, grasp 2 to 3 sprigs of herb at a time (or a few stems of chive), immerse them in the boiling water for 3 seconds to blanch, and immediately hold them under cold running water for 10 seconds.

Set the herbs between sheets of paper towels for a few minutes to dry.

Remove the leaves from the stems and chop (just chop the chive). Distribute the chopped leaves on a flat plate or tray in a single layer, cover with plastic wrap, and place in the freezer for 2 hours.

Herbal Teas

"Many say that tea is very hurtful, but we all know it causes cheerfulness, clearness of mind— and is a welcome accessory to every table," a Victorian author advises. "Tea is recommended in the following cases: after a full meal, when the system is oppressed; for the corpulent; for hot climates, and especially for those who, living there, eat freely, or drink milk or alcohol; for soldiers and others marching in hot climates . . . By promoting evaporation and cooling the body, it prevents in a degree the effects of too much food as of too great heat."

Herbal teas, which our Victorian author would have viewed only as a medicinal aid for the invalid, are free of even the rumor of ill effects. They're soothing and invigorating at once!

We provide recipes for several that make use of *Home Made* dried herbs, including lavender, as well as one for a unique tea made from *Home Made* Dried Sour Cherries. Our blends yield about 2 tablespoons herbal tea leaves, or enough to make 6 cups.

Before making tea, pour very hot tap water into a china, ceramic, or glass teapot and swirl it around to warm the pot. For every 8 ounces of boiling water, add 1 teaspoon tea leaves. Put the lid on and allow the tea to steep for 5 to 10 minutes before serving.

For the dried orange or lemon zest in some recipes, let the zest sit out overnight until dry and brittle, then chop (this can be done in advance and stored in an airtight container).

SOME OF OUR FAVORITE HERBAL TEA MIXTURES:

2½ teaspoons air- or microwave-dried mint, 2½ teaspoons dried orange zest, ½ teaspoon whole cloves, crushed, and 1 cinnamon stick, crushed

5 teaspoons Dried Sour Cherries, ½ teaspoon ground allspice, and 1 cinnamon stick, crushed

2 teaspoons air- or microwave-dried sage, 2 teaspoons ground cinnamon, and 2 teaspoons ground nutmeg

1 tablespoon dried rosemary, 2 teaspoons dried lemon zest, and 1 teaspoon ground cinnamon

2½ teaspoons dried lavender, 2½ teaspoons dried rosemary, and 1 teaspoon dried lemon zest

Transfer the herbs to an airtight container and return them to the freezer.

To freezer dry chopped basil, dill, and sage for use in soups and stews, remove the leaves from the stems and chop. Put 2 tablespoons chopped leaves in each slot of a clean ice cube tray. Cover with boiling water to fill the slots. Freeze for at least 4 hours, until frozen solid.

Pop the cubes out of the tray, transfer to an airtight plastic bag, squeeze out the excess air, seal, and return the herbs to the freezer.

To freezer dry chopped parsley, remove the leaves from the stems and chop. Distribute the chopped parsley on a flat plate or tray in a single layer, cover with plastic wrap, and place in the freezer for 2 hours.

Transfer the parsley to an airtight container and return it to the freezer.

Dried Mushroom Medley

The author of one 1894 magazine article on "economical living" expounds upon "the vast amount of wholesome and nutritious food that lies at the door of every country dweller.

"City people pay at least a dollar a pound for mushrooms," he notes, "which are served at the finest dinners, and are considered among the best articles for use in high-class cooking."

Most of us forsake mushroom gathering for the bounty stocked by our urban markets—which, unfortunately, somewhat exceed "a dollar a pound"—but we can still make the most of mushrooms by preserving them.

Drying is an excellent way to preserve seasonal mushrooms for use all year, and to keep a manageable supply of any kind on hand for cooking.

Drying intensifies the flavor of mushrooms. Once dried mushrooms have been reconstituted, you don't need to sauté before adding them to recipes, as you would fresh mushrooms.

White mushrooms, shiitakes, and portobellos can be dried either in the oven or in a dehydrator. Since mushrooms dried in a dehydrator hold their shape better, we prefer to dry them this way for soups and sauces, where appearance counts; oven drying works well for stews and other long-simmered recipes, where the mushrooms will break up anyway. At twenty-five dollars a pound and up, we entrust morels only to the dehydrator.

OVEN DRYING:

> 1 pound large white button mushrooms, cleaned, stemmed, and halved, *and/or*
>
> 1 pound shiitake mushrooms, cleaned, and trimmed, *and/or*
>
> 1 pound portobello mushrooms, cleaned, stemmed, and cut into ½-inch slices

Preheat the oven to 140° F.

Line a baking sheet with baker's parchment. Distribute the mushrooms on the sheet in a single layer, placing white button mushrooms cut side up and shiitake mushrooms stem side up. Put

Mushroom Risotto

Mushroom risotto is a delectable way to show off the wild mushrooms you dried a few weeks ago.

> 2 ounces dried mushrooms (any variety or combination)
> 2 cups hot water
> 2½ cups chicken stock
> 2 tablespoons olive oil
> 2 large shallots, peeled and chopped
> 1 cup uncooked arborio rice
> ½ cup dry white wine
> Salt
> Freshly ground black pepper
> 1 tablespoon chopped flat-leaf parsley
> 2 tablespoons freshly grated Parmesan cheese

Combine the mushrooms with the hot water in a bowl and soak for 15 to 30 minutes, until they are soft. Slice the mushrooms if you are using one of the varieties dried whole.

Bring the chicken stock to a boil in a small saucepan over medium heat. Reduce the heat to low and maintain at a simmer.

Remove the mushrooms from the soaking water and strain 1 cup of the water through a fine sieve into a measuring cup.

Heat the oil in a large, heavy saucepan over low heat. Add the shallots and cook for about 4 minutes, stirring constantly until translucent. Add the rice and cook for 3 minutes, stirring constantly. While still stirring, slowly add 1 cup of the stock and bring to a simmer. Once the stock has been absorbed, add the cup of strained soaking water. Bring back to a simmer while stirring. When this liquid has been absorbed, stir in the mushrooms and wine.

Add the remaining 1½ cups stock, ½ cup at a time, stirring constantly, until the rice is creamy. Season with salt and pepper to taste, and stir in the parsley. Garnish with the Parmesan cheese and serve immediately.

Yield = 4 servings

✧ ✧ ✧ *O*ne of the niftiest discoveries we made while researching this book is the availability of easy home mushroom-growing kits (see Source Guide). They allow you to produce a bumper crop within a box barely larger than a shoe box. The only requirement is that you have a space where the temperature can be maintained at 50 to 65° F.

The mushrooms grow in a bag that fits into the box in which they are delivered, which contains the compost and the mushroom spawn. You also receive a small quantity of a peat moss and limestone mix, which gets added to the compost. A little bit of attention to watering, and you have up to 10 pounds of mushrooms popping up over the next 60 to 90 days. We grow portobellos; the source we use also provides kits for white button mushrooms and Bavarian browns. ✧ ✧ ✧

the baking sheet into the oven, leaving the door slightly ajar.

Dry the shiitakes for about 7 hours, until hard, but still pliable, and the portobellos and white button mushrooms for about 8 hours, until papery.

As the mushrooms are done, remove them from the oven, cool for about 30 minutes, and store in an airtight container.

DEHYDRATOR DRYING:

> ½ pound morel mushrooms, *and/or*
> 1 pound portobello mushrooms, cleaned, outer layer peeled, stemmed, and cut into ½-inch slices, *and/or*
> 1 pound shiitake mushrooms, cleaned and trimmed, *and/or*
> 1 pound large white button mushrooms, cleaned, stemmed, and thinly sliced

Layer the mushrooms on trays of a dehydrator. Dry the morels for about 2 hours, until hard and hollow-sounding when tapped; the portobellos for about 4 hours, until papery; the shiitakes for about 9 hours, until hard, but still pliable, and the white button mushrooms for about 9 hours, until papery.

Remove the mushrooms from the dehydrator as they are done, let them cool for about 30 minutes, and store in an airtight container. (Do not let the first batches done sit out while longer-drying mushrooms are still in the dehydrator.)

REFRIGERATOR DRYING:

> 1 pound white button mushrooms, cleaned and stemmed

Place the mushrooms, whole, into an unwaxed brown paper bag and fold the bag closed. Refrigerate for 10 to 14 days, until the mushrooms are dry but still slightly pliable. Transfer to an airtight container for storing.

Yield = 1 pound of white button mushrooms, shiitakes, or portobellos yields about 2 ounces dried mushrooms; ½ pound morels yields between 1 and 1½ ounces dried mushrooms.

Trail Mix

We make this healthy treat in a dehydrator, since it works better than oven drying for some of its components. If your own household doesn't devour the Trail Mix first, it makes a great gift.

4¾ cups water
1 pound seedless green grapes, stemmed
Juice of 1 lemon
2 pounds (12 to 14) apricots, halved and pitted
2 pounds (about 8) freestone peaches, halved and pitted
1 medium pineapple, peeled, cored, and thinly sliced
½ cup whole almonds

Bring 4 cups of the water to a boil in a medium saucepan over high heat. Throw in the grapes and boil for 3 minutes, then drain and rinse them under cold running water. Lay them aside on paper towels to dry.

Combine the lemon juice and the remaining ¾ cup water in a bowl. Add the apricots in batches and soak them for 1 to 2 minutes to prevent discoloration. Drain, but do not dry, the apricots.

Put the grapes, apricots, peaches, and pineapple on trays of a dehydrator; place the apricots and peaches skin side down. Dry the pineapple for about 9 hours, until moisture-free, but still pliable; the peaches for about 11 hours, until dry but still pliable; the grapes

◇ ◇ ◇ **For a Dried Fruit Gift Assortment, dry the apricots, peaches, and pineapple; arrange in a *Home Made* Saltbread Breadbasket (page 160), Edible Gingerbread Bowl (page 164), or Edible Chocolate Gift Box (page 140). For a ready supply of golden raisins, dry any quantity of seedless green grapes by themselves.** ◇ ◇ ◇

for 12 hours, until they turn into golden raisins; and the apricots for 12 to 13 hours, until dry but still pliable.

As it is done, remove the fruit from the dehydrator, set it aside to cool for about 30 minutes, and transfer immediately to an airtight container. (The pineapple will become tough and inedible if left out until the apricots are done.)

When all the fruit is dried, chop the peaches, apricots, and pineapple into bite-size chunks. Combine with the raisins and the nuts and mix thoroughly. Return the mix to the airtight container to store.

Yield = About 21 ounces

Turkey Jerky

This dehydrator-dried snack is a lighter rendition of classic beef jerky, equally suited to the campsite, the hiking trail, or the bicycle path. The teriyaki marinade adds an interesting twist.

> 6 tablespoons low-sodium teriyaki sauce
> 1 tablespoon dark brown sugar
> 1 teaspoon hickory salt
> 1 pound uncooked skinless turkey breast, thinly sliced

Put the teriyaki sauce, brown sugar, and hickory salt into a tightly sealing plastic bag. Seal and shake the bag to mix. Add the turkey, reseal the bag, and shake to coat the turkey. Set the bag aside for 20 minutes for the flavors to meld.

Put the turkey onto a dehydrator tray in a single layer and dry for about 8 hours, until leathery. Remove the jerky and set it aside to cool for 20 to 30 minutes. Store in an airtight container.

Yield = About 6¼ ounces

Dried Sour Cherries

These little delicacies can be substituted for raisins in baking, lending a distinctive tart accent. Home drying is easily done in the oven and well worth the minimal effort. Although frozen or canned sour cherries are readily available out of season, the dried variety are hard to find and usually quite pricey.

2½ pounds stemmed and pitted sour cherries

Preheat the oven to 140° F. Line a baking sheet with aluminum foil.

Spread the sour cherries in a single layer on the baking sheet and put it into the oven for about 14 hours. Remove any cherries that are dry and moisture-free (cut one open and look inside for wet spots), but still pliable and dark red in color.

Turn the remaining cherries over and raise the oven temperature to 170° F. If you are drying more than 1 baking sheet at once, rotate the sheets at this time to ensure even distribution of heat. Dry the cherries for another 1 hour to 1 hour and 15 minutes.

Remove the baking sheet from the oven and allow the dried cherries to cool for about 30 minutes. Store in an airtight container.

Yield = ½ pound dried sour cherries

"Sun-Dried" Tomatoes Indoors

The prized taste of sun-dried tomatoes can be obtained in one of three ways. If you happen to live in a place that has a climate approximating that of southern Italy and have days to spare, you can set up and monitor sun drying in your backyard or on your terrace. Or you can buy them for an outrageous price from gourmet shops in major

❖ ❖ ❖ **V**ariations: Substitute 2 pints blueberries or raspberries, picked over, for the sour cherries. Follow directions for drying sour cherries, but leave the oven door slightly ajar.
❖ ❖ ❖

Reconstituting

Dried tomatoes and dried mushrooms should be reconstituted before use in recipes other than long-cooking soups and stews.

Reconstituting involves covering the dried vegetables with a liquid and soaking them until they are soft, which usually takes 15 to 30 minutes. The more papery or brittle the vegetable, the longer it will take to reconstitute; brittle dried morels take the longest.

Reconstitute dried tomatoes or mushrooms in plain boiling water. Dried mushrooms can also be reconstituted in boiling chicken stock or chicken or beef bouillon.

Dried tomatoes are particularly good reconstituted in oil, especially when they are to be eaten plain, in salads, or on pizza. Put 6 to 8 dried tomatoes into a Mason jar and top with *Home Made* Garlic Oil (page 38) or any other variety of *Home Made* oil (pages 39–41), or with olive oil. If using plain olive oil, add 1 garlic clove, peeled and thinly sliced, and 1 small sprig fresh or dried rosemary. Refrigerate for at least 3 hours and up to 1 month.

A side benefit to reconstituting is that the intensely flavored reconstituting liquid can be used in cooking. Use mushroom liquid for making rice, in beurre blanc or other sauces, and in soup stocks. (If you soaked morels, strain the liquid through a fine sieve before using.) Tomato reconstituting oil can be used for cooking pasta, sprinkling atop cooked pasta, or brushing over the top of *Home Made* Focaccia dough (page 171).

Quick Corn Chowder

- ½ cup dried corn
- 1 cup boiling water
- 2 tablespoons unsalted butter
- ½ cup diced yellow onion
- ¼ cup diced red bell pepper
- ½ tablespoon chopped poblano chili
- 1 garlic clove, peeled and minced
- ¼ teaspoon salt
- ⅛ teaspoon ground white pepper
- 1 cup milk

Combine the dried corn and the boiling water in a bowl and set it aside.

Melt the butter in a medium saucepan over medium heat. Add the onion, peppers, and garlic. Saute for 7 to 8 minutes, stirring occasionally, until the onion has wilted. Add the corn and water mixture. Stir in the salt and white pepper. Reduce the heat to low, cover, and simmer for 20 minutes.

Stir in the milk, re-cover, and cook for 10 minutes more.

Yield = 4 servings

cities. *Or you can stock up on plum tomatoes in season and dry a supply in your oven, following the directions below.*

5 pounds Italian plum tomatoes

Wash and thoroughly dry the tomatoes.

Preheat the oven to 170° F. Line a baking sheet with aluminum foil. Cut the tomatoes in half lengthwise and place them on the baking sheet, cut side up.

Dry the tomatoes in the oven for about 6 hours, then remove any tomatoes that are moisture-free, but still pliable (you do not want them to become brittle or to blacken).

If you are drying more than 1 baking sheet of tomatoes at once, rotate the sheets at this time to ensure even distribution of heat. Dry the remaining tomatoes for about 1 hour longer.

Remove the baking sheet from the oven and allow the dried tomatoes to cool for about 30 minutes. Store in an airtight container.

Yield = 1 pound dried tomatoes

Dried Corn for Quick Chowder

We dry corn in a dehydrator when it's juicy and succulent and keep it on hand for chowder, a hearty and nutritious one-pot meal that can be whipped up in a few minutes after a long day's work. Dried corn holds its shape much better than frozen or canned; and even when corn's in season, who wants to be bothered shucking it at the last minute?

2 large ears corn, husked

Microwave the corn for 2 minutes at full power, turning the ears after 1 minute, or steam them for 2 minutes. Remove the corn kernels from the cob with a sharp knife or a corn shucker.

Cut a sheet of baker's parchment to fit a dehydrator tray, making sure to cut around the well in the center. Put the corn kernels onto the parchment. Dry for about 8 hours, until leathery.

Remove the corn from the dehydrator and set it aside for about 30 minutes to cool. Store in an airtight container.

Yield = ½ cup dried corn

Source Guide

Chapter 1: Pickles and Preserves

Ceramic Supply of New York
534 La Guardia Place
New York, NY 10012
(212) 475-7236
ceramic paints and supplies

Laguna Clay Co.
14400 Lomitas Ave.
City of Industry, CA 91746
(818) 330-7694
*ceramic paints and supplies;
white ceramic pottery*

Maryland China Co.
54 Main St.
Reisterstown, MD 21136
800-638-3880
white ceramic pottery

Tom Thumb Crafts
1026 Davis St.
Evanston, IL 60201
(708) 869-9573
*ceramic, fabric, and glass paints
and supplies*

Chapter 2: Oils, Vinegars, & Condiments

Beer & Winemaking Supplies,
Inc.
154 King St.
Northampton, MA 01060
(413) 586-0150
vinegar mother starters

Dean & Deluca
560 Broadway
New York, NY 10012
(212) 431-1691
dried herbs and spices

Food Animal Concerns Trust
P.O. Box 14599
Chicago, IL 60614
(312) 525-4952
Nest Eggs® brand eggs

E. C. Kraus
9001 East 24 Highway
P.O. Box 7850
Independence, MO 64054
(816) 254-7448
vinegar mother starters

Spiceland, Inc.
3206 N. Major
Chicago, IL 60634
(312) 736-1000
dried herbs and spices

Tom Thumb Crafts
1026 Davis St.
Evanston, IL 60201
(708) 869-9573
acrylic paints in squirt bottles

Chapter 3: Beverages

Beer & Winemaking Supplies,
Inc.
154 King St.
Northampton, MA 01060
(413) 586-0150
*beer and wine kits; champagne
yeast; corks; soda extracts*

Ceramic Supply of New Jersey
10 Dell Glen Ave.
Lodi, NJ 07644
(201) 340-3005
lettering brushes

Inlet, Inc.
One Saunders Ave.
San Anselmo, CA 94960
800-786-5665
English ale kits

E. C. Kraus
9001 East 24 Highway
P.O. Box 7850
Independence, MO 64054
(816) 254-7448
*beer and wine kits; champagne
yeast; corks; crown caps;
food grade glycerin; soda
extracts*

Montague Associates, Ltd.
Reception House
34 Montague Rd.
Richmond, Surrey TW10 6QJ,
England
English ale kits

Semplex of U.S.A.
4159 Thomas Ave., No.
Minneapolis, MN 55412
(612) 522-0500
*beer and wine kits; corks; soda
extracts*

Webs Yarn
P.O. Box 147
Service Center
Northampton, MA 01061
(413) 584-2225
silk cord

Chapter 4: Dairy Products

Food Animal Concerns Trust
P.O. Box 14599
Chicago, IL 60614
(312) 525-4952
Nest Eggs® brand eggs

International Yogurt Co.
628 N. Doheny Dr.
Los Angeles, CA 90069
(310) 274-9917
soft cheese and yogurt cultures

Maid of Scandinavia
3244 Raleigh Ave.
Minneapolis, MN 55416
800-328-6722
butter molds; dairy thermometers

Nasco
901 Jamesville Ave.
Fort Atkinson, WI 53538
(414) 563-2446
*rennet tablets; simple cheese
kits*

New England Cheesemaking
Supply Co.
85 Main St.
Ashfield, MA 01330
(413) 628-3808
*cheese molds; cheesecloth; citric
acid; dairy thermometers; rennet
tablets; tartaric acid; cheese and
yogurt kits*

Wilton Enterprises
22440 West 75th St.
Woodridge, IL 60517
(708) 963-7100
*small candy molds for
decoratively shaped butter*

*Chapter 5: Smoked Foods &
Sausages*

CM International
P.O. Box 60127
Colorado Springs, CO 80960
(303) 390-0505
*portable indoor hot smokers
(Cameron smoker cooker)*

Chapter 6: Candy

Love Chocolate Factory
P.O. Box 1010
Hartville, OH 44632
(216) 877-3322
*plastic candy and lollipop
molds*

Maid of Scandinavia
3244 Raleigh Ave.
Minneapolis, MN 55416
800-328-6722
candy thermometers

Wilton Enterprises
22440 West 75th St.
Woodridge, IL 60517
(708) 963-7100
*candy dipping sets; candy
thermometers; foil cups; lollipop
sticks and wrapper bags; metal
lollipop molds; oil-based candy
flavorings*

*Chapter 8: Kitchen Growing &
Drying*

Far West Fungi
P.O. Box 428
South San Francisco, CA
94083
(415) 871-0786
*indoor and outdoor mushroom
kits*

Field & Forest Products, Inc.
N3296 Kozuzek Rd.
Peshtigo, WI 54157
(715) 582-4997
*indoor and outdoor mushroom
kits*

The Walter T. Kelley Co.
Clarkson, KY 42726
(502) 242-2012
*beeswax; general candle-making
supplies*

Pourette Co.
6818 Roosevelt Way
P.O. Box 15220
Seattle, WA 98115
(206) 525-4488
general candle-making supplies

River Valley Ranch
P.O. Box 898
New Munster, WI 53152
800-SHROOMS
simple indoor mushroom kits

Yankee Candle Co.
Rts. 5 & 10
South Deerfield, MA 01373
(413) 665-8306
*professional candle-making wax;
stearic acid; wicks and wick
bases*

Index